WORKING PAPERS

Reflections on Teachers, Schools, and Communities

WORKING PAPERS

Reflections on Teachers, Schools, and Communities

VITO PERRONE

Teachers College, Columbia University
New York and London

Published by Teachers College Press, 1234 Amsterdam Avenue,
New York, NY 10027

Library of Congress Cataloging-in-Publication Data

Perrone, Vito.
  Working papers : reflections on teachers, schools, and communities
/ Vito Perrone.
     p.   cm.
  Bibliography: p.
  Includes index.
  ISBN 0-8077-2945-0.—ISBN 0-8077-2944-2 (pbk.)
  1. Education—United States.   2. Educational equalization—United
States.   3. Teachers—Training of—United States.   4. Education and
state—United States.   I. Title.
LA217.P466 1989   88-33361
370'.973—dc19   CIP

ISBN 0-8077-2945-0
ISBN 0-8077-2944-2 (pbk.)

Manufactured in the United States of America

94   93   92   91   90   89   1   2   3   4   5   6

Contents

Acknowledgments

The papers included in this book grow out of my experience in and around schools. This places me in great debt to the many teachers and school administrators who shared their classrooms and schools and engaged in countless hours of discussions with me. I am also indebted to my colleagues at the University of North Dakota and within the North Dakota Study Group on Evaluation who have provided me enormous support and encouragement. Their extraordinary commitments to teachers, schools, and communities have been continually inspiring. I also wish to acknowledge the assistance of colleagues at the Carnegie Foundation for the Advancement of Teaching, especially with regard to the final manuscript. And finally, I wish to recognize Carmel Perrone, my loving spouse of thirty-two years. It was she, in the end, who convinced me that these papers should be brought together. I dedicate the book to her.

Introduction

This collection of papers covers a span of 20 years, from 1968 to the present. These 20 years encompass two quite diverse reform periods in American education, the more experimental, open-ended, curriculum-oriented, student-centered, and decentralized 1960s and early 1970s and the more traditional, regulatory, teacher-information-centered and centralized years associated with the late 1970s and 1980s. In an important way, then, the papers provide a significant historical perspective on the issues that filled the discourse of schools in these years.

For the most part, the papers were written as speeches, essentially sets of ideas, expressions of thought about various aspects of education. I did not view them at the time as final, definitive statements. Often written quickly, they were conceived as *working papers* designed to stimulate further discussion and active response among those in and around schools and teacher education institutions.

My largest task in bringing this particular collection together has involved selection. For each paper included, 10 others had to be rejected. Several that I liked a great deal personally, and proved at the time to be especially provocative, focused directly on issues specific to North Dakota, my home for most of the 20 years covered by this collection. While they may well have had some social interest for a national audience, I judged them inappropriate for this collection. Others were connected to particular events such as the Bicentennial, celebrations relating to specific schools and individuals, and then-pending federal legislation. While each contained an important historical perspective and social context and addressed critical aspects of educational practice, they would all have needed fairly extensive contextual statements to make them fully accessible.

In the end, I selected papers that relate to some of the continuing discourse of American education, believing that the older statements might make the current discussion more productive. I also felt obligated to provide in this collection some connection to aspects of my experience having ongoing historical interest. That is the reason, for example, for including the discussion of the New School and the Center for Teaching and Learning, distinctive North Dakota institutions of national importance.

The papers have been grouped around the six basic themes— equity and pluralism, progressivism in education, teacher education, school testing, curriculum, and education and policy—that have filled virtually the whole of my professional life. These themes have formed natural groupings for much of my educational writing over the years.

Going back through a couple of decades of talks about schools, teaching, and learning proved to be an interesting experience. While the issues changed somewhat, I believe a consistent point of view and a reasonable degree of optimism was maintained. I *thought* that would be the case, but it was good to find it was indeed so.

As we move toward the 1990s, the basic discourse related to schools, teaching, and learning is beginning to change again. There is, for example, renewed talk of integrated curriculum, active learning, school-site decision making, parent involvement, experimentation, a broader use of community resources, teacher empowerment, and language as a cultural phenomenon. I understand well these directions and beliefs. While counter to much that has prevailed in the aftermath of *A Nation at Risk* (National Commission on Excellence in Education, 1983), they have a long history and may move us toward the kinds of change in schools that can make a constructive difference to students and teachers. It seems clear that the regulatory and narrowing directions of the 1980s have produced too little of consequence. The working papers included in this collection should contribute to the renewed discussion about how to conceptualize schools as powerful centers for learning on the part of teachers and students alike. They have been brought together with such a purpose in mind.

In concluding this introduction, it should be noted that colleagues have for a number of years encouraged me to bring together some of my talks, believing they would be useful to college students, classroom teachers, school administrators, parents, and policy makers. It took a good deal of time, however, to convince myself that I should do it.

My hope is that these papers will contribute to ongoing deliberations about education—and that through our discussions we will find ourselves as educators more prepared in the decade ahead than in the decade past to commit ourselves to structures and practices that make learning powerful and sustaining for children and young people. Anything less is a disservice to them and to society.

WORKING PAPERS

Reflections on Teachers, Schools, and Communities

Part I
EQUITY AND PLURALISM

CHAPTER ONE

The World's Children: Valuing Diversity

"The World's Children: Valuing Diversity" was the theme of the Association for Childhood Education International's national conference for 1972 and the title of my keynote address. It was published in the October 1972 issue of Childhood Education. *Cultural pluralism was one of the democratic themes that filled the reform literature of the 1960s. While we have long lived with diversity, we have tended to struggle with its implications. At the present time, as immigration has reached the high levels existing at the turn of the century, diversity has become again a subject of particularly intense debate.*

Not long ago I asked several teachers, college students, and children to close their eyes and describe what they "saw" when I said: "We are going to discuss the world's children." The pictures evoked by those words tended to have their settings in Africa, Mexico, the Philippines, and Vietnam. And the pictures were of children who were ill clad, undernourished, and solemn in appearance. But the "world's children," in reality, are never that far away. They are closer to home. They live next door, right in our neighborhoods. They are in the streets where we walk and the schools where we teach. They are the individuals we often wish would make less noise. They are persons many adults in our society have forgotten how to talk with or listen to. Without them there would be little continuity in our lives. There would likely even be less joy and hope about the future.

The Melting Pot—A Perspective

To speak of children and diversity brings me naturally to our country's history as a land of immigrants. But the belief in America as a crucible, a "melting pot," that grew richer through the alchemy of cultural integration has always been more rhetorical than real.

Nathan Glazer and Daniel Patrick Moynihan in *Beyond the Melting Pot* (1963) described a limited mobility for America's minorities and educational systems that more often restricted than encouraged growth, labeling large numbers of individuals as inferior. And Oscar Handlin (1959a) depicts economic misery, discrimination, psychological depression, and unhappiness for vast numbers of America's immigrants who lived "beyond the melting pot" for most of their lives, being unable to adapt to or assimilate easily the expectations of the dominant culture.

My mother, an Italian immigrant in Yankee America, in her last days shared with me, not in bitterness but in a state of calm reflection, her "American cross" and how she often wished she had never come to this country. The uniquenesses she brought were seldom capitalized upon by the schools or the community. Her language, basic to her cultural heritage, was a detriment, a symbol of her difference and alienation. And she was not alone.

The rhetoric that supported the melting pot was essentially liberal—a vision of immigrant peoples changing together to form a new type of person, uniquely American. The practice was nativist, demanding that individuals turn their backs upon their non-Anglo pasts. Despite a professed respect for the uniqueness of various individuals, the educational systems that developed had preferred modes of communicating, relating, motivating, and teaching that were characteristic of the Anglo-American middle-class culture. While it worked for some, it was for too many—possibly most—a clear path to failure in school.

Alfredo Castaneda (1972) argues that the "preferred modes [of learning] are considered by virtue of one form or another of melting pot ideology, to be the ideal modes which all children must acquire. If the child pursues different modes he is then viewed as 'culturally different,' 'culturally impoverished,' 'passive,' 'lacking in achievement motivation'" (p. 114).

Such reaction to cultural difference is understandable. The outsider, the person who is different, is typically viewed with suspicion, not just in America but in most parts of the world. Individuals are considerably more comfortable in settings where their belief systems and racial identification are supported. Most of us, I suspect, understand the psychological basis for the foregoing: We have often experienced a sense of belonging as well as isolation. To say that it is understandable, however, does not justify it or make it acceptable. The legacy has, in fact, been quite costly—not just for those who were asked to take on the lifestyle of the dominant culture but for those who were denied the full measure of other cultures' contributions to their own lives.

While the melting-pot ideology and practice always had its critics, it received its greatest challenge in the post–World War II period from blacks, Puerto Ricans, Mexican-Americans, and Native Americans who demanded an equitable share of America's promise along with the maintenance of a distinctive lifestyle. All the talk of equal educational opportunity—or democracy writ large—had, over the years, little practical meaning for these populations. It still means too little. Fifty percent of black youngsters who live in our cities do not complete high school. The average Mexican-American child in the Southwest drops out of school by the seventh grade; in Texas alone, 89 percent of children with Spanish surnames who start school do not finish. Over 70 percent of Native American children drop out of school. These statistics represent a terrible loss of human potential. That such conditions are tolerated, not seen as the basis for massive and focused educational and economic reform, is shameful.

Failure of the melting-pot ideology and an appeal for cultural pluralism are encompassed today in active discussions about community control of schools, educational voucher systems, various ethnic studies programs, and multiculturalism. Concerns about pluralism are also evident in the large numbers of court cases dealing with education and non-Anglo minorities. While the changing discourse and active civil rights litigation create unease for many who see only divisiveness in pluralism, I believe that differences need to be acknowledged and respected and in the long run can and will enrich our lives, creating a wonderful and complementary human mosaic.

A residual issue relates to these comments about differences. A vast amount of curriculum materials and related literature published after World War II dealt with intercultural, international, and interracial understanding. Their purpose—essentially well-meaning—was to ameliorate the "negative" effects of differences. A common admonition to teachers in the literature and curriculum materials was to "focus on similarities and not on differences." While none of us would deny that there are similarities among all people, across all cultures—part of our common humanity—it is not through the study of similarities that the uniqueness of individuals from diverse cultures becomes manifest and our lives potentially enriched.

Thinking that encourages a preoccupation with similarities, seeing them as positive and differences as negative, also strikes hard at educational areas beyond intercultural, international, and interracial understanding. Children viewed as too active, for example, are often removed from regular classrooms or placed on medication to reduce their activity levels and produce greater conformity. Originality too frequently is neither expected nor encouraged, and efforts are made to reduce the range of differences through a variety of special-grouping patterns. Alternatives become restricted; everyone follows a similar systemwide program—the same books, the same narrow frame of acceptable behavior.

Despite the uncertainty of the future, support of what Castaneda calls "democratic cultural pluralism" remains one of America's great needs. Without such a view, we can have no genuine *valuing* of *diversity* in our society and in our schools.

Schools and Communities

Valuing diversity in our schools calls for beginning with the child—acting on the assumptions that learning is a personal matter, varies for different children, proceeds best when children are actively engaged in their own learning, takes place in a variety of environments in and out of school, and is enhanced in a supportive setting where children are taken seriously. To act on these assumptions would mean challenging the ways most teachers, schools, and classrooms now function. Normative orientations, which include predetermined expectations for children at prescribed ages, would, for example, begin to collapse, as would most standardized testing. A diversity of options for learning would be available. As most teachers have come to understand, the opportunities for successful experience and increasing levels of self-esteem are related to the range of options available to children.

If we acted on a belief in the value of diversity, the clock would not determine to such a large degree when children started and ended learning activities; there would be enlarged potential for integrity and intensity in learning. Peer interaction—communication—would be encouraged. Learning would be cooperative rather than competitive. Integral rather than peripheral to a child's life in the classroom would be the creative and expressive arts: dancing, singing, painting, and improvising—all the expressive forms of communication that have the capacity for developing feeling, the most personal of human possessions. Distinctions between work and play, as they relate to learning, would be less sharp. Children's interests and strengths would be essential starting points for learning.

The environment beyond the classroom would become an accessible arena for learning. There would be increased interaction between young and old. Parents, in particular, would play active roles in the classrooms and in the learning that takes place in the community.

Personalization or Individualization

To value diversity, as the foregoing suggests, is to commit the school and its personnel to personalization. And because so many people still view personalization as synonymous with individualized instruction, some clarification of the latter is called for. As commonly practiced, individualized instruction often provides children with alternatives about how they are going to learn and at what pace; however, what is to be learned is typically predetermined. Such a one-dimensional model loses the essential quality of human action or purpose as distinguished from behavior. Children's own intentions are not honored.

I read, a year ago, some school district proposals that had been submitted to the U.S. Office of Education. One described the three years of effort in developing an "individualized program" that had now reached, as the proposal stated, a "high" level and was supported by "an extensive library of instructional packages." After describing in great detail the foregoing program and the ways teachers and aides functioned, the proposal discussed the school district's principal problem: "It is taking so much effort just to maintain the system (all of the paperwork and recording) that the teachers don't have the time to interact personally with the children." Not to interact personally and intensively with children is hardly a means for observing or supporting uniqueness.

Buckminster Fuller addressed a similar issue in a recent PBS television interview. He noted that schools "receive comprehensivists who think in wholes and quickly break their learning into parts, which reduces their capacity for the kind of learning that might make a difference in their individual lives and in our society . . . rather than continuity in learning, [the schools] provide discontinuity. " If we valued children's learning we would have made similar observations long ago. Integrity would still be a central focus.

Personalizing education—beginning with children, their strengths and intentions—opens up broad learning possibilities, especially in settings where children are encouraged to ask their own questions rather than waiting to find out from the teacher what questions they ought to ask. This goal is especially important if we want children to have sufficient opportunities in school to achieve success rather than experience any kind of continuing failure. In discussing this point, I have often been reminded that "large numbers of children are not motivated," hence not successful. But children as well as adults are never unmotivated. All individuals are motivated to enhance a sense of personal adequacy. How many children lose interest in school and eventually drop out because of too many success experiences or too many opportunities for enhancing personal adequacy?

Diversity with Dignity

Dignity, a sense of worth, is another self-enhancing concept to which we need to give greater attention. How often do we concern ourselves with the meanings children bring to experience, the ways they feel about themselves? In a popular ACEI publication, Ira Gordon (1972) suggests that children's views of themselves are often limited, artificially imposed by adults' lack of support for their personal identity. He reminds us further:

> Acceptance of not only the fact that children differ but the right of children to remain different will aid the teacher to plan . . . so that each child feels challenged to learn along with being valued as a person. (p. 33)

I was deeply moved by the young 13-year-old Mississippi boy who led the following chant during a 1968 demonstration at the Republican National Convention:

> I may be black
> But I am somebody,
>
> I may be poor
> But I am somebody,
>
> I may be hungry
> But I am somebody.

To be black, poor, and hungry in America and remain conscious about being somebody demands extraordinary inner strength. Without the strength to be somebody—regardless of race or socioeconomic status—is to live Thoreau's "life of quiet desperation."

Treating children with dignity demonstrates a belief in each child's ability to learn. Paulo Freire (1971) says that dialogue, the encounter of persons engaged in a process of learning, "requires an intense faith in man, faith in his power to make and remake, to create and recreate. . . . Dialogue cannot exist without hope" (p. 76). Dialogue and dignity are connected.

I recently visited some magnificent classrooms in Sedro Woolley, Ferndale, and Burlington, north of Seattle, Washington. Several interactions that stood out for me are related to the issue of dignity—children's respect for each other and themselves.

- In one classroom, I was sitting with an eight-year-old who was sharing her song book with me. I asked her if she would read "Blowin' in the Wind" to me. She began and then stopped and said: "You know, I am a very good reader." I asked her how she knew and she replied: "I just know." She also knew that the teacher knew, and the teacher had never told her that she knew.
- In the same classroom a young fellow was preparing a model of an intricate but wild-looking race car. Obviously pleased with the quality of what he was doing, he asked me if I knew anything about the racing circuit—the cars and the drivers. He knew a great deal—I knew practically nothing. After some extended discussion, when I asked him about his use of time in the classroom, he was prompted to show me some crocheting that he had completed the previous day and was on the wall for display. In a classroom where respect for individuality is not present, boys would not so publicly engage in crocheting.
- In another classroom, I was reading a family story to a group of first-grade children and in the course of the reading asked some questions about the children's families. As I began to talk with Alessandro, a young girl said with warmth and pride: "Alessandro doesn't speak English; he only speaks Spanish." I carried on a limited discussion with Alessandro in Spanish, and we then began to list all the Spanish words that children in the class knew. They had learned many from Alessandro.
- In yet another primary classroom, where children were all "authors," a youngster brought me to David, an Asian child, so I could see his drawings. My young guide was obviously proud of David's drawings—they *were* spectacular—and also told me that David was teaching him how to draw.

Obviously, these were classrooms that supported learning, valued diversity, and treated children with genuine dignity.

The Fallacy of Misplaced Concreteness

The foregoing brings me quite directly to a concern—shared by a growing number of people—about the increasing number of achievement and intelligence tests to which children (and teachers) are subjected, the normative character of which represents an antithesis to uniqueness or to the valuing of diversity. They tend to get in the way of productive human relationships in the classroom. Henry Dyer (1971), formerly of the Educational Testing Service (ETS), makes the following observations about IQ and grade-level equivalency scores:

> [They are] psychological and statistical monstrosities. I have defined the IQ as a dubious normative scale wrapped up in a ratio that is based upon an impossible assumption about the equivalence of human experience and the opportunity to learn. A grade level equivalency score has many of the same properties, and as such it lures educational practitioners to succumb to what Alfred N. Whitehead called the "fallacy of misplaced concreteness." (p. 15)

In this regard, James L. Hymes, Jr. (1972) suggests that we will not deal effectively with diversity until we stop our use of standardized tests that "confuse the measurable with the meaningful" (p. 117). Many of us have been trapped by "misplaced concreteness" and the "measurable." Word calling has become equated with reading; manipulation of mathematical symbols, with concept formation.

The critique of standardized tests is becoming sharper. Deborah Meier (1973), in a paper on "Reading Failure and the Tests," analyzes large numbers of questions appearing in the more popular tests. That they work against minorities, the poor, and less conventional thinkers is quite apparent. That they are not supportive of what schools should be about, if supporting diversity is important, is also obvious.

Regarding a child's progress, Meier states:

> Let us try to leave *accountability* for a child's progress as a matter between the child, his teacher, and his own parents. Let us demand *only* that the teacher and school be able to demonstrate that they are aware of each child, that they are planning for each child, that their plans are being continuously reassessed and modified, and that they are always prepared to change the structure of the school and class if necessary to meet the needs of a child. (pp. 30–31)

Normative tests are hardly necessary to respond to such questions as: To what degree do individual children initiate their own learning? What have individual children accomplished? What have they understood of their experience? In what ways have they extended their learning? Teachers who are engaged in good documentation can answer such questions well.

Reversing the Concept of Irreversibility

The concept of irreversibility—the belief that children deprived of particular learning stimulation in the early years come to school with a deficit that may well be "irreversible"—has been placed before parents for a number of years. While it has, by and large, been accepted, I doubt that it has ever really been believed. It is a disparaging concept falling hard on those from less advantaged environments.

My basic intuition, which had long rejected such a premise, was bolstered by Jerome Kagan's research (1972), which calls into serious question the concept of irreversibility and also gives support to the naturalness of growth. When I enthusiastically shared Kagan's conclusions with my wife, she responded: "Any mother knows that. He really didn't have to go to so much trouble." My wife is correct. Basic intuition and belief in one's experience and direct observation are in need of revival. Professionals need to take increasing cues from parents and children as well as put more trust in their own understandings, those natural thoughts that give a measure of reality to what they do.

Parents and Community

The foregoing raises another important point. What is the role of parents and community people in the life of schools? Clearly, parent and community participation relates directly to the question of uniqueness, diversity, and dignity. Schools have too long kept parents at arms' length—safely within the confines of passive parent-teacher associations. Parents' lack of knowledge and sense of helplessness vis-à-vis schools and educational programs are frightening. I meet few parents and community people who feel comfortable about their interactions with the school. They are typically placed on the defensive, with limited opportunity to take part in planning or evaluating school practices. Their alienation is growing, with unhappy effects on their children. We need desperately to reverse such conditions.

What must children feel when their parents are so far removed? In what way is the school related to the community when the people who live in the community have so little interaction with the school? How much important learning are children deprived of when the full range of human resources that exist in every community are not accessible? When the rich cultural resources are not made integral to the school's ongoing work?

The Diversity and Dignity of Teachers

To value diversity is also to ask serious questions about teachers—their racial-cultural-economic backgrounds and their lifestyles, as well as their academic and experiential backgrounds. For a long time, teachers have come from a narrow range of the population. The need for more black, Chicano, and Native American teachers is clear if we are to provide a sense of personal identification to large numbers of minority children and give support to political and cultural pluralism. But our schools need more than ethnic/racial minorities. How many practicing dancers, actors, painters, sculptors, musicians, writers, artisans, and craftspersons can one find associated with our elementary schools? Such diversity of personnel from across many age groups could provide an increasing diversity to help children deal more effectively with the world beyond the school.

It would be unfair not to extend this discussion to practicing teachers. Teachers, too, need to be treated with dignity. They, too, need to be encouraged to cultivate their personal uniqueness, to bring more of their personal interests and enthusiasms into the classroom, to be themselves. The roles teachers are asked to assume and the classroom structures they are asked to maintain are typically antithetical to the values that support diversity. Decisions about what is to be "covered" in a classroom, what books will be used, the nature and style of evaluation, and the organization of the day are often made by persons far removed from teachers and children in the classroom. Little wonder that teachers' enthusiasm for teaching and for children does not remain high. School systems often produce rhetoric about children's learning but give little thought to opportunities for teachers' learning—witness the decreasing amounts of money available for inservice education or other staff-support measures. For all the concern voiced about children's communication, little opportunity is offered for teachers to communicate, to engage in collective thought. Valuing diversity among children demands the corollary of valuing diversity among teachers.

Further Implications

The mutuality of the foregoing suggests several things. The school needs to be developed as a community in order for diversity to bloom. And this condition is more possible in a small school setting than in a massive one. The United States, unlike England and Sweden, for example, persists in a tendency to build very large schools believing that they provide more learning opportunities. The reality is that the larger a school becomes, the more control and standardization of procedures it requires.

Hallmarks of most of our massive elementary schools are anonymity and alienation—hardly characteristics that invite parent and community participation and the teacher-child commitments that are basic to the building of a community in its more traditional forms. And these large schools are not the most appropriate settings for children, who should be learning to be decision makers, to take responsibility. While I prefer school buildings with 8–10 teachers and 200–250 children, I know that most communities are beyond that possibility. But large schools can be broken down into smaller units of 100 students and 4–5 teachers occupying a particular geographic area of a school as a base. Within such a setting, a program with integrity can be built, one that provides support to its members.

I commented earlier on basic intuition. I'd like to conclude with some moving interviews with children by Robert Coles (1969). Their words relate also to my comments about scale. Margie, from an inner city setting, said:

> I'd have the teacher be better. She could laugh a lot and there wouldn't be a clock up there, making noise every minute that goes by. We would open and close the windows. . . . We could have a big rug in the room. . . . And they could have some . . . big sofas maybe, where if you didn't feel too good you could lie down, or you could just sit in them sometimes and you'd be more comfortable. . . . You'd think [people would] want to change it around, and have us spend the day better. . . . My older brother, he's in the sixth grade and it's like he's across the country from me. I never see him except when school's out. Then everyone wakes up. (pp. 48–49)

And Margie's brother, Arthur:

> The windows, no one ever looks in them or out of them. . . . I'd like
> comfortable chairs. . . . I'd like us sitting around—you know, looking
> at each other, not always in a line, not lined up. . . . You know what?
> I'd like to be able to take off my shoes and relax. . . . [In my home-
> room] there might even be curtains and a magazine stand and lamps
> . . . and plants and flowers. (pp. 50–51)

Susan, 8 years old, lives in the suburbs:

> If I could build a school . . . I'd make [it] warm and small. I'd have a lot
> of little schools. Then there wouldn't be all those big buildings, and you
> get lost in them. . . . You can tell when [the teacher] gets angry be-
> cause her chair squeaks a lot, because she moves around more. They
> should get rid of that chair. . . . And I think we should have places to
> play, not just the halls and classrooms and nothing else. Yes, we have
> the gym, but that's for games and it's too big and I mean a room like
> we have at home, a playroom, for our class; and other classes, they could
> have theirs, too. (pp. 52–53)

And Billy, in the same school:

> They should divide schools up, so you get to know the part you're in,
> as if it was your home or your friend's home. . . . They should have it
> more like home when you eat lunch and not like it is, with . . . every-
> one trying to eat at once [in the cafeteria] . . . and when you get [a seat]
> it's no good anyway—those benches. . . . They could build nicer and
> friendlier [buildings]. I'll bet I could. . . . [If I could build a school
> building] it would beckon and welcome and reach out and say hello and
> a big goodbye. (p. 53)

Children could teach us much if we listened, really listened to
them, and observed them carefully. Valuing diversity would then
become common, because diversity would be so apparent and such
an asset.

CHAPTER TWO

Accessibility to Schools and Communities

This paper was originally presented as a faculty lecture at the University of North Dakota in 1972 and later published in a joint publication of the National Association of Elementary School Principals and the Association for Childhood Education International entitled New Views of School and Community *(1973). I include it here for its discussion of teachers, communities, and schools, a subject receiving considerable attention in this era of teacher education and school reform. In this sense, it seems timely.*

Public confidence in our schools continues to decline at an accelerating rate. The growing and serious public discussion of such educational alternatives as free schools and the use of entire cities as schools, as well as provisions for parent vouchers is only one of many indications. In historical terms, these are all rather radical proposals.

A decade of promise, in which billions of new dollars have been expended for education, has borne limited fruit for large numbers of Americans. Not only have too many schools failed to assist children in their learning of basic skills, they have also failed to provide a vision of a humane and sensitive life. And they have not encouraged broad participation in civic and community affairs. The need for change in public education is acknowledged quite broadly (see Goodlad, 1968; Kerensky & Melby, 1971; Martin & Harrison, 1972). Yet the typical response is to suggest a little more of the same thing: a new reading series, more time for mathematics, more grouping of children by some perception of ability. Few people are questioning the assumptions that underlie our existing modes of schooling or the purposes that motivate them; but to do less may not bring about the kinds of changes that are demanded if schools are to regain significant public support and serve more consistently the needs of young people.

15

I would certainly acknowledge that some of the contemporary critiques of schools are exceedingly harsh. Expecting the schools to remake American society, for example, may well be unrealistic. But the issues that critics most frequently raise are more basic, far short of remaking American society.

What could be more basic than the nine-year-old girl who appeared before the Illinois state superintendent of public instruction during one of a series of public hearings on education (*Action Goals*, 1972, p. 2) and said: "I usually receive good grades from teachers I like and poor grades from teachers I don't like. Why can't I have the right to choose my own teachers?" No one at the hearing could answer the question. Illinois State Superintendent Michael Bakalis asked, on the basis of the public hearings: "Can we say that education is adequate when so many of our young people find unenjoyable an experience that should be among the most meaningful in their lives, and when most of our older citizens [cannot return to elementary and secondary schools and] are deprived of the chance to understand our fast changing world?" (*Action Goals*, 1972, p. 7). Bakalis also related in his public statements that the depth of discontent, the overwhelming feeling that the schools were not working, came as a surprise to the educational leadership of the state.

Those who look at education nationally are finding a similar depth of discontent. A day does not pass for me without a letter or telephone call from a parent group—black, Native American, and white, across a broad socioeconomic spectrum—wanting assistance in organizing an alternative school, one that, if necessary, is separate from the public school system. The concerns raised by these parent groups seldom have anything to do with remaking American society; rather, they revolve primarily around their high hopes for their children. Parents are also concerned about the quality of teachers in the schools and their relationships with children, their lifestyle commonality, and their demographic sameness—the fact that they are mostly white and are principally women in the elementary schools and men in the secondary schools. Parents also question the practice of uniform instruction, testing, and tracking; the preoccupation with order and control, credit hours and courses, routines, and schedules; and the schools' seeming lack of commitment to encouraging creativity.

Schools and school personnel are on the defensive. And they should be. They have been less than open in the conduct of their enterprise. The desire to keep parents at arm's length, safely within the confines of the PTA, is only one expression. Other expressions are the narrow manner in which those in schools discuss purposes and the ways they discuss outcomes. Because schools have been essentially closed institutions, they have survived; but they have not prospered in any universal manner. They have often tinkered with change, but they have remained the same. Goodlad and Klein (1970) have written convincingly about how little schools have changed in spite of their rhetoric of change. I am becoming more convinced that they will change only as they become more accessible to varied human resources, materials, and environments as well as to fresh ways of looking at teaching and learning.

I will outline briefly several dimensions of accessibility that have the potential of promoting significant changes in schools. In general, they call on schools to affirm in practice what most educators acknowledge in the vast literature of education and human development.

Increasing Diversity in the Teaching Population

Schools are dominated by teachers who come out of middle-class backgrounds, have wanted to be teachers since the third grade, and are white. There is a need to bring into the schools more minority peoples—black, Chicano, Native American—in order to provide a sense of personal identification to large numbers of minority children and give positive support to political and cultural pluralism. But we need more than ethnic and racial minorities. We also need individuals from more diverse economic, social, and academic backgrounds in schools.

How many individuals with outstanding preparation and experience in mathematics, engineering, medical science, or various laboratory sciences are not available for teaching in schools because they lack traditional credentials—the required courses in education? How many practicing dancers, actors, painters, sculptors, musicians, writers, artisans, and craftspersons can one find associated with elementary schools? Such people have the potential of bringing some new life to schools because of their particular experience. They could also bring an enriching cultural and intellectual dimension to the schools.

Teachers in the schools need intellectual stimulation and fresh—if not unorthodox—perspectives to grow personally and professionally. But schools typically offer little support for such growth. Accessibility to a more diverse teaching population, part-time or full-time, can be such a support system, providing fresh opportunities for ongoing learning. The Teachers and Writers Collaborative[1] in New York City, for example, has stimulated writing among elementary school children who "were not supposed to be able to write." A number of school personnel, after seeing the quality of writing produced by children involved with the Teachers and Writers Collaborative, have said to me: "They should get that kind of writing from children; after all, they are professional writers." And they often say it without thinking about the implications for themselves, children, and schools.

To speak about new people in teaching raises, of course, the issue of certification. It seems clear, at least to me, that changes in the education and employment of school personnel can be brought about most economically and rapidly by changes in licensing requirements. Because social institutions, such as schools, reflect their membership, changes in personnel represent the most lasting and direct way to change the character of institutions. As it is, the laws that govern the certification of teachers neither guarantee that children will be protected from incompetent teachers and administrators nor provide enough incentives to attract the most able on a consistent basis. Furthermore, they tend to keep out many persons who might do a better job than many of those already there.

I recently described to some educators our experience at a Native American community in the Southwest, where an elder was taking walks each morning with small groups of primary-age children. He told them stories of "other days," described the vegetation and its religious significance, and related to the children some of the historical background for various place names. Among the questions I received was: "But the man isn't a qualified teacher. What about the school's liability?" What is a teacher? The Native American elder's real authority (as opposed to the more typical vested authority) is unquestioned. Not a single certified teacher in that community could match his credentials.

To speak of accessibility to new kinds of teachers at a time when a teacher surplus supposedly exists raises additional questions. Many are advocating that fewer individuals be admitted to teacher education programs, that academic standards be raised (which is usually thought about in terms of entrance examinations and grade point averages), and that certification requirements be made more stringent. While such advocacy is understandable, it supports "where we

---

1. The Teachers and Writers Collaborative's address is: 244 Vanderbilt Ave., Brooklyn, NY 11205.

are," not "where we ought to be." Sufficient evidence exists already to show that present practices of selection, collegiate requirements, and awarding credentials keep many people out of the teaching profession. To add other obstacles only intensifies the problem, potentially making schools even more inaccessible to minority peoples for whom traditional selection measures and requirements are still discriminatory, favoring those who come from middle-class backgrounds. And such advocacy fails to acknowledge that large numbers of people who do not now have the required background will not engage in a credential system built around required courses in education even if they have the qualities that might help revitalize the schools.

Drawing on Community People

Closely related to the issue of accessibility to culturally diverse people as teachers is accessibility to parents, to other community people, and to the environment beyond the schoolhouse. Schools that have depended on teachers alone have always been limited by the experience base that teachers bring to their classrooms. Every community has persons with experience who could further enrich life in the schools.

I discussed this point recently with a young teacher-intern who was employed in a small community of 175 people. The young man had a good academic background in mathematics and psychology, but he knew considerably less about grains than the local farmers. He knew far less about machines than the man at the garage. And he did not have the access to the riches of the wildlife refuge that the conservation officer possessed. While he could organize the baking of cookies, he lacked the style and the knowledge of national cuisine of the Japanese woman who had married a local man during his tour of military duty in Japan. This young teacher was in a small rural community; it takes little imagination to see the educational potential of the large human resource base in larger communities.

Opening the school to parents and others in the community increases the opportunities for children to interact with a broader range of adults. It also provides young people more meaningful contact with various lifestyles. Jerome Bruner (1971) addresses that question well, contending that schools are too isolated and are not dealing effectively with the growing reality of lifestyle diversity:

> Could it be that in our stratified and segmented society, our students
> simply do not know about local grocers and their styles, local doctors
> and their styles, local taxi drivers and theirs, local political activists and
> theirs. . . . I really believe our young have become so isolated [in school]
> that they do not know the roles available in society and the variety of
> styles in which they are played. I would urge that we find some way of
> connecting the diversity of the society to the phenomenon of school, to
> keep the latter from becoming so isolated and the former so suspicious.
> (p. 7)

Seeking broad participation may also provide children a more
realistic view of the world of work. Vocational choices are limited
for large numbers of young people because of the attitudes that
schools often foster; for example, that lawyers are more important,
more skilled, than mechanics. It just is not true. But while schools
often invite lawyers to visit schools and share their knowledge, mechanics are not often given the same opportunities or shown the
same level of respect.

Accessibility of the schools to "outside people" also provides
increased opportunities for individualization. For example, parents
and community volunteers can undertake such activities as reading
to children, listening to children read, preparing and assisting in the
use of manipulative and instructional materials, supervising small
groups on field trips related to children's interests, assuming responsibility for various learning centers, and sharing unique cultural backgrounds, hobbies, and work. Such efforts enlarge the potential for parents to relate the home to the school and the school
more directly to the home. Schools typically lack this quality. The
separation of home and school, the isolation of one segment of a
child's life from the other, has contributed significantly to our educational failures.

Another important dimension of such accessibility is the increased possibilities for creating a more responsive educational
community in which individuals can gain a deeper understanding
of schools, become participants in decision making, and develop
more intense commitments to the process of schooling. In many
communities, as schools have become more accessible, parent-
teacher councils are becoming active in shaping the direction and
practice of individual schools. It is surprising that such developments are taking so long. For a nation committed to the practice of
democratic participation, we have shown little capacity to establish
the mechanisms in schools to nurture it.

Involvement in the Community

And what about life beyond the school? The school as a fortress is not only a metaphor; it is real. In too many cases the school has become an institution with a life of its own, rarely impinging on or having much relationship to the world outside. Philip Jackson (1968) observes that

> There is a social intimacy in schools that is unmatched elsewhere in our society. Buses and movie theaters may be more crowded than classrooms, but people rarely stay in such densely populated settings for extended periods of time. While there they usually are not expected to concentrate on work or to interact with each other. Even factory workers are not clustered as closely together as students in a standard classroom. . . . Only in schools do thirty or more people spend several hours each day literally side by side. Once we leave the classroom we seldom again are required to have contact with so many people for so long a time. (p. 8)

The environment beyond the school is clearly too rich to be ignored. Not only can the outside community serve as an excellent base for children to gain significant skills in observing, recording, and interpreting what goes on in their world, it can, in addition, provide teachers with increased opportunities for personal and professional growth. Liza and Casey Murrow, in a marvelous work entitled *Children Come First* (1971), comment on a variety of schools they visited in England that were no longer "inward looking" regarding the use of space:

> They now look beyond the walls of the school itself, and beyond the grounds. . . . Teachers want their children to participate fully in firsthand experience that can be brought into the school. They also realize that the child has another life outside the building which is equally important to his growth. For schools which have opened themselves to learning more about children, the natural step beyond is to take the children into the community. (p. 205)

The movement toward schools without walls in several American cities is an attempt to use the local environment more fully and to develop higher levels of personalization. While it would be good to report that such schools are increasing rapidly, the reality is that they are looked on principally as experiments.

Encouraging Initiative Among Children

It is becoming increasingly evident that children's learning is enhanced if it is centered on a child's own experiences, needs, and interests and if children participate in some of the directions for their own learning. Most schools do not function on the basis of that understanding. The provincial government of Ontario reports in its recent study of schools, *Living and Learning* (1968), that

> At the present time, in most schools, many controlled stipulations must be accepted by everyone who enters their portals. Basically, the school's learning experiences are imposed, involuntary, and structured. The pupil becomes a captive audience from the day of entry. His hours are regulated; his movements in the building and within the classroom are controlled; his right to speak out freely is curtailed. He is subject to countless restrictions about the days to attend, hours to fill, when to talk, where to sit, length of teaching periods, and countless other rules. (p. 54)

Critics of American schools concur. But schools can be more than that. They can be places where children are given back initiative and potency, a real desire to learn. This does not call for any radical thinking. In part it asks only for schools to put into practice what educators commonly assent to intellectually; namely, that learning is a personal matter and varies for different children, proceeds best when children are actively engaged in their own learning, takes place in a variety of environments in and out of the school, and is enhanced in a supportive environment where children and their intentions as learners are taken seriously. Many educators have told me that I make too much out of starting points, children's questions, children's intentions. Yet it seems clear that they are not ends. As Robert King (1971) has said, they are interests that end somewhere,

> either in the area of self-enjoyment, appreciation, or self-development, or in practical results such as the learning of a craft or perhaps the achievement of a desired social action. The interests of the people [students] are not the enemies of real education, they are the essence of it. (p. 12)

Capitalizing on the creative initiatives that young people bring to the learning environment is the teacher's task. Children's initiatives are critical starting points and open up broad learning possibilities, especially in settings in which children are encouraged to ask their own questions rather than waiting to find out from the teacher what questions they ought to ask. This is particularly important if we are concerned about children's having sufficient opportunities to achieve success.

To achieve a success experience, Arthur Jersild (1952) suggests that children need to be reminded more often in school of their ability to be successful. While he believes that in learning more about themselves young people should come to understand their limitations and shortcomings, such learning needs to be real rather than artificial. To understand the lack of dignity afforded to children and the continued climate for failure in the schools, all one has to do is look at the labeling, the separating of children into "bluebirds and buzzards," the *A*s and *F*s, and the large numbers of poor, Chicano, Native American, and black children who have been closed off to learning and hope.

Children's potential for extended learning also increases in an environment where the distinction between work and play is not so sharp. Those who currently write about the need for informality in schools—from Charles Silberman, to Joseph Featherstone, to Lillian Weber, to George Frein—take quite seriously the often quoted statement from the Plowden report (*Children and Their Primary Schools,* 1967): "The distinction between work and play is false, possibly throughout life, certainly in the primary schools" (p. 193). Parents have generally and quite intuitively looked on their children's play activities as central sources for learning. Developmental psychologists such as Jean Piaget also give support to the direct relationship of play and learning. Yet the school syndrome is: "Stop playing. We have to get back to work (learning)."

What are the possibilities for peer teaching? Can children share with each other in ways that are productive to learning? Can older children assist younger children? Can we build in schools an ethos in which cooperation—cooperative learning—is dominant? The evidence is overwhelmingly positive. For peer teaching to function, children need to have supportive access to each other. Mobility and interaction must be valued and facilitated. Closely related to mobility is the degree to which storage systems, for example, are accessible to children. It is important that children know what learning materials are available, where they are stored, and that they have access to them. If children must ask for permission, which usually means waiting, and do not know what is available, they may well lose interest or have limited opportunities for exploring new learning areas.

Supporting Teachers' Initiative

Teachers have too long been intermediaries between curriculum developers and children. Decisions about what subjects will be covered in a given classroom, what books will be used, the nature and style of the evaluations, and the organization of the day are often made by persons outside the classroom, oftentimes by faceless and nameless people. It is little wonder that teachers' enthusiasm for teaching, and for children, tends to decline with experience (Hector, 1971). Classroom teachers need to be decision makers about curriculum and learning. They need to be free from standardized curriculum and basic textbooks, free to respond to the individual interests that children bring to school and to actively participate in the making of a learning community. At a practical level, teachers should be entrusted with keys to the schools in which they teach. It seems wasteful, if not disgraceful, to prevent teachers from being in their "workshop" except at prescribed times.

Needless to say, the plea to support the creative initiatives of teachers is also a plea to relax the pressures of growing numbers of achievement and intelligence tests. That they are instruments contributing to the discouragement that prevails in many schools, characterized by children's growing loss of self-esteem and by self-fulfilling prophecies, is reasonably well documented. That they are in the way of teachers' establishing the kinds of personal relationships with children that make creative learning more possible becomes quite clear as one interacts with teachers.

Another impediment to the creative initiative of teachers is the roles we have defined for them. Those roles have been authoritarian and call for significant detachment. They have an external, distanced quality. "Don't smile until Christmas" is a common admonition that greets too many new teachers. Richard Foster, superintendent of schools in Berkeley, California, comments that teachers often ask him: "When I start to teach, should I start tough and get easy, or should I start easy and get tough?" Foster replies, "Why don't you start? Why don't you be you?" (quoted in Olson, 1968, p. 40). It ought to be as simple as that! Teachers need opportunities to be different, to risk alternative directions in the ways they meet children and the community. Teachers find it easier to be themselves as they move off center stage and create more open, diverse learning environments.

One experienced teacher who had returned to our program at the

University of North Dakota to complete her baccalaureate degree expressed her first month's frustration in this way: "People around here continually ask me about my personal interests. Of course I have interests; they are things I engage in after five o'clock. I came here to learn more about teaching reading, writing, and arithmetic." Such an attitude is not uncommon among teachers pursuing advanced work or some form of inservice training. A teacher's personal interests, though, ought to be integral to his or her life in the classroom. Classrooms that are not accessible to such interests will not sustain the continued extension of a teacher's learning. And teachers who are not learners will not foster the kind of learning in classrooms that is possible and demanded if schools are to thrive.

Enabling Principals to Exert Leadership

Much of what I have said about teachers is also true of principals. If they are not active participants in the life of the classrooms, maintaining their enthusiasm for children and learning, they will not be in a good position to exercise educational leadership. Educational leadership is not promoted in settings in which the principal is outside, acting as an intermediary between a central administration and teachers and between parents and teachers. The organizational pattern of many school systems is such, though, that principals cannot be decision makers. Establishing a unique school that adapts itself to the particular community it serves rather than the district as a whole is unusual. Individual schools should be more autonomous than they are. To the degree that principals and their schools have little independence, their potential for educational leadership is diminished and the potential for school reform is blunted.

One of the primary tasks of principals is to create a climate in which teachers, children, and parents make significant contributions to the life of the school. In this sense they are facilitators of group process. And the goal of group process is to assist teachers in their personal and professional growth, to provide support and encouragement for their efforts at change, and to encourage their role as disseminators of ideas, which means their staying alert to what is happening educationally beyond the school.

Surveys relating to how principals use their time continually report that administrative-managerial tasks are dominant. Yet human leadership is more critical; it provides encouragement to children, parents, and teachers. Managerial leadership, on the other hand, tends to promote discouragement.

Goethe wrote: "Everything has been thought of before, but the difficulty is to think of it again." As our knowledge about learning increases, much of the longstanding education literature, based largely on a variety of personal experiences, feelings, and intuition, is finding legitimacy again. To affirm in practice what we now know or feel to be true will not be a simple task in our overorganized, curriculum-heavy schools, but some new beginnings can surely be made. The plea for accessibility is a plea for some fresh beginnings—a base for educational renewal.

CHAPTER THREE

A Perspective on Educational Equity

This paper was prepared initially for a ceremony in Ann Arbor, Michigan (Spring 1984), to honor the twenty Michigan schools that had received Office of Education awards for excellence. It was modified for a presentation to students and faculty at the University of North Dakota in April 1985 and later published in Insights *(May 1985) and in* Challenge & Responsibility *(Association for Supervision and Curriculum Development, 1987). It was meant as a partial response to many of the education reports of the 1980s that tended to be quite silent on longstanding equity concerns.*

We live in an age of "educational reform," a time in which "improving the quality of our schools" is a matter receiving great public attention. Such a focus is salutary. Our children, young people, and their communities need and deserve better schools—settings with thoughtful, carefully articulated purposes; committed, intellectually alert teachers and administrators; powerful literacy programs; expansive curricula; high expectations; close connections to important community resources; and more open and accessible public accountability procedures.

But despite the many constructive hopes and possibilities, there are some disturbing elements in the reform discourse; namely, a language and related public policy of constraint, limits, competition, and punitiveness, as well as an enlarging pessimism about our increasingly pluralistic society. Such negative themes may well assume precedence if not vigorously challenged by every person who cares deeply about children, schools, and communities. I will share in this paper some of what I view as the troublesome side of the current reform effort, my way of easing into a perspective on educational equity, a subject being given too little attention.

Historical Background

I believe it is important to begin with a brief historical excursion. Implicit in *A Nation at Risk* (National Commission, 1983), among other recent education reports, and given considerable encouragement in the popular media as well, is the belief that schools were once uniformly better than they are today, that there was at some earlier time—certainly before 1960—an idyllic age in which everyone learned to read and write effectively, studied physics and foreign languages, and gained a strong historical and cultural background. That is clearly a distorted history in need of constant challenge. It just was not the case that everyone learned to read and write effectively. And at its peak, physics was only studied by a small percentage of high school seniors. Further, efforts to promote citizenship education suffered as much at the turn of the century as today. More importantly, however, in relation to the past, we should feel particularly obligated to ask how many blacks, Native Americans, children of the poor, immigrant and cultural minorities, children with special needs were in the schools in 1900, 1920, 1940, 1960. There was large-scale *de facto* as well as *de jure* exclusion well into the 1950s, in spite of our longstanding rhetoric of democratic education. And for most of these groups, prejudice, misplacement, and miseducation have been more the case than not. However one wishes to rationalize about these earlier exclusion-dominant, prejudice-oriented years, they ought *never* to receive the accolade "idyllic." They do not represent models to which we should now aspire.

Related to this thread about an idyllic past is the complementary belief that we tried equity in the 1960s and early 1970s and it cost quality. In many ways this belief and its related public policy discourse represents a serious and unacceptable attack on the Civil Rights movement of the 1960s and the corresponding desire for a truly democratic society. Title I and Head Start worked. Desegregation was right. Nutrition and health programs were needed. Attention to curriculum relevance was logical. Women's equality was long overdue. But the denigration of these reforms has become a constant theme of many educational leaders and public officials.

Secretary of Education William Bennett, for example, characterizes the 1960s as a time when *all* standards fell, when schools "lost their way." He makes this point quite forcefully in his report on the humanities and higher education (1984), issued a year before he assumed his cabinet position. While not a report on elementary and secondary schools, its implications are closely connected. Bennett suggests, for example, that the 1960s inclusion of ethnic, non-Western, and women's literature and history is one of the important reasons for the decline of the humanities and a loss of "the best that has been said, thought, written and otherwise expressed about the human experience" (p. 3). He is critical in this report of "our eagerness to assert the virtues of pluralism" (p. 29). Bennett has continued, as secretary of education, to keep such beliefs in high profile.

To suggest that these efforts at inclusion were the reasons for some mythical loss of quality is to pose a false problem. To state, as many educational and political leaders do, that equity and quality are competing goals or distinct formulations is a massive abuse of our social language. The 1960s effort to include all children, young people, and their families in the schools has not yet been completed. In spite of some significant gains, we have, unfortunately, a very long way to go to achieve the longstanding promise of universalism. For every school with a universalist commitment there are hundreds of others in which such commitments have been forgotten or compromised.

Some of the Problems

In relation to universalism, the percentage of young people of high school age completing high school declined annually from 1972 to 1983, representing a major shift of direction after a century of keeping more students through high school graduation. The percentage of high school students graduating reached its peak in 1967 (76.7%), with that percentage remaining relatively stable until 1972. The overall percentage of graduates is now below 72; and in some of our minority communities, the completion rate is well below 40 percent. I have shed a number of tears during the last year reading dropout reports from Chicago, Boston, New York, and Los Angeles. Unfortunately, these reports get little constructive public policy attention. It is almost as if such dropout rates are to be expected, almost as if the lives of the young people involved do not matter. In light of dropout statistics, and our past neglect, how ought we to react when hearing about a state's enlarging greatly its graduation requirements when its schools are already losing a very large number of its students *before* graduation?

My home state, North Dakota, and our neighboring state of Minnesota have long led the nation in the numbers of their students who complete high school. Their 90+ percent figures are the subject of pride and positive comment in the media. But who are those who do not complete high school in North Dakota and Minnesota (and in other states with similarly high graduation rates)? And who are those who stay in school but struggle with learning, who lack the skills and knowledge to go on successfully to a full range of postsecondary educational settings? Race and social class are undoubtedly powerful factors in the educational success of students in these states, as they are elsewhere. But in these apparently more stable, more favorable settings, the effects of social and economic class are not often part of the ongoing discourse.

In settings where 85–90 percent of young people complete high school, too little time is spent asking about the 10–15 percent who do not. I can assure you, though, that they look a great deal like the 40–50 percent who do not complete high school in New York City and Boston and Los Angeles and Chicago. We speak with pride in North Dakota, as I know people do in many other places, about "our advanced placement programs" and "our superior math and science and arts programs" without asking often enough about the students who are and are not represented in them. We should be more troubled than we are when we see only one woman for every eight men, or one black or Hispanic for every ten whites in a calculus class, or, as was shown in Michigan State University research (Bell, 1979), that ninth grade general math classes are filled with minority students and white females.

What seems to characterize the proposals aimed at this 1980s "return to quality" reform? We are seeing more testing mechanisms, more state curriculum requirements that seek greater standardization, increased centralization regarding text and materials selection, time-on-task mandates that foster increased minutes of worksheets, pedagogical admonitions that equate discrete skills with whole meaning, and rule making that confuses the constructs of discipline and responsibility. Such directions have not in the past brought much improvement to the schools, and there is no reason to believe that the future will be different. Such regulatory efforts will surely discourage those young men and women most intellectually able and socially committed from considering teaching at a time when the demand for teachers is growing. And they will also demoralize large numbers of those thoughtful teachers we most need to continue in the schools. Over the long run, they will most likely discourage students and parents as well.

How should we respond to issues relating to fairness, access, and economic well-being, issues that are receiving too little attention in the discourse of educational reform? For example, only 18 percent of those who qualify for Head Start services are being served in spite of the carefully researched and reported benefits. Bilingual programs, guaranteed by legal and legislative actions, serve fewer than 25 percent who qualify. Special education support still does not reach a large percentage of those who need such services. And within special education there is the paradox of blacks and other cultural minorities being overplaced through misclassification, thus unnecessarily straining an already underfinanced system. Black students, for example, are about four times as likely as white students to be in a class for the mentally retarded or emotionally disturbed. Why is this not understood as a problem within the schools? Why do teachers, counselors, and school administrators not wonder how such discrepancies could happen?

Title I services, which have proven successful in many realms of school achievement, reach just over 50 percent of those eligible. And very few secondary students receive any assistance from Title I. Further, in regard to Title I, the requirements for parent advisory councils, a vehicle for encouraging parents to take an important role in the substance of their children's education, have been relaxed significantly, seen within this current national administration as burdensome and unnecessary. Even our states are beginning to drop parent advisory requirements in their compensatory programs.

Vigorous enforcement of the Civil Rights Act and of Title IX has virtually come to an end. With the loss of women's equity coordinators, for example, the related curricular efforts of the early to mid-1970s have virtually collapsed. Enormous inequities of resources and curriculum exist between school districts and in schools within school districts. Anyone taking time to visit diverse schools—an activity almost always enlightening—will notice quickly the enormous differences in the chemistry labs, libraries, and general aesthetic character of the schools. Overall services for children—nutrition, child care, housing—are more inadequate than they have been since the years of the Great Depression. Females are still heavily concentrated in vocational programs aimed at the lowest-paying jobs in our economy, contributing to the increasing feminization of poverty. Tracking mechanisms that have long worked against the interests of those most vulnerable in the schools have expanded, and new sources of exclusion are being encouraged in the name of quality. These are critical issues—tests of our commitment to equity, pluralism, and social democracy.

Children at Risk

In regard to this democratic commitment, my experience in helping put together *Barriers to Excellence: Our Children at Risk* (1985) is pertinent. The report is based to a large degree on the testimony of teachers, school administrators, students, parents, and political leaders.

At our first hearing in Boston, a witness urged us to ask ourselves one question: "Which children matter and to whom?" We tried to apply this critical question throughout our inquiry and came to the conclusion that large numbers of children do not matter enough to too many of those who set the educational and economic policies of this nation and its states and localities. Minority children, it seems, do not matter as much as nonminority children; poor children are considered less important than nonpoor children. Non-English-speaking children are not as important as English-speaking children; and girls matter less than boys. Most educators tend, in the press of their educational lives, to see the schools differently. But how are different conclusions really possible?

A young man in New York City testified as follows:

> I hated the school. It was overcrowded; teachers didn't care; students walked out and acted up and no one did anything to help the situation. I never knew who my counselor was, and he wasn't available for me. In the year that I attended, I saw him once about working papers. One 10-minute interview period. That was all. After awhile, I began spending my time sleeping in class or walking the halls. Finally, I decided to hang out on the streets. I did this for two years. During this entire time, I received about three cards in the mail asking where I was. Luckily, I always got the mail before anyone in my family did. That was it. End of school. (*Barriers to Excellence*, pp. 2–3)

That young man's story proved to be fairly common in many urban communities.

There are a large number of young people in Boston who are on the school rolls but have never been seen and have never been contacted. The argument is that they are 16 years of age and "we have no legal responsibility to make sure they are in school." But what of the moral responsibility?

In Massachusetts, a teacher reported to us that when she tried to get enough textbooks for all of her students, she was told to have students share the books because half the class would leave anyway. Still another teacher, whose principal responsibility was to teach writing, told us her school's policy was to hand out half-sheets of paper to students, no matter what the assignment. She did not understand how she could expect her students to take writing seriously if the initial message to them was they would not have more than a half-page worth to say anyway. But she was told often, sometimes even directly, not to have expectations greater than this.

A parent who described herself as "an average middle-class citizen" of Seattle told us of her reaction to the gifted option program established in that city—a program that drained off a fairly large number of students from each of the neighborhood schools. It was a powerful statement given with great passion and corroborated by several other white, middle-class women.

> Every time I read, or hear, how much somebody loves the Seattle School District, how they love the special program their child is enrolled in, how they applaud the job of educating the school district is doing, I don't have to read any further. I know the next sentence will read, "My child is enrolled in the 'gifted' program. . . ." No one with a child in a nongifted classroom in Seattle, with one or two exceptions, would ever think of writing such a letter of praise. (*Barriers to Excellence*, p. 21)

She concluded: "If the regular classroom is not good enough for the gifted, perhaps it is not good enough for those left in it either" (p. 21). I tend to agree with such a conclusion. I have yet to observe an activity in a "gifted classroom" or specialized magnet school that could not easily be accessible to *all* children. And *all* children should be our focus of attention.

Others in Seattle also talked about the depressing effects the "creaming" of kids (and parents)—mostly white and middle class—has had on the regular schools. The parent I quoted above asked: "What are my children—all in the gifted magnet that is almost exclusively white and middle class—learning about the values of democracy?" (p. 22). But how often do we talk in schools about democracy? It seems that democracy is a radical concept in American schools.

A number of witnesses noted how little is done in most schools to retain or bring back pregnant or parenting teens, either in terms of providing support services or creating a more welcoming school climate. As one presenter testified: "Even if she is granted medical maternity leave, she will probably fall behind in her studies . . . because home tutoring is not readily accessible and schools for pregnant girls do not have a full curriculum" (p. 23).

Lack of daycare also appears to be a principal reason teen parents have difficulty returning to school. With child care sporadic or uncertain, many of those who do return are unable to meet the attendance requirements and end up suspended from school. The director of a continuing-education program for girls in Michigan noted that "teens returning to school after delivery fear being judged immoral, delinquent, or promiscuous by school personnel" (p. 23). Already frightened at the prospect of being different and of not fitting into a classroom situation, these young women often lose heart and stay at home. As a social worker in Chicago put it: "When there are problems with reregistering and when administrative officials at the school are not supportive, it is hard to feel wanted" (p. 23).

In effect, many of our schools have all but written off this population of young women. Having allocated few resources, schools offer little help once a student becomes a young parent. The negative effects on children and the society are too large for such ambivalence and lack of support.

What else did we learn, relearn, get pushed to comprehend once more? The kaleidoscopic nature of what follows reflects more of what we heard and had to think about again:

- The average child from a family whose income is in the top quarter of the income range gets four years more schooling than the average child whose family income is in the bottom quarter; this gap has remained rather static for several decades.
- In 1977, 50% of all black high school graduates went to college. In 1981 the rate had fallen to 40%, and in October 1982 it fell to 36%. The percentage for whites has continued at between 51 and 54%.

Thirty years after the *Brown* v. *Board of Education* decision:

- Fully 62.9% of black students attend predominantly minority schools.
- Only 8.5% of all teachers are minorities—and this number is declining.

- At the high school level, blacks are suspended three times as often as whites; while minority students comprise about 25% of the school population, they constitute about 40% of all suspended and expelled students.
- The national dropout rate for blacks in high schools is nearly twice that of whites.

Women face considerable educational and economic discrimination. By the time they reach young adulthood, females are often at a disadvantage relative to males in basic skills, in academic options and aspirations, in vocational and career opportunities, and in anticipated economic security.

- Vocational education programs remain overwhelmingly segregated by sex, with females clustered in those programs that prepare them for the lowest-paying jobs. Females comprise 92% of those studying to be secretaries or cosmetologists but only 5% of those in electrical technology.
- Women are less likely than men to complete four years of college.
- At all educational levels, women have higher unemployment rates than men.
- Women college graduates on the average earn less than men with an eighth-grade education. The average woman worker earns about 59% of what a man does, even when both work full-time; minority women earn less than any other group of workers. (Women in the workplace, by the way, were doing about as well or better in 1882.)
- Pregnancy is the major known cause of dropping out of school among school-age females. Three-fifths of women at or below the poverty level in 1982 were high school dropouts.

School finance has long been a major issue. The *Serrano* case in California in the early 1970s brought the issue of fiscal inequity to the level of critical public discourse. Yet enormous inequities persist.

- Funding varies widely among states. In 1982, New York spent $2,769 per pupil, while Mississippi spent $1,685.
- Funding varies widely within states as well. In Massachusetts, for example, annual per-pupil spending reaches a high of $5,013 in Roe and a low of $1,637 in Athol. In Texas, the top

100 districts spend on average four times more per child than the bottom 100 school districts. Some school districts spend two or three times as much as do neighboring districts. This sort of inequity is repeated in many other states.

Conclusion

The need for difficult questions to be raised is great. This is not to say that all that appears negative is consciously or overtly pernicious. Nor does it say that many of the issues that I have outlined are not being seriously addressed in many settings by thoughtful and courageous persons. Nonetheless, we have far to go to assure a democratic, fully equitable, and accessible system of education. But we will not get there unless we continue to raise our voices and keep our commitments vital—asking hard questions, challenging simple answers, creating and risking the implementation of new structures.

Much of what I have said here has a negative quality. That was purposeful. I presented it because it represents a dimension of American education that has been put aside by too many—forgotten in the glow of talk about standards, quality, and excellence.

Increasingly I meet individuals who argue that the quality we need may well have to come at the expense of a commitment to a fully equitable and democratic system of education. I refuse to accept that. It seems that many of us in education have become spectators: voicing too few concerns about the loss of minority teachers to the ax of some technical formulation of competence; or watching kindergartners in record numbers being held back and more students failing to complete high school than has been the case for two decades; or accepting funds for more specialized schools for the privileged while inadequate funding is the general rule; or spending even more money on testing mechanisms when we cannot provide the funds necessary to support bilingual education at minimal levels; or developing larger statewide mandates that diminish even further the potential of individual schools and their teachers, parents, and students for becoming sufficiently empowered to develop responsible programs; or choosing not to protest very loudly the loss of arts funds or library resources or jobs programs. We need to be more than spectators. We need to encourage louder voices from many more of our school administrators, teachers, students, and parents. All need to be more powerful advocates for educational and social equity. We cannot continue as we are.

CHAPTER FOUR

Effective Schools, Teaching, and Learning

Originally a talk at the Minnesota State Conference on Leadership in Special Education in November 1982, this paper was later published in Insights *(April 1983) and* Outlook *(Winter 1983). In large measure it represented a response to the then growing popularity of the Effective Schools movement and its formulas for school improvement. My belief then, as now, is that this movement has contributed to the narrowing of education, that it does not inspire teachers or students.*

We in education have long had an unrequited love affair with a science of sorts, leading us to search for "the one best system," that particular technology that we hope will assure a closer match between the very large expectations we have set for education and the ever-present realities. This orientation was given added strength in the late 1960s and early 1970s by both James Coleman (1966) and Christopher Jencks (1972), who challenged longstanding notions about the value of schools, especially in relation to the poor and minorities. While most thoughtful individuals were able to dismiss the Coleman/Jencks line of work fairly easily, having considerable observational data that were contradictory, there were others who took it as a challenge for additional research. The Effective-Schools research, that search for schools where poor and minority children were successful, is one outgrowth. The prescriptions growing out of that research represent, in many respects, the new technology, the fresh definers of current educational discourse, the guiding outline of a burgeoning literature. But, in spite of the relative simplicity of the message, there *are* tensions, a number of which I shall discuss here.

As a way of engaging the challenge of the Effective-Schools literature, I will begin with an assertion about teachers and then make use of the 1960s as a cultural benchmark for commenting on our current situation. This may, at the outset, appear somewhat removed from my topic, but its connection should become more clear as my concerns are more fully developed.

I continue to believe that teachers, not programs, make the critical difference in schools. The higher the quality of teachers—intellectually, socially, academically, and morally—the greater the potential for schools to be successful with children and young people. That may be conventional wisdom, but I will argue that many of our current conceptions of school organization and practice, as well as what appears philosophically to be emerging from much of the Effective-Schools research, have qualities that tend to impede our progress in the directions such conventional wisdom calls for. This perspective should be kept in mind as I proceed now to construct a personal, and largely autobiographical, context within which to place the current discourse about Effective Schools.

The Watershed Years: A Personal Perspective

I will begin with the 1960s, inasmuch as this decade is viewed in a number of ways as a benchmark for much of the current discourse. Just as importantly, however, it represents for me my entry into the world of teacher education and a more conscious examination of teachers *in* schools and society.

I have come to view the 1960s as a cultural watershed, a decade to measure events against. It was clearly a period in which change was visible, when longstanding values as well as social, political, and economic beliefs were under challenge. In the aftermath, which is our present, this decade is seen, not unsurprisingly, as generative as well as degenerate, a flowering as well as an aberration of our culture. The expansion of political democracy and common schools in the 1830s and 1840s, the populist revival of the 1880s and 1890s, and the social revolution associated with the early twentieth century were viewed similarly. I cite these earlier progressive reform periods that affected schools, values, literature, the arts, and popular culture as a way of suggesting that the years of the 1960s, rather than being unique, were part of a longstanding strand within the American experience. The ethos of the 1960s cannot be dismissed, as many would like to do; and these years likely will not be the last such progressive benchmark period in our history.

The 1960s were a time when commitments to equal educational opportunity in all areas of human endeavor were high and when large numbers of people of *all* ages believed that through their individual and collective efforts the quality of life in their communities and in the country as a whole could be improved. It was a time when cultural pluralism—diversity in the broadest sense—as a process for active commitment and participation became an understandable goal and when significant political, social, and educational reform appeared possible. Such beliefs are under enormous challenge today. And, disappointingly, the response is rather impotent.

I was especially encouraged by many of the young people who entered education in the 1960s, individuals who genuinely believed that within the schools there would be support for creative attention to the social and intellectual needs of children and young people, room for significant integration of academic and community interests, education in the broadest sense rather than schooling as it is often defined. The Peace Corps in those years attracted similarly motivated individuals.

We still have at our various institutions many fine young men and women preparing for careers in teaching, and my purpose is not to suggest otherwise; however, they tend now, it seems, to be less diverse in their backgrounds, interests, and talents. There are many fewer dancers, artists, musicians, philosophers, poets, and social activists, as well as National Merit Scholars. And how many of those socially and intellectually alive 1960s people remained in teaching? Obviously many did—but too many, unfortunately, did not. I have met with many of our University of North Dakota graduates from those years who left teaching for a wide range of alternative careers. Most have continued their social and political commitments and maintain, as well, their broad array of avocational interests. But teaching lost its attraction for them as they perceived testing, tracking, labeling, a narrowing and distancing—essentially technical approaches to education—gaining dominance.

In the fall of 1980, the *Boston Globe* carried an education feature on Master of Arts in Teaching (MAT) graduates. Needless to say, the feature spoke to me, reminding me of the interactions I was having with our own graduates who had left teaching. These MATs, essentially 1960s and early 1970s graduates of Harvard, Yale, Dartmouth, Wesleyan, and Columbia, were described as bright, articulate, energetic young people with high ideals and considerable commitment—persons who symbolized the 1960s interest in diversity and educational reform. That few were left in schools in 1980 was, for the writer of the feature, a visible sign that schools had lost a good deal of their intellectual base. I heard from, and interacted with, many public school parents who read the article. They were eloquent in their belief that children had been abandoned by too many bright and socially committed young people and were faced increasingly with technicians who appeared uninterested in their struggles to learn. In following the educational literature of the last few years, one would come to believe that technicians were desired, that education, the larger hope engendered by our culture, was again giving way to schooling, a minimalist position.

During the past couple of years, I have been rereading a good deal of the progressive literature—in large measure articles, books, and diaries from the 1830–1940 period, much of it written by classroom teachers or close observers of classrooms. While this literature is not representative of the schools in the largest sense, it is part of the fuller view of education that seems always somehow to remain alive. I am impressed by the richness and clarity of the language in these accounts, by the obvious love and familiarity of the writers with a breadth of classical and contemporary literature and thought, by the quality of teachers' expectations for young people and that of the teaching-learning activities they supported. For example, not only was Caroline Pratt, a producer of much of this literature, an educator, a keen observer of children's development, a curriculum builder and researcher, she was also a social reformer. There were many like her—Bronson Alcott, Horace Mann, Susan Blow, Francis Parker, Lelia Partridge, John Dewey, Margaret Naumberg, Marietta Johnson, Ella Flagg Young, Lucy Sprague Mitchell, Julia Weber Gordon, and Myles Horton, to mention just a very small number of persons about whom no one would build a caricature of blandness and limited intellectualism. The 1960s produced a similar spirit and sense of intellectual ferment, a reaffirmation of our best definitions of a powerful education.

During this past year, and I believe it relates, I had occasion to engage in a discussion with Dorothy Ross, a University of Virginia social historian, about some research she was doing on the social sciences and higher education. She asked me if I would hazard a guess about the fields that attracted the largest share of Harvard College graduates during the 1915–1920 period. Knowing that this represented a major reform period in American life, I suggested that education and social services were likely high on the list. In fact, they were near the top and ahead of law. Not surprisingly, education and the social services now hardly show up as preferences for graduates of Harvard College. The same would be the case for graduates of similar institutions, public and private, across the country. I take no joy from this, since I do not believe it bodes well for children and young people in schools.

Are the schools becoming, as they have at other times, possibly even unwittingly, places that discourage, as many of our 1960s graduates suggest, professionalism in its more traditional and progressive forms? While I am not prepared to accept this formulation in any absolute sense, in part because I know of too many places where it is not the case, I believe that there are a number of discouraging tendencies, pressures, practices, and conditions that do not, in fact, encourage the most intellectually able to go into or remain in teaching.

In relation to the foregoing, Gerald Grant (1981) suggests that technical values have come to dominate schools—teachers and administrators who know how to use various management and testing systems being more valued than persons of significant intellect, persons willing to follow prescriptions being more valued than persons who wish to develop their own curricula. My experience suggests he is correct.

As an illustration of this, Frank Smith, a psycholinguist of note, tells the following story of his work with reading specialists (cited by Meier in Perrone, 1975). It parallels some of my own recent experience with a group of special educators. It relates to his account of a child presented with the passage "He lives in a house." One child read the sentence as "He lives in an apartment," while a second read it as "He lives in a horse." Asking if either of the children might be having difficulty with reading, Smith found that many of the specialists thought the first was having the most difficulty. The second, after all, was off by only one consonant, while the first was off by an entire word. Unfortunately, such a view of reading is being increasingly supported. It is certainly the orientation of most of the programs I see being used with children labeled learning-disabled or language-deficient. It clearly speaks to the power of our technical approach to education.

In relation to this growing attachment to technical considerations in educational practice, the special education field has made a particularly heavy investment that needs critical review. The testing/clinical prescription apparatus is a particularly potent example. Psychological tests, projective tests, skills tests, and aptitude tests have in many cases become the principal arsenal of special educators. By gaining a monopoly on the interpretive language and the vested authority accompanying this language, special educators have too often set themselves apart from their colleagues in schools. But toward what ends? Why, for example, did it take poor Mexican-American parents in Santa Ana, California, to ask why so many Mexican-American and black children were in educable mentally retarded (EMR) classes—three to five times their actual percentages in the schools? Why did it not occur to the professional special educators that something might be awry in the testing, interpretation, and placement procedures. Why did it take parents in the more recent *Larry P.* case to challenge the continuing use of an IQ test score as the principal base for EMR placement in San Francisco? Again, why was the lead not taken by special educators? Surely they had to know that something was wrong. When one is tied too closely to elaborate placement procedures emanating from some distant source—whether the federal government, state government, or school district office—it is very difficult to be thoughtful instigators of discussion about what it means to grow and learn, advocates for careful observation and interaction, or students of content and process, teaching and learning, system and program. But that is increasingly the pattern.

Schooling or Education?

We are at present in the midst of an unparalleled schooling, rather than education, race. Such phrases as *direct instruction, time on task, high basic skills expectations, management systems,* and *competency testing* are becoming the dominant definers of the current discourse. They reflect the ascendancy of a technical rather than a liberating view of schools and education.

The most potent school-related descriptor today is *Effective Schools,* a construct associated with the research on Effective Schools carried out by Wilbur Brookover (1979), Ron Edmonds (1979), Barak Rosenshine (1979), and Michael Rutter (1979) and described quite extensively by Beverly Caffee-Glen (1981), Richard Hersch (1981), and Donald Medley (1979), among others. Almost every journal in education has given space to this formulation in the last two years. To see it in print and hear it discussed, one would think that after centuries of fumbling about, we now know scientifically what makes schools work—ergo, it should be fairly easy to make every school work. (Now I am using the advocates' language rather than my own.)

The Effective-Schools literature has a lot of appeal: it grows out of the dominant forms of social science research; it provides unambiguous direction and, hence, appears authoritative; it encourages many who have lost hope in the schools to hope again; it seems congruent with much of the emphasis on the schools as centers for maintaining minimum levels of achievement in basic skills (another kind of safety net); it stresses orderliness, uniformity, and adherence—values viewed by many as paramount to societal progress; and it reasserts the importance of hierarchical leadership. But, however appealing, simple, and straightforward—and I personally support its reaffirmation of the importance of individual schools as the focus for change and of the critical nature of purposefulness, high expectations, and curriculum continuity—it is, nonetheless, a strange script. I have difficulty reading it, as it has no voice for me. Potent in its assertions, it is weak in its descriptive qualities.

In *Fifteen Thousand Hours*, for example, Rutter (1979), whose work is a bit more appealing than most, reports that "the provision of school outings was significantly correlated with examination success" (p. 127) but neglects to produce *any* description of the circumstances, purposes, or length of the outings; likewise, he does not mention whether they related to what was being studied or whether they were followed up. It is as if the content did not matter. Seldom in this literature do we learn about the content of curriculum. Further, we receive little acknowledgment of the complexity of schools, communities, teaching, and learning, an oversight that I fear encourages too many educators to view school improvement as little more than the application of a five-step formula that usually begins with a "strong principal." Knowing that the remaining themes are familiar—orderly school climate; focus on academic, basic skills instruction; time on task; homework; direct teaching; clear academic goals; carefully sequenced, generally predetermined curricula—I'll comment on some of the challenges of this particular wave of thought to education, broadly defined, and to my interest in assuring that teaching is interesting, engaging, intellectually stimulating, and attractive to the most thoughtful, intellectually alive, committed persons among us. If teaching is not all of this, children and their communities will get far less than they deserve.

Carl Bereiter (1972) provides a glimpse into our current tension. His essential message is that skill training and custodial care are the only legitimate functions of elementary schools—that we need to rid ourselves of the belief that schools can educate. Bereiter, it must be noted, argued his case quite persuasively, just as those currently promoting Effective Schools do.

Beverly Caffee-Glen (1981), a major Effective-Schools analyst, writes: "Whether or not the emphasis on the narrow range of school skills measurable by multiple-choice tests is correct, Effective Schools focus on raising test scores" (p. 55). Effective Schools, indeed, focus their energy on instruction and learning in those areas measured by tests. That is how they define *all* growth in learning. I do not find this particularly uplifting. School districts almost everywhere—Boston, New York, Richmond, Des Moines—are reporting enormous test-score gains over the past two years (and, by the way, on fewer real dollars). Has the ability of children to read, as reading is commonly understood in the culture at large, actually improved by 30–40 percent—which are the kinds of increases being reported? Or are we seeing little more than what we would expect from situations where programs are geared heavily to the tests? What will it be like when every school district in America reports above-average test scores? Will we then say we have succeeded in the educational arena? Or will we still talk about having a literacy problem? Thinking more about testing, how should we respond to the National Assessment of Educational Progress (1981) report that students are scoring better on basic skills tests in reading/language arts but are declining in what are being called higher-level skills—analysis, inference, critical thought? Analysts of this data suggest that so much instructional activity is geared toward the requirements of a vast array of narrowly formulated multiple-choice tests that such a result should have been anticipated. Could we really have expected any more?

There is another strain within the Effective-Schools literature that also warrants attention—essentially the social-class, ethnic-racial differentiations.

Donald Medley (1979) reports that effective teachers of lower socio-economic status children ask more low level questions—facts, names, dates; are less likely to pick up and amplify students responses; have fewer student initiated questions and comments and give less feedback on student questions. He claims further that effective teachers devote most of their time to large group or whole group instruction. George Cureton (1978) agrees, noting that "strongly teacher centered learning environments are most effective for poor children" (p. 754). And Rosenshine (1979), with another dose of corroboration, concludes that "in the elementary grades, effectiveness comes with questions that are at a low cognitive level" (p. 38). Is there anything uplifting about this, even if test scores increase?

In related research discussed by Deborah Meier (1980), researchers differentiated between instruction for the middle classes and for the poor. Schools for the middle classes had a lot of what most of us have supported for all children—challenge, a wide assortment of materials, individualization, open-ended questions, analysis and synthesis, trade books, art and music. Schools for the poor, by contrast, featured low-level questions, group instruction, a narrow range of materials, carefully sequenced step-by-step reading materials, and so forth. To maintain that certain kinds of education are appropriate—even effective—for certain classes of children and not for others is not particularly inspiring; it might even be immoral, however simple and straightforward, whether put forth by persons of liberal or conservative persuasion. Disastrously, such views have helped support an increasing array of tracking mechanisms in schools. We all know where the best resources go in these tracking activities. That tracking works to the detriment of *all* students is not often acknowledged, though careful observational research carried out by Mary Metz (1982) in Milwaukee makes this point quite clearly.

What does not make a difference in the Effective-Schools research? The variables that *did not* relate to school effectiveness as determined by test-score measurements are, among others, the size of the school, variations in class size, age and experience of teachers, internal forms of organization, amount of teacher preparation time, staying with the same children for more than a year, and level of parent participation. One cannot spend a lot of time in schools and really believe that these are not qualitatively significant. One also has to know that such conclusions are likely to work against many of our more valued commitments. New regulations written for Title I, for example, eliminate most of the requirements relating to parents. Such decisions are buttressed by some of the Effective-Schools research.

And what about issues that were not examined in the Effective-Schools research and not discussed substantially in the related literature—issues that apparently were not considered consequential even though I would argue that they are critical issues if education rather than schooling is viewed as paramount? How one views childhood is not considered. Is childhood viewed as important, a time for exploration, evoking memory, imagining, gathering, and playing? If teachers in a school consider childhood as a unique, important period of time, might they not be expected to act in particular ways? Should they? Does it even matter what teachers' beliefs are? Is it important in a school to have music, art, drama, dance, storytelling, opportunities for creative endeavor, support for expressing feelings, searching for personal meanings? Such curricular issues are apparently of little consequence for Effective Schools. Does it matter whether students have intense interest in what they do or whether interests serve as starting points for curriculum development or whether significant choice is available? Apparently not. How important is the physical environment, its aesthetic qualities? Not very important. Is the content being studied particularly critical? Are trade books more or less valued than basal readers? How significant is it to have attribute blocks, cuisinaire rods, sand or water, games, diverse literature? Does it matter very much whether what one studies in social studies is related to what one studies in language arts or science? Is there concern about the quality of children's work, the stories and poems they write, the paintings they create, the questions they ask? Is it important to have children engage in cooperative learning activities, to socialize?[1]

Note that despite the length and scope of this list, I have only touched the surface of activities, directions, and qualities that have *not* been considered important to Effective Schools, which is why I find it to be such a contentless literature. This recognition has given me greater encouragement to go back again to that earlier progressive literature. It has also caused me to be more vigorous in my encouragement of careful descriptions of practice written by current classroom teachers and observers, unfettered by any predetermined construct.

If education, as I have outlined it, rather than schooling, were the critical concern, much of the current discourse would assume a different shape. The focus on testing, for example, would likely not be so dominant. It would be too apparent that tests as a measurement of growing and learning would be incapable of describing what is important for children and young people, too insensitive to capture the diversity that ought to characterize the schools. A narrow construct of competence rooted in test-score designations can be talked about today only because the focus of education *is* narrowing. Likewise, in our current environment, observation schedules for evaluation purposes can concentrate almost exclusively on the five or six major Effective-Schools research findings—how many minutes are children on-task, is there homework? Remember, of course, that the *content* of the skill sheets children are working on-task on or of the homework they are asked to complete is not a significant focus of attention in these observations, nor is the quality of the questions framed by teachers or students. The fact that what is being worked on may well be mindless does not matter. Researchers at

---

1. I am indebted to Vincent Rogers, from the University of Connecticut, for several of these questions and some of this line of thought.

Michigan State University's Institute for Research on Teaching note in this regard that much of what is called reading time in the primary grades is devoted to worksheets that demand rote reaction rather than thinking and contribute little to reading improvement.

There are other issues not made particularly clear in the Effective-Schools literature that I will comment on briefly. Let us take, for example, the issue of leadership. We read that Effective Schools have strong principals. What does that mean in practice? What do our thousands of principals need to learn to be such principals? There is little help to be found in the Effective-Schools literature.

The schools I have found over the years to be the most productive—most supportive of learning—are those in which *all* parties participate in decision making, where leadership is provided by everyone. In contrast, much of the Effective-Schools literature tends to encourage more authoritarian models. Do we really believe that authoritarian models will contribute to excellent schools, encourage the most able to enter and remain in teaching, and encourage teachers and students to exert their best, most creative efforts? Schools I have found to be the most productive are also schools in which teachers are energized through interactive, community-oriented processes; in addition, they emphasize localized curriculum development, to which teacher commitment is high, rather than depend on externally organized and standardized curriculum. But can any of these directior.s be mandated? What does it take to bring a school to this point?

In the Effective-Schools literature, good school climate is the most important of all the factors identified. But a good school climate, like leadership, cannot be mandated. It, too, is the end product of a process that takes time and effort, involves teachers, students, and parents, and has, as well, a number of idiosyncratic qualities.

I wish to bring all of this back to teachers, where I began. Is it any wonder that so many teachers are discouraged? And they are! Is it surprising that so many who came to teaching with particular education-writ-large beliefs have departed, given up, or need to struggle so much? I have to acknowledge that within the current climate it *would* be easier in a number of ways for teachers in many settings to accept current wisdom and use a single text with a predetermined sequence for most instructional areas than to examine a broad range of literature and devise in an ongoing manner fresh curriculum materials that relate to specific children and young people. But the latter is necessary, of course, if student learning at the highest levels—education rather than schooling—is the goal. It would certainly be easier to adopt the latest checklist for student

evaluation or accept the current drive toward test-score improvement than to continue an evaluation process demanding careful observation, record keeping, and sharing among teachers. And it is also
easier to accept the structure of relatively linear thought than to
struggle to become a personal theory builder, the student of teaching that a developmental philosophy demands.

Yet within the schools there are those still struggling to put forth
a more liberal and liberating view; these teachers deserve support,
and it is to their concerns that the energy now being dissipated in
drives for simple solutions to complex human issues should be devoted. They need some thoughtful reaffirmation, support for the formulation that teachers can be, must be, decision makers, curriculum builders, knowledge generators, persons who think and write,
who bring to their efforts their individual enthusiasms, high expectations, and powerful commitments to the educability of all persons. And it is through such a reaffirmation that we might rekindle
among a larger number of the most intellectually alert and socially
committed of our university student population a renewed interest
in teaching and the schools, a commitment to join that continuing
corps of teachers in the schools who have not yet given up on the
best definitions of education that we can devise.

And for those still struggling to affirm what is historically education in its richest sense, there are a number of important expectations. I will discuss them briefly in relation to evaluation inasmuch
as the argument is often posited that the reliance on testing and the
drive for teacher accountability in the form of competency tests and
competency standards stem from teachers' inadequate evaluation
efforts. While I accept this to some degree, I believe the impetus is
larger and in many cases unrelated to teacher performance in this
regard.

Teachers need to communicate clearly, both to parents and to the
communities, their educational purposes regarding the expressive
arts, language, and the basic skills; they must also explain how they
propose to achieve those purposes, the procedures they plan to use
to assure children's acquisition of and growth in the various learning areas, and how they will report to parents. Teachers can be ex-
plicit about all of this. While this is not a new challenge, it is one
needing greater attention if those who wish to affirm the best practice are to maintain, even regain, the confidence of those who support them. Teachers need to enter into a systematic process of
informal assessment, observation, and record keeping as a means of
getting close to children's learning, developing and sustaining in the

process a capacity to organize curriculum in response to what is made increasingly visible. Such directions were eloquently described in the progressive literature of earlier days and affirmed again in the 1960s: within the more recent literature I am particularly impressed by the writing of Patricia Carini (1971, 1972, 1975, 1979, 1984), who has carried this traditional, more phenomenological view to a very high level.

To push oneself close to children's learning qualitatively is to become in the process more knowledgeable about children and learning, to become the student of teaching that schools need and parents desire, to become the potential producer of a new literature on teaching and learning. Teachers able to describe children's learning in great detail are teachers who are trusted, who gain authority and are capable of helping reestablish parent and public confidence. We need room for these kinds of teachers. If we push too hard to implement the Effective-Schools direction—with its technical formulations, focus on schooling, and call for more tests and narrowly defined standards—we are likely to cause discouragement among our most able teachers, push out many more, encourage too few of those we need, and assure that the diversity so vital to American culture is rendered even more difficult. We will also be even more disappointed in the educational outcomes for children and young people.

Part II
PROGRESSIVISM
IN EDUCATION

CHAPTER FIVE

Open Education and Educational Reform

This paper brings together material from a variety of talks about aspects of open education given to parents and teachers between 1968 and 1972. These notes were consolidated for the Phi Delta Kappa Education Foundation Fastback entitled, Open Education: Promise and Problems *(1972). While open education as an educational movement has gone through difficult times, its basic formulations are timeworn and proven. As we move into the 1990s and a new round of reform, much that was basic to the discourse and practice of open education is being revived, seen as critical to higher quality, more personally engaging education for children and young people.*

Unlike the curriculum reform effort of the early post-Sputnik years, open education raises fundamental questions about the nature of childhood, learning, and the roles of teachers and schools. It represents a challenge to many current assumptions about the organization and purposes of schooling, reaffirming in its related practices that learning is a personal matter that varies for different children, proceeds at many different rates, develops best when children are actively engaged in their own learning, takes place in a variety of settings in and out of school, and gains intensity in an environment where children—and childhood—are taken seriously.

Regarding curriculum, practitioners of open education are exploring the more integrative qualities of knowledge, skills, appreciations, and understandings, seeing the conventional separation of these qualities—knowledge and skills in particular—as unnatural, even wasteful. They have come to understand that the integration of learning, its wholeness, is an essential base for personalizing the educational process. While the traditional basic skills are considered fundamental, practitioners do not view them in isolation from other aspects of learning. For example, the skills of literacy—reading, writing, speaking, thinking—are not treated as academic exercises taught in a vacuum, as ends. They are taught in a learning context that stimulates children's imagination and thought, thus fostering a desire to communicate.

Practitioners of more open directions in education would not generally specify a *particular* body of information as absolutely essential for all children to learn. Their concern is not so much the specific content of instruction as it is the process by which powerful subject matter content is taught and the conditions under which children learn. They believe that it is particularly important that children be able to initiate activities, that they become more self-directed and more able to take responsibility for their own learning as they grow in their understandings of the power of cooperative action and collective thought. They believe further that children should be intensely involved in their learning and that such intensity should arise out of their wonder, imagination, and curiosity, leading ultimately to concern and commitment.

Open education has many historical roots. In fact, many of the attitudes and philosophical assumptions that are basic to its formulations are consistent with the language that fills our most thoughtful literature of education. In addition to the accounts of progressive education as it was practiced in the early decades of this century, students of open education turn for support to the philosophical and psychological writings of Jean Jacques Rousseau, Leo Tolstoi, Johann Pestalozzi, Maria Montessori, Friederich Froebel, and John Dewey, as well as the more contemporary works of Jean Piaget, Nathan and Susan Isaacs, Jerome Bruner, John Holt, Bill Hull, Joseph Featherstone, Lillian Weber, Herbert Kohl, and James Herndon, among others.

While Piaget may well have the most currency at the present time, it is also clear that much of the thrust of open education in the United States preceded the important support that his writings now provide. As is often true in the field of education, good practice seems to outdistance the theoretical underpinnings.

While many people think of the open classroom movement as radical, large numbers view it as a return to the educational practice of the "little red schoolhouse." The *New York Times Magazine* (Griffith, 1971) featured an article entitled "A Daring Educational Experiment: The One Room Schoolhouse," which described openness, more intellectually able children assisting those less able, independent study, children progressing at their own rate, extensive use of the out-of-doors environment, child-initiated activity, an integrated curriculum, and the teacher functioning as a guide and facilitator of learning. Many individuals who attended one-room schools can appreciate these characteristics; such was their experience. There were obvious limitations—teacher turnover was high and teacher quality was often low, materials were in short supply, there was limited interaction for older children, and little assistance for those with special needs was available. Yet large numbers of individuals who had their schooling in such settings still look back on the experience as a sound preparation for learning how to learn.

The young and gifted teacher described in the *New York Times* article was far removed from the discussions about open education; in fact, she had not heard about it. Still, her comments are quite similar to those that have been made and quoted extensively by teachers in open classrooms. For example:

> The children and I are learning together. I don't have any big philosophy about teaching and I don't have the time to prepare individual lessons for each of the [children] in advance. We just take it a day at a time. All I want to do is help each of them learn as much as possible every moment of the day. (p. 19)

> I guess they feel respected here because I really listen to them. That's easy to do though, because they are so naturally curious. . . . The best thing about these little country schools . . . is that we all learn together. (p. 19)

> There's too much going on inside the class for the children to stare out the window or at the clock. It's sort of like a seven ring educational circus. (p. 16)

> Despite the steady chatter of voices in the room, they learn to study independently and privately. They have to. I can't give lectures to a class of such mixed ages and [abilities]. (pp. 15–16)

Undoubtedly there are many teachers in many different communities who, like the teacher quoted above, have experimented with a more open classroom and are experiencing success without the benefit of formal understanding of the developmental theory that is often cited to buttress open classroom activities or the vast practice-oriented literature on open education.

The English Influence

English primary schools have had a particularly strong influence on the development of open education practices in America. Movement toward more informal styles of teaching and learning took place in England over a 40-year period, blossoming first in the "infant schools" housing children from five to seven years of age. The successful practice in the infant schools, as well as a renewed interest in child development, fostered changes in the Junior schools (serving eight-to-eleven-year-olds), and in the 1960s informal approaches became more common there as well.

The quiet movement toward informal education might not have mushroomed so rapidly and with such glowing press accounts had it not been for *Children and Their Primary Schools,* a report of the Central Advisory Council for Education, published in England in January 1967. Popularly called the Plowden report after Lady Plowden, who chaired the council, it called British and worldwide attention to the informal practices occurring in large numbers of infant and junior schools throughout England. Importantly, it gave official support to the pioneering work of large numbers of teachers, headmasters and headmistresses, and local Advisories.[1]

The Plowden report was enthusiastic in its reaffirmation of the importance of organizing primary education around the needs of children, their patterns of growth, their interests, and their play. While it would be impossible to capture the spirit of the Plowden report (two lengthy volumes) in a short space, the following extracts are particularly exemplary of its philosophical tone.

> At the heart of the education process lies the child. Children need to be themselves . . . to enjoy the present, to get ready for the future, to create and to love, to learn to face adversity, to behave responsibly . . . to be human. (p. 7)

> The best preparation for being a happy and useful man or woman is to live fully as a child. (p. 188)

> The distinction between work and play is false, possibly throughout life, certainly in the primary school . . . play is the principal means of learning in early childhood. It is the way through which children reconcile their inner lives with external reality. (p. 193)

> Good teaching practice insists that knowledge does not fall into neatly separate compartments and that work and play are not opposite but complementary. (p. 198)

---

1. We have no absolute counterpart for the English advisory in the United States. An advisory, supported by a local education authority, is made up of persons who function in support of teachers yet are not burdened with administrative-supervisory functions. The increasing number of teacher centers in the United States are attempts to develop a support system that is similar to the English advisory.

The strength of the report rested not only in its careful review of what is known about child development and its formulation of what is good for children but also in the documentation that large numbers of primary schools were already putting such beliefs into practice.

Although many Americans had been watching what was happening in England, it was not until the Plowden report that large-scale attention was generated. Articles by Joseph Featherstone, which appeared in *The New Republic* in 1967 and were widely distributed, brought widespread interest (these were gathered together in a book and published in 1971). And *Crisis in the Classroom*, the Carnegie Corporation–financed study by Charles Silberman (1970), added further impetus to more informal practices. The bandwagon has been gaining momentum since.

A Description of an Open Classroom

Because teachers and children are at many different stages in their development and have different levels of experience and diverse personal interests, open classrooms tend to develop their own unique qualities. Space and materials, as well as particular school/community environments, also make a difference. Still, there tend to be a number of common attributes that are given greater or lesser emphases by different advocates and practitioners of open classrooms. The different emphases represent one of the strengths of open education to date. The tendency to reject an orthodoxy regarding how to organize for more open processes of education has been healthy. If there is an orthodoxy, it has to do with the belief that a child's growth—personal and intellectual—is paramount and it is toward that end that the school exists.

A person's first look at an open classroom may well bring the response that "it doesn't look like school should look." I have heard many initial responses of that kind. It is common to see a variety of learning activities going on at the same time. Some children may be reading, others playing musical instruments, weaving, acting out a play, working at math, or painting. The mobility of children is obvious. The classroom will typically be decentralized into a variety of learning areas, and there will generally be no "front of the room." Desks, if there are any, will most often be grouped in clusters, and commercial and homemade materials of considerable range and diversity will be found in abundance. Children will be conversing, with the noise level typically higher than most observers have experienced. Learning is viewed as cooperative. In addition, the classroom atmosphere is relaxed, there is a sense of real enjoyment in learning, and the teacher may not always be immediately visible (he or she may be behind a bookcase reading to two or three children).

A short visit for the first-time visitor might raise concerns; it would be much better to remain a good part of the day or take part in an instructional activity to gain a clear picture of what is happening.[2] For only after some time does it become apparent that there are few barriers between most subject-matter areas and very few restrictions determined by the clock, thus providing a fluid schedule that permits more natural beginning and ending points for a child's learning activity. Children who are intensively engaged in an activity, such as constructing a tetrahedron or reading a book, would not stop "because it is now time for writing." Visitors would also find themselves quickly involved in learning activities with children. Adults and older children are typically looked upon as resources. And teachers generally see others in the classroom as additional individuals with whom children can interact.

Parents are frequent classroom participants. In such classrooms, where the goals are less dominated by precise curriculum objectives, specialized training for parents is less important. It is also easier for a parent to enter into the life of the classroom. As a result, parents are often found in open classrooms taking part in such activities as woodworking, cooking, sewing, arts and crafts, reading stories, listening to children read, and just conversing with children. If the school, as opposed to a classroom, is moving in such directions, there will be more interaction between classrooms, children will move quite freely from one setting to another, hallways will be extensions of the classrooms, and the environment outside will be integral to the life of the school.

The decentralized character of the classroom facilitates the learning efforts of individuals and small groups. Teachers are able to respond more sensitively to individual children and *their* starting points. They can converse naturally with children, and they in turn

---

2. Parents who visited open classrooms in North Dakota for less than an hour and did not actively participate in a learning activity with children were generally negative. Parents who made several visits, remained longer than an hour, or participated in a learning activity with the children were almost always positive (Patton, 1973b).

with others, and children are provided a broader range of alternatives for learning. While the various learning areas, or centers, may be prepared initially by a teacher, they undergo change throughout a school year. Children add considerably to them as their interests change, as their starting points extend themselves in many diverse directions, and as the teacher gains greater insights into the learning patterns established by individual children.

Arrangement of Room

Figure 5.1 depicts the decentralized character of a classroom, serving eight-and-nine-year-olds, that I have frequently visited. The areas are broken up by a variety of dividers, such as movable screens (which also serve as display space), bookcases, and planters. There are tables in the room that comfortably seat five to six children; seldom, however, are all of the tables occupied. Shelves have been built to accommodate plastic storage trays in which children keep their personal belongings, such as pencils, notebooks, crayons, and rulers. While the room changes in organization from time to time, most of the learning centers, as physical locations, remain in some form.

The art area contains three easels, which can serve six children; aprons; paints (water and tempera); jars; brushes; paper of various

Fig. 5.1 A Decentralized Classroom

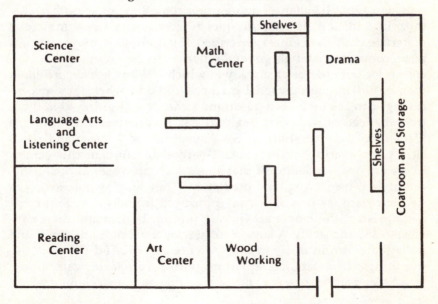

sizes, shapes, and textures; clay; chalk; scissors; and a variety of scraps, such as egg cartons, glue, string, vinyl tile, wood chips, yarn, wallpaper, and magazines. There are times, because of particular interests, that the art center contains leaves, starch, styrofoam, rubber, twigs, dyes, and looms.

The reading corner is particularly inviting. It is brightly carpeted, has a rocking chair, several pillows on the floor, and large numbers of books and magazines that are freely accessible to the children. The reading materials cover a broad range of subjects and ability levels and include large numbers of books written by the children. On display are "ideas for sharing," "new books in the center," and "books I especially liked." Such descriptions are all written by the children.

The language arts/listening center is adjacent to the reading corner and contains materials and equipment relating to the broad area of communications. There are a typewriter, a tape recorder and record player equipped with headsets, records and tapes containing music for enjoyment, stories (sometimes associated with programmed readers), and skill lessons in such areas as listening and spelling. There are also a variety of reading and spelling games (most of them made by the teacher), puzzles, a reading-skills kit, and a box containing pictures and ideas for writing. Displayed are children's poetry, stories, and new words with some "fascinating" uses.

The science area is designed for active involvement with materials and typically changes more often than most of the other centers. In addition, it contains more "common," noncommercial materials than the centers described thus far. This movement toward common materials generally occurs in classrooms when science is looked upon as an activity in which children learn more about their world through personal investigation and when they are encouraged to ask their own questions rather than waiting to find out from the teacher what they ought to ask. A variety of units from the Elementary Science Study (ESS)—"small things," "peas and particles," "structures," "pendulums"—are also found in this center. These are open-ended units that stress such processes as analyzing, classifying, measuring, and predicting. They employ balances, lenses, microscopes (the $2 variety produced initially by ESS), magnets, prisms, thermometers, plastic tubing, bottles and jugs, candles, rocks, and shells. A large incubator, motors, nuts and bolts, and pulleys are also in this particular science center. And there are living things: hamsters, an aquarium with a variety of water life, a snake. An electric fry pan is made available once a week for cooking projects. Cooking produces enormous enthusiasm because everyone can be successful at it. In addition, it provides an excellent opportunity for integrating the various curriculum areas. There are also science reference books on animals, plants, insects, rocks, astronomy, and engines. A filmstrip projector is available for use with the large numbers of commercial filmstrips pertaining to the physical and natural sciences. On display are projects that have been completed by individuals or groups of children.

The math area also stresses active involvement with materials and thinking. Measuring devices are prominent (tape measures, string, rulers, jars of various sizes), as are counters (buttons, washers, abacuses), cuisinaire rods, blocks (multicolored and multishaped), geo-boards, catalogs, tangrams, dice, math games, puzzles and flash cards, and a variety of math textbooks and workbooks. The teacher has prepared a large number of "activity cards," which give some sequential nature to a variety of mathematical concepts that serve as starting points for children. The influence of the Elementary Science Study and the Madison, Minnemast, and Nuffield Mathematics Projects (the latter developed in England) is particularly visible. Evidence of their influence can be seen in the extensive measuring, weighing, graphing, sorting, and classifying activities in which children engage. Chess also is played extensively, seen by the teacher as a good game for stimulating thinking, strategy, and logic.

The drama area serves a broad range of the expressive arts, from pantomiming, role playing, and puppetry to some limited forms of movement and music. There is a puppet theater and materials for making puppets. There are dress-up clothes, records, several recorders and drums, an autoharp, and a variety of rhythm instruments constructed by the children. Improvisation is strongly encouraged. The broad opportunities children have for engaging intensively in the creative and expressive arts are in sharp contrast to what is available in most formal elementary classrooms.

The woodworking area attracts girls as well as boys. Local lumberyards supply scraps of wood that children use to construct boxes, boats, rockets, and geometric designs. (In a classroom staffed by one of our intern-teachers, eight- and nine-year-old children designed and constructed a 6' × 8' × 6' playhouse; they even shingled the roof.) An old table serves as a workbench. There are hammers, saws, screwdrivers, pliers, nails, rulers, glue, wire, and sandpaper stored on a pegboard and in plastic containers.

A rich environment and easily accessible learning materials form an important dimension of the open classroom. Teachers in such settings consider it important that children know what learning materials—paints, brushes, wood, paper, scissors, batteries, masking tape, wire, audiotapes, filmstrips—are available and where they are stored as well as understand that they have virtually complete access to them. If children must ask permission to use the items, which usually involves waiting, or do not know what is available, they may well lose interest or have limited opportunities for exploring new areas. It should be noted, too, that the children do things for themselves—mix paints, clean brushes, and operate tape recorders, filmstrip projectors, and record players. These simple chores are part of the process of learning self-reliance and responsibility.

Organization of the Day

How does the teacher organize? What does he or she do? The teacher in the setting described above is in her second year of teaching in a more open classroom[3] and her first year with this particular group of children. The initial period of the day is generally devoted to "free activities." Children pick up where they left off the previous day or begin something else. After approximately 40 minutes, the class gathers for a planning session. The teacher takes a few minutes to describe many of the activities going on in various parts of the room. Several children are asked to describe what they are doing that may be of interest to others, and a few others outline their plans for the remainder of the school day. In the planning session everyone draws up a personal plan for the day. The teacher generally uses this occasion to call attention to new additions to the learning centers and new possibilities for using outside resources. She also takes this opportunity to organize a specific time to meet with particular groups of children (she names them) to work on a specific skill; for example, using reference materials, using context in reading, or number facts. These groupings come about as a result of her observations and discussions with children. They seldom are permanent, changing from week to week. She also indicates the times she will have individual conferences with particular children.

---

3. I tend to use such phrases as *more open classroom* or *less formal classroom* inasmuch as I view the movement toward open education as a process. Teachers and children advance, generally along a jagged front, from their present levels of independence and experience with active learning. The rate and quality of the progress varies from setting to setting.

In this classroom there are some teacher expectations that children include in their planning. At a minimum, children are expected to engage in reading, making sure that they record for the teacher any new books they have begun, work in the math area, and do some writing. While these may appear to be rather separate activities, and the learning centers may well seem a reinforcement, encouragement is always given for integration of learning. For the house-building project, for example, the children visited a lumberyard and arranged to get some old plywood. They developed elaborate plans that involved measurement and geometry. An architect demonstrated model making, which the children then tried. They viewed a variety of films on house building. A tape-recorded lesson provided additional information on the use of tools—the lever, plane, and gear. And two retired carpenters in the community gave some practical demonstrations. Individual children pursued many different interests in relation to the house-building project. They wrote letters telling others of their experience. They took up individual projects, including Native American homes, termites, trees, creatures that live in trees, homes around the world, workers who build homes, old and modern tools, skyscrapers, and doll houses. Such projects quite naturally move across the artificial separation of subject matter.

After the planning session, the children go into the various learning centers. The teacher then moves about the room, working with individual children and small groups. She asks questions, suggests other resources for extension of a particular activity, encourages, listens, and learns.

At the end of the day, the children come together again to evaluate and share what they have learned or found particularly interesting. At times there are dramatic presentations and readings of favorite poems. Often, the teacher uses part of the time to read a story.

There is direction—a structure—in this classroom, and it becomes obvious to most observers who remain for any length of time. Teacher direction and child direction are clearly balanced. Early in the year, teacher direction was greater, but it decreased during the course of the year. By the end of the school year, the balance had shifted even more toward child direction. In subsequent years, as the teacher and children become more adjusted to an open setting, progress toward greater child direction should become more rapid. As all of the classrooms in this particular school become more open, such progress would be facilitated, of course, because movement from one classroom to another would not require major adjustments by the children or teachers. While observers will easily take notice of the fact that children are very active in this classroom, it should be noted that the teacher is also extremely active. Her personal interests in movement, poetry, and artistic display are much in evidence.

Knowing the Children

What does this particular teacher feel is important for her? Because she believes that her ability to assist the various children in their personal and intellectual growth depends on the degree to which she knows them as individuals, she devotes a good deal of her time to observing individual children, their learning choices, and their interaction with materials and with others. She converses often with children, listens well, and is willing to accept their ideas. As she has said to me: "*Knowing* the children means more than knowing their names. It means knowing their styles of learning, their interests, their feelings about a variety of issues and things, and establishing a relationship of trust and respect."

One of her major tasks is record keeping. This is important to her because the children are at so many different levels and working on so many diverse topics. Planning and provisioning would be less constructive, less focused without a careful record-keeping system. She attempts to write something each day about each child. And the children also maintain a variety of records. They record their activities for the day and place some of their writing, math, and other projects into files for the teacher to review. An outgrowth of the extensive record keeping is the teacher's ability to describe to parents precisely how their child is doing, in what ways the child's interests have broadened, and how the child meets his or her commitments. In this particular setting, parents have been enormously impressed by the fact that "the teacher knows our child so well."

Implications for the Teacher

Many teachers who observe an open classroom for the first time raise questions about planning. Carefully drawn lesson plans, so much a part of the more formal classroom, are not found. Planning takes on a different form. The teacher I am describing talks about the hours she spends thinking about materials, resources that might extend the learning of various children who are pursuing different interests, need (or skill) groupings, trying to find new books rich in language, and recording children's learning.

It is an exhausting endeavor for the teacher. Almost everyone I know who is working in an open classroom setting speaks about the physical and psychological drain. It clearly demands more from the teacher than a more formal setting. But there are obvious rewards. The teacher above speaks about it as "keeping me alive intellectually; the classroom provides many opportunities for me to be a learner." Without the domination of a formal curriculum developed outside of her classroom, she can bring more of herself and her life into the setting.

One of the exciting things for me is to hear experienced teachers describe children's learning as they (the teachers) have moved toward more open settings. Invariably they talk about children's achieving at levels they would not have anticipated or assuming responsibilities they did not believe children were capable of. We have, it seems to me, vastly underestimated children. That realization alone brings many real opportunities for reestablishing oneself as a learner.

An Additional Note on Materials

In describing the classroom above, I made some mention of materials. It seems appropriate to comment further, because a rich environment is so important to the open classroom. Teachers do make use of many commercial materials, for example, textbooks, listening centers, tape recorders, and individualized learning kits that have come from many of the major curriculum projects of the past decade. But open classroom teachers also recognize that such materials generally have "predetermined routes" and do not really encourage broad exploration.

A stimulating aspect of the effective open classroom is the large reservoir of common materials from the local community. Some of the best materials I have seen are those developed by teachers, children, and parents. Many teachers quite literally invite parents to bring their junk—milk cartons, plastic containers, cardboard, wood, wire, brushes, and magazines—to school. Such materials have not only been useful for arts and crafts activities; they have also served as a good base for developing attribute blocks, tangrams, classification exercises (used in science and math), and puzzles, word games, and writing exercises (used in the language arts).

Use of common materials tends to serve another useful purpose, that of increasing the integration of the school and home environments. Parents visiting a classroom and viewing vast stores of expensive commercial equipment and materials often resign themselves to being able to contribute little to a significant learning environment at home. And children will be less likely to involve themselves in really creative enterprises at home, which may grow out of or into experiences at school, if there is not greater overlap of materials inside and outside the school.

Teachers who are conscious of materials and their potential for learning have also tapped good sources of materials in the business community. Such materials have included old radios, adding machines, typewriters, wallpaper, ceramic tile, and cloth. These contacts have also had the additional effect of broadening the range of people who gain an interest in visiting the classroom to see "what's going on."

A Note on the Outside Environment

Along with the use of common materials, open classroom teachers place stress on the outside environment, viewing it as too rich to be ignored. It certainly serves as an excellent base for children to gain significant skills in observing, recording, and interpreting what goes on in the world. Attempts to bring "the world" into the classroom are, at best, limiting. Moving out of the classroom into the world holds more promise. Parents have been particularly helpful in many schools by making themselves available to take small groups of children into the community to extend a particular interest.

Reading in the Open Classroom

Reading, for large numbers of people, is what the elementary school is about. And, realistically, the open classroom must address itself to reading if it is to gain long-term support; hence, it seems appropriate to outline the ways in which reading is typically approached in open classrooms.

Teachers in such settings view "healthy attitudes toward reading" as paramount. Teaching "appropriate skills," while critical, is a secondary concern. (In most formal classrooms the latter is stressed almost to the exclusion of the former.) They tend to support the belief that many children are pushed into formal reading too soon, producing frustrations that multiply at a rapid rate, convincing children quite early that they cannot read well. Open classroom teachers also typically reject debates about "whole-word" vs. "phonics" approaches to reading, feeling that such debates in the past were wasteful of time and energy. They are quite eclectic, accepting a variety of approaches to reading. This view is quite consistent with their belief that the teacher must respond to the particular learning styles of individual children, knowing that children enter reading in a variety of ways.

Basal readers are often used as supplementary materials in open classrooms; the general pattern is to have a few copies from several reading series at many different levels rather than having a single, graded series. Reading workbooks are also seen in many of the classrooms; however, they, too, represent a variety of programs and are not followed in any particular sequence. Some children will work through many pages; others may not use them at all.

Reading-skill kits, such as those produced by Science Research Associates (SRA) and the McGraw-Hill Reading Laboratories, are commonly found and are available for use by children. But none of the aforementioned materials are considered central to the reading program.

Communication in all its forms is stressed as the base for reading, not only in the primary years but beyond. Children listen to records and tapes, talk to one another, and listen to stories read by the teacher, older children, or parents who come to the classroom especially for that purpose. There is a great deal of support for what Bill Martin (1967), who writes many delightful books for children, often says: "Reading is learned through the ear." It is through hearing language that children gain a sense of structure and rhythm.

Stories read by the teacher are often acted out, and these activities link oral language and feeling. In addition, people, settings, and sequences from the stories may well become the context for painting that children might do. Such activities are a critical beginning for thinking skills, which are important to reading comprehension.

Because the opportunities to explore a variety of materials are broad, children have more to communicate about. And the early reading that children do grows out of *their* talking, the personal language that they bring to school. Using what is commonly called "language experience," teachers (or older children) record children's descriptions of a particular experience or a story they wish to tell. This establishes a direct link between oral language and print. It is a positive indication to children that their speaking can be written. And the written material can be read back exactly as it was originally told. In the process of such experiences, children learn to identify some words. In the initial stages of reading, these words become the "child's words." The child may keep them in a notebook or on cards, adding "favorite words" and "key words." Using these known words, a youngster can build sentences. And the teacher will extend this beginning by asking: "What other words sound like *bake*? It begins with a *B* sound. Do you know other words that begin with that sound?" It is through language-experience activities also that the child is introduced to writing, beginning by forming the letters the teacher has printed. As the child learns to recognize words visually, he or she also begins writing them.

Children often dictate stories into a tape recorder and hear them played back. As their writing vocabulary and skill increases, they write more stories. In the kind of environment provided in open classrooms, this kind of communication is more than an exercise.

The environment is rich with reading materials. This is important. Classrooms and schools without books and magazines in profusion can hardly be serious about reading. And a teacher who does not serve as a constant model for good attitudes about reading by demonstrating a personal love of language and books can hardly be serious about teaching reading.

As children's ability to identify a larger number of words increases, the teacher begins to provide assistance with sounds, letter and word discrimination, use of context to assist with decoding, and so forth. Because children make progress at different rates, the teacher organizes need groupings for working through specific skills. Being sensitive to individual needs, the teacher occasionally introduces reading games and puzzles made by himself/herself or, at times, by the children. The teacher also prepares audiotapes that children can listen to as they follow printed matter.

By conferencing often with individual children, listening to them read, and reading their writing, a skillful teacher can begin to provide individual assistance where it is necessary. While children learn to read, they also come to enjoy reading.

Evaluation

There has been little intensive evaluation of open classrooms. Part of the difficulty in evaluation is the lack of instruments that measure adequately the goals of open education, that is, critical thinking, independence in learning, trust, ability to face new problems with confidence, commitment to reading, and positive attitudes about learning. A number of observational instruments are being developed, but they tend to call for qualitative judgments by the observers and end up as descriptions. Sadly, these kinds of efforts carry less weight in traditional evaluation circles than do "objective" assessments based on standardized achievement tests. One can only hope that this will not remain the case. Giving credence to standardized tests is a limited and limiting direction in evaluation.

Evaluation completed in England, though limited, gives support to the informal practices, noting that children achieve at about the same levels in typical subject-matter areas as do children in formal schools. In five years of monitoring achievement test scores here in North Dakota, we have also found that children in the more open classrooms tend to achieve at levels equal to, sometimes better than, children in reference populations. Given the fact that traditional, more formal schools pay more attention to tests and actually prepare children for taking them, we actually expected that a gap might exist.

On less conventional measures, research has been conducted in several North Dakota school districts (in such areas as interest in science) that reveals significant differences favoring children in the more open settings. Data relating to interest in and enjoyment of school, parental attitudes about their children's classrooms, school attendance, and teacher attitudes also tend to favor the more open settings at significant levels.

The Promise of Open Education

In many ways, the promise has already been touched upon. Classrooms that foster initiative and responsibility, address themselves to what is known about children, childhood, and learning, extend children's intellectual growth, prepare children to deal more confidently with new problems, and are more humane have to be promising. An orientation toward schooling that can give back initiative and potency, a desire to learn, to young people is urgently needed. Within that context open education represents a positive direction.

As was noted earlier, as a philosophic orientation open education is encouraging a serious reexamination of our educational assumptions. And because open education and its basic formulations are being practiced quite extensively in many parts of the country—

from urban centers such as Boston, New York, Los Angeles, and Washington to a variety of more rural communities in New Mexico, Arizona, Oregon, and North Dakota—there is a chance to sustain this reexamination.

Open education can serve as a catalyst to redefine our understanding of what are acceptable and significant areas of involvement for children, causing schools to move away from the narrow focus on learning objectives that can be easily measured over short periods of time. Such a redefinition may bring increased opportunities for personalization of learning. And the possibility of that learning's having integrity—a wholeness—should increase.

Open education can also cause those of us in the field of education to reestablish the school's essential tie to the outside community. In the process, the school may well become a resource base from which children go out rather than *the* place where all *real* learning goes on.

Because open education gives support to the use of diverse learning environments, in and out of the school, parents and other community people are encouraged to participate at ever-increasing levels. This is a promising development, not just in its potential for reviving public interest and support for schools—which is needed badly—but in its possibilities for enriching the lives of children. Inasmuch as teachers in open classrooms feel the latter point is particularly important, it may be appropriate to develop it further.

The teacher in the classroom is limited by his or her experience. The larger the experience base is, the better. But regardless of scale, the lives of children can be further enriched by the use of other human resources that exist in every community. There are many community people, with varied interests, talents, and vocations, who could make numerous contributions to children—and teachers—in and out of the school.

The opportunities for increased levels of individualization grow as parents and other community people participate in the school. The house-building project, discussed earlier, is an excellent example. There are, though, some obvious difficulties in opening a school to active participation by "outside people." Many teachers and principals find it threatening, feeling that it calls into question the professional competence of the schools. Such attitudes represent one of the challenges of open education. For if our concern is to enlarge the educational potential of children, such anxieties need to be confronted, such distances closed.

An outgrowth of the open education movement that is particularly encouraging has been the sharp increase in what I tend to call "new kinds of people" who are committing themselves to education. With the redefinitions of what are acceptable areas of learning for children, talented individuals in the arts, for example, are becoming enthusiastic about elementary schools and are increasingly willing to devote some of their time to children. One only has to follow the efforts of the Teachers and Writers Collaborative in New York City to gain a sense of what is possible in classrooms that are more open to fresh approaches to language. As noted in chapter 3, children who "were not supposed to be able to write" are doing some exemplary writing. Two recent publications, *Imaginary Worlds* (Murphy, 1974) and *A Day Dream I Had at Night* (Landrum, 1971), are examples.

Our program at the New School, an experimental program in teacher education at the University of North Dakota, addressed the same issue. We worked with large numbers of individuals who sought elementary teacher certification after having completed degrees in such areas as art, dance, music, theater, philosophy, literature, and foreign languages. They were not the typical elementary school teacher population. Because they saw in the formulations of open education an opportunity to work creatively with children, without the restraints of a prescribed curriculum and without having to give up their personal interests, they turned to teaching. In addition to the foregoing, it should be noted that almost 40 percent of those preparing for teaching in the New School are men. Nationally, fewer than 4 percent of those in elementary programs are men.

But what does open education hold for the experienced teacher? One of the major dilemmas in the field of education is a decline over time of teachers' interest in learning and the rapid process by which many teachers become locked into fixed practices (Hector, 1971). Such a process is not difficult to understand, given the constraints imposed by large numbers of school systems and by standardized curricula. In contrast, open education holds considerable promise as a renewing force, revitalizing teachers and, in the process, schools. It provides teachers a fresh opportunity to become learners and decision makers about learning. Our experience at the New School has been particularly rewarding in this respect. Teachers with 10 to 20 years of teaching experience have dramatically changed their behavior in classrooms. They have become aware of interesting possibilities for learning beyond paper-and-pencil activities; they have learned to trust children and themselves; and they have become enthusiastic again about learning. As one teacher with 15 years of experience wrote to me: "It's been almost like starting a new profession."

The movement toward open education is causing many educators to reaffirm the need for a human scale in schools. Anonymity prevails in many of our schools because they are too large. Individuals and physical resources are isolated. Communication becomes, of necessity, over organized and highly formal. I am personally appalled at the judgment of educators who were responsible for developing elementary schools that have 50–100 teachers and 1,000–2,000 children. Such schools typically have hallways fit for an indoor track meet, but they hardly provide a human dimension for a learning environment.

What is an ideal size? I prefer schools of 8–10 teachers and 200–250 children (and so do large numbers of parents who are gaining access to schools). In such settings the principal and most of the staff come to know every child. The principal and staff also come to know each other well. Communication is quite simple—sound systems become much less necessary. Such settings are large enough to provide children access to a variety of resources; they are also small enough to encourage a sense of community.

What can be done about schools that are already too large? It is possible to decentralize such schools into smaller clusters of teachers and children, schools within schools. Lillian Weber's Open Corridors Program in New York City (described by Norris & Hazelwood, 1971) represents a successful effort at such decentralization within a larger school building. Several large schools have been broken down into clusters of 4–5 teachers and approximately 125–150 children. The teachers within the cluster, or "family," plan together and carry out a reasonably integrated program.

Before closing this section, I should add another potential outgrowth of open education. It is clearly having an effect on elementary schools. Yet many educators argue that the real problems are at the secondary and college levels. Developments in the elementary schools are beginning to cause reexaminations of our assumptions about schooling at the secondary and college levels as well. And the expectation that education in the latter settings might become more supportive of learning and strive for individualization is growing.

The Problems of Open Education

There are many difficulties ahead for those who see open education as a positive response to the problems that plague American schools. In the closing section of this paper, I will address several of the issues that practitioners themselves are raising.

In their eagerness to transform America's schools along the lines of the English primary schools, many enthusiasts tend to forget that informal practices in the primary schools of England were developed over several decades. This need not suggest that such a long developmental period is essential; however, it should suggest that good practice may not be with us tomorrow.

Open education is not a package to be introduced like the older curriculum models. It will not happen because school principals or superintendents announce that "beginning next week, we will do *it* [open education]." Unfortunately, there are numerous reports of school administrators making such announcements. It does not take a serious student of American education to know the results of such rapid, uninformed adoption of a serious educational orientation stripped of its substance and made into a slick package, the latest fad.

Advocates of open education may well be a part of the problem. In their enthusiasm they have tended not to share the problems, the hard work that is necessary, the skills that need to be learned, the kind of support and changes in attitudes that are necessary.

Along with the enthusiasm for open education, considerable myth-making has developed; for example, the belief that if all the more traditional classroom structures were removed children would create an environment assuring personal and intellectual growth. And further, if teachers would remove themselves, stepping into the background, children would quite rapidly go about their own learning. These two beliefs have led several teachers down a chaotic path. They have also given support to the anti-intellectualism that surfaces occasionally within the open education movement. I have often cringed as I have heard teachers report that: "Children will learn to read if they have any particular need to read—encouragement is unnecessary." Or: "My positive relationship with a child would be damaged if I suggested that he read a particular book." Fortunately, such attitudes are becoming less prevalent, and teachers who tend toward such positions are rapidly finding that learning needs intellectual stimulation, encouragement, and support and that freedom alone does not guarantee such stimulation. Children need structures that provide a sense of order and meaningful options in order to establish a sustaining direction for learning. It is also clear that the teacher must be an active agent, not only as a provisioner but as a stimulator and catalyst for extended learning.

Many teachers have rid themselves of authoritarian modes. Their classrooms are relaxed, and children are involved in a myriad of activities. This is an important step, and with assistance and support, sensitive teachers seem to arrive at that point within a few months. The extension and deepening of learning, critical to the success of open education, is a much more complex and engaging task. I meet few teachers who feel comfortable about this dimension of their work. (I should note that formal, traditional classroom teachers are no more successful in the extension and deepening of children's learning. I rarely find such concerns discussed in these settings.) Considerable physical and intellectual efforts on the part of the teacher, as well as many new skills, are essential for children's learning to be extended in positive ways. An environment where support services are available is also critical. Both the preparation available for teachers to gain new skills and ongoing support systems are currently problems.

There are very few colleges and universities in the United States with significant experience in open education. (The most extensive efforts are being made by the Educational Development Center and its Follow Through Program, Wheelock College, Bank Street, the University of Connecticut, the City College of New York, the University of Illinois, the University of Colorado, and the University of North Dakota.) And there are very few school systems with sufficient experience to assist large numbers of teachers. A support system must be developed out of the same underdeveloped resources.

The principal in a school, assuming that a teacher has had some initial assistance and has volunteered to move in more open directions, is a critical person. He or she is in the best position to provide support through the early stages, when teachers sometimes develop doubts. But for principals to be effective, they must be active classroom participants, willing to be involved in the teacher's struggle. Unfortunately, schools have placed principals in roles that remove them from active participation in classrooms; as a result, they have often lost their personal enthusiasm for children and learning.

It should be noted, especially before I leave the subject of teachers, that where open education is functioning at a high level, or is progressing in a positive direction, in England and the United States, teachers have volunteered to pursue more open directions. The orientation has not been imposed upon them. In those situations, teachers have had time to work out their own routes. They have been able to begin where they are, not where outsiders felt they should be. They have been able to take small steps. Such a condition may not exist in the future, as the movement spreads more rapidly and as educators latch on to it, as often happens, as a means of remaining "current with educational trends."[4]

A problem that parents are raising is: "What will happen when my son reaches junior high school (or senior high school, or gets Mr. Jones), where the setting is strict and very traditional?" The concern about continuity is understandable. Open education advocates typically respond that "children are adaptable" or that "being independent learners, they should fare well regardless of how traditional the secondary school." Still, there is little significant evaluation that deals specifically with that issue.

I commented earlier on the potential for change at the secondary level. It is, from my perspective, high. The assumptions that underlie open education are equally applicable to secondary schools. Given the history of education at that level, however, I am also ready to acknowledge that it may be many years before there is good articulation between the more open processes of the elementary schools and similar developments at the secondary level. Unless such a development occurs, open education may not reach its promise.

A Closing Note

While not extensively discussed in the literature, it is certainly implied that open education will not thrive in a society that does not support openness, individuality, participation, and trust. And most of those people I know who are struggling with more open forms of education are also actively challenging the closed nature of most social institutions in America. They understand quite well the relationship between schools and society.

---

4. In retrospect, while open education practices did not enlarge to the degree I expected, what I expressed concern about—teachers being pushed to take steps they did not understand well or feel comfortable about—did occur in many settings. It was not helpful.

CHAPTER SIX

Open Education:
Where Has It Been?
Where Is It Going?

Originally a presentation to a meeting of the North Dakota Study Group on Evaluation, this paper was published in Insights *in November 1974 and reprinted in* City College Notes, *Winter 1974–75. It is included in this collection for historical purposes, principally to provide contemporary readers with a fuller introduction to the critical literature.*

Many people ask where open education is today. Is it a passing phase in the history of American education? Or is the movement still before us? I wish to present some of my reflections about these questions, shaped in large measure by my personal experience over the past decade. These reflections are organized in two parts: the first being a brief review of the literature of open education and the second a series of personal thoughts about some selected aspects of open education.

A Perspective on the Literature of Open Education

The literature on open education has expanded rapidly since 1967, when Joseph Featherstone wrote a series of articles for *The New Republic* on informal education in English primary schools. Featherstone's lively descriptions of *Schools Where Children Learn* (1971), the title of the book that contains his *New Republic* articles, attracted many Americans to England, including Charles Silberman. With the publication of Silberman's popular and influential *Crisis in the Classroom* (1970), the English experience became popularized even further and small informal education ventures in the United States gained considerable visibility.[1] Though not well understood at the time, open education was proclaimed after Silberman's work as a means of responding to the mounting criticism of the schools, especially in urban communities, and to the growing alienation of young people. In some respects, Silberman's descriptions held out some of the promise outlined in John and Evelyn Dewey's *Schools of Tomorrow* (1915/1962).

The literature on open education has gone through at least four distinct phases since Featherstone. Between 1967 and 1971, it drew heavily on the English experience; in fact, much was provided by English educators, such as Leonard Sealey, John Blackie, Sir Alec Clegg, Mary Brown and Norman Precious, Leonard Marsh, Sybil Marshall, Lorna Ridgway and Irene Lawton, Charity James, and Alice Yardley. Closely related to this "English" phase of the literature was greater attention to the work of Jean Piaget. While nursery school and kindergarten educators in the United States had discovered Piaget long before and were committed to many of his developmental ideas, the fact that Piaget's work was becoming a rationale for English practice brought his work to a larger audience of American educators.

Americans whose names were prominent in the literature of this early period (Joseph Featherstone, Lillian Weber, Vincent Rogers, Ann Cook and Herb Mack, Casey and Liza Murrow) drew heavily on their observations in English schools. To a large degree, this was to be expected. The English schools were clear demonstrations that schools could, for example, *begin with children*, provide more integrated study, place increased emphasis on the creative arts and cooperative learning, and enlarge the use of concrete materials. If English schools and teachers were committed to informal schooling and could put more open processes of education into practice successfully, "Americans could too."

Since about 1971, there has been increasingly less emphasis in the literature on the English experience. The growth in practice in American schools has been responsible for producing an independent direction. Even the English advisors who dominated open education workshops, especially on the East Coast, have virtually disappeared from the scene. Lillian Weber's writing, for example, is now focused almost exclusively on informal school settings in New

---

1. I have included within the bibliography a large number of the more popular books that appeared in the 1967–1974 period.

York City. Betsye Sargeant's fine publication, *The Integrated Day in an American School* (1970), is another particularly clear example of the changing pattern. The important work of Patricia Carini (1971, 1972) at the Prospect School, North Bennington, Vermont, especially in regard to evaluation and documentation, makes no reference to English schools. Virgil Howes (1974), once highly influenced by English schools, now draws almost all of his material from American settings, and the titles of Roland Barth's popular *Open Education in an American School* (1972) and Kathleen Devaney's *Developing Open Education in America* (1974) speak for themselves.

A third phase, only beginning to take shape and reflecting an interest in historical roots, draws upon the literature of the older progressive movement. *The Dewey School* (1936/1966), written by two former teachers, Katherine Camp Mayhew and Anna Camp Edwards, is being referred to increasingly in the literature. Further, John Dewey's writing, especially *School and Society* (1899/1956), *Schools of Tomorrow* (1915/1962), *Democracy and Education* (1916/1961), and *Experience and Education* (1938/1963), are once more being studied for their insights into the present practice of open education. (I have personally found Dewey's work to be particularly provocative now that my experience with open education has enlarged.) So, too, is *The Story of the Eight Year Study* (1942) by Wilford Aiken, a follow-up study of some 1,400 students who had attended 30 progressive schools. And the *Diary of a Country School Teacher* (1946/1970), a classic progressive statement by Julia Weber Gordon, is being read with renewed interest.

A fourth phase, also in its infancy, is the literature on "how-to-do-it." Lillian Stephens's *The Teacher's Guide to Open Education* (1974) and *Organizing the Open Classroom: A Teacher's Guide to the Integrated Day* (1972) by Joy Taylor are but two examples. "How-to-do-it" books, most of which are not of the quality of those produced by Stephens and Taylor, are unfortunately likely to proliferate. This is a phase in the literature that most people involved in open education knew would come but have been apprehensive about. The view posited by much of the "how-to-do-it" literature is that open education is a *model*, a *method* to be followed. The advertisement for one new book in this genre reads: "You can do it too. How to implement open education in easy to follow steps."

In closing this section, I wish to comment on two areas—evaluation and accounts of practicing teachers—in which an expanded literature would be enormously helpful. Inasmuch as both, in large measure, reflect some of my personal concerns, they provide a natural transition to the second part of this reflection.

Evaluation is an issue that poses considerable difficulty for many teachers moving in more open directions. It ought to be a positive factor in schools and classrooms, a process through which teachers and children increase the quality of their learning and their capacity for growth. But evaluation has tended, in schools, to assume a narrow "accountability" orientation, a process that restricts the potential range and quality of learning for teachers as well as children.

Standardized tests, which provide support for that narrow focus and have little relationship to the important goals of teachers and schools wishing to move in more open directions, are, unfortunately, deeply entrenched in most schools. Even where decision makers in schools acknowledge the serious limitations of the standardized tests, understanding that they do not get very close to children's learning and finding few educational arguments for their use, they are, nonetheless, often forced to ask: "Do we really have any alternatives that will be understood popularly as credible?" I understand that question.

There are evaluation alternatives that can support teachers in their efforts to respond more effectively to children (see e.g., Bussis & Chittenden, 1970; Carini, 1971, 1972; Duckworth, 1973/1987; Hein, 1975; Macdonald, 1974; Meier, 1973; Patton, 1975; Perrone, 1975; Perrone & Strandberg, 1972; Shapiro, 1973; Stake, 1973; Tobier, 1973; Zimiles, 1973). But the literature supporting these alternatives is disparate and not easily accessible. This gap needs to be filled.

Another body of literature that is needed, and not yet broadly available because it tends to be unpublished, is documentation of classroom practice written by classroom teachers and advisors who are internal to school settings. In large measure this literature is closely related to the alternative modes of evaluation discussed earlier. Such documentations have the potential of enlarging our understanding of learning, space, materials, growth over time, language acquisition, teacher roles, support mechanisms, and the like. This literature can extend our understanding of what many of the earlier progressives only speculated about. It also has the capacity to link discussions of theory and practice more closely as well as to sustain an important level of intellectual vitality in open education.

Comments on Selected Aspects of Open Education

In response to the question raised in the introduction about the state of open education, *I believe it remains vital, and good practice is becoming more common.*

The issues being raised by those moving in more open directions—including, for example, the nature of childhood, intensity in learning, the meaning of curriculum, processes of evaluation, and the role of the community, as well as the alternative practices being developed—are attracting greater levels of support from increasing numbers of teachers and parents. This has occurred in large measure because teachers have begun to understand open education not as a model but as a stimulus, even legitimization, for reexamining their practices; assuming increased responsibility for their individual classrooms, its materials, and operational patterns; and reestablishing themselves as learners rather than continuing to follow predetermined, external models (as they were asked to do with so much of what came out of the curriculum development efforts of the 1950s and early 1960s). The focus on children and children's growth—personal and intellectual—rather than on the efficacy of another new social studies program, for example, has helped bring many teachers back to where they have really wanted to concentrate their attention. In addition, the enlarged importance attached to community and parent resources in open education's child-centered orientation has increased the quantity and quality of the schools' contact with parents, causing parents to reestablish some commitment to the schools.

William Hull (1971), in a provocative statement on "The Case for the Experimental School," suggested that the language of open education had grown faster than the practice. I tended to agree at the time. To hurry and make the practice fit the language, many teachers took steps they and the children were unprepared for. For example, they got rid of the basal readers without understanding alternative strategies; they decentralized their classrooms (learning centers became almost faddish) without understanding the relationships between such decentralization and children's learning; and they tried to foster freedom and responsibility without sufficient materials or structures to support such goals.

The language used was often not precise enough. It assumed at times euphoric, even mystical, tones. In the hands of some of its advocates it took on a revolutionary cast, encompassing a new orthodoxy. Ann and Harold Berlak (Berlak, Berlak, Bagenstos, & Mikel, 1975), in an article in *School Review*, argue quite convincingly, I believe, that much of the language used to describe open education in the early period did not provide teachers sufficient assistance, and when put into practice, in literal terms, caused, for many, enormous frustrations.

I understand quite well why a teacher *might* say that "children will go about their learning more rapidly and with higher quality if I just step into the background and get out of their way." Much of the language of open education could easily have led to such understandings, though such views seem much less prevalent today as teachers have found, through experience, that learning needs ongoing intellectual stimulation and that freedom alone does not guarantee such stimulation. They have learned, too, that children need structures that provide a sense of order and meaningful options in order to establish a sustaining direction for learning.

Further, there was a great deal in the early language that stressed dichotomies. *A classroom was open or it was not.* More traditional forms of education were barraged with criticism, at times indiscriminately, regardless of the variations within traditional educational structures. It was often a language of excess not yet tempered sufficiently by experience. John Dewey (1938/1963) noted a parallel in some of the early progressivism, expressing concern about the tendency to derive "its principles negatively rather than positively and constructively" (p. 20).

None of this, in retrospect, is surprising. And it was not without some positive outcomes. It drew attention to many of the problems of more traditional schooling, helped enlist into education a broader range of people with some commitment to reform, and gave impetus to many of the reformulations of teaching and learning that provide a base for current open education practice.

As teachers have gained in their experience, good practice has begun to form the basis for a clearer articulation of open education. Advocates are now better able to explain what they are doing—how they organize for learning, how they use materials and space, and the importance of establishing a positive relationship with children. They are not dissipating their energy attacking traditional education. This is a sign of strength, though it might not fit the current interests of the popular media. Inasmuch as the popular press, for example, does not carry as many articles about open education as it once did, there is a view that "open education must be declining." A survey of the professional journals, however, would reveal a different reality. Open education has been quite prominent in the past three years in such journals as *Childhood Education, National Elementary Principal, Phi Delta Kappan, School Review, Elementary School Journal, Insights, Learning Magazine, Teachers College Record*, and *Outlook*, among others.

When I indicated earlier that open education remains vital and

good practice is becoming more common, I did not want to imply
that anything close to a majority of schools are organizing more open
classrooms. We are very far from a situation wherein open classroom processes are dominant. What encourages me, however, is an
increased willingness of teachers to reassess their practice and to
make changes, small as they might be, in the ways they respond to
children and organize their classrooms. There is less defensiveness
than most of us experienced several years ago.

As individuals and groups fostering open classroom practice
have grown in *their* experience, they have begun to provide greater
support to teachers *where they are* as opposed to *where someone external to the classroom or school* believes they ought to be. The only
requisite for support has become the teacher's desire to engage in a
process of change. To support such a position is to acknowledge that
the development of open education practice is a long-term process
demanding continued teacher opportunities for personal and
professional growth. While some teachers make very rapid gains, we
have found a three- to five-year developmental pattern more usual.

During this developmental period, we have observed a number
of growth points that seem relatively common; for example, aware-
ness/information gathering (a period of initial reflection), alteration
of space, an enormous amount of energy devoted to gaining practical classroom ideas, changing patterns of relationships with children, introduction of a more diverse range of materials, and an
increased interest in theoretical underpinnings, including how children grow. At the latter stage, teachers have tended to become far
more discriminating about what they hear and read and appear far
more able to sustain their own growth, having more limited need
for outside resources.

Support, through the developmental process outlined above, is,
on the basis of our experience, critical. And the persons or institutions providing the support need to be particularly attentive to where
the teachers are, beginning with their basic strengths, without, as
stated earlier, making judgments about where they think the teachers ought to be.

Six to eight years ago, when open education began to surface as
a serious educational development, there was little organized support available for teachers. While support mechanisms remain
underdeveloped, considerable progress has been made. Increasing
numbers of colleges and universities have organized open education programs at both the pre- and inservice levels. And to a large
degree, such programs are being staffed by individuals with some
practical experience in American schools. Teacher centers, orga-

nized in a variety of ways, have expanded rapidly to provide supportive services to teachers who are engaged in opening up their classrooms. And the continued existence of good open classrooms and schools also provides enormous support. All of the foregoing give some additional reason for optimism.

Administrative support for teachers moving in more open directions, as almost everyone working in open education has come to understand, is crucial. If principals are active participants in the instructional aspects of the school, they are in an excellent position to provide needed support through the early stages of developing a more open classroom. It is at this time that teachers develop some doubts about themselves and the children's learning, when traditional academic activities are undergoing modification (sometimes complete redirection), as children struggle (as they often do) with new expectations, and as teachers come to the conclusion (as they invariably seem to) that standardized processes of evaluation have little relation to the children's learning or their enlarging educational goals. But schools have, during the past decade, tended to place principals in roles that remove them from active participation in classrooms, lessening in the process their personal enthusiasm for children and learning and their ability to provide teachers very much support. (The practice in many communities of giving principals responsibility for two or three different schools is hardly a direction that can support improved teaching or learning.)

An assessment of open education, even the cursory one I am outlining, needs to speak to some of the problems that exist—issues that need to be responded to if open education is to be sustained in an optimal manner. In spite of the increasing number of alternative schools and schools within schools, as well as some inquiry-oriented, integrated curriculum programs beginning to arise at the secondary level, open education remains predominately an elementary school effort. The assumptions that underlie open education at the elementary school level are equally applicable in the secondary schools. But who is working with secondary teachers? Many parents and teachers who are actively involved in organizing open classrooms are concerned about continuity: "What will happen to the youngsters when they reach the junior high or high school?" While this is not yet a critical issue, it is likely to become one as larger numbers of children complete their elementary education in open classrooms.

One of the major goals of more open processes of education is integration in learning. Integration, in large measure, relates not only to more horizontal learning—less tied to typical curriculum definitions—but to intensity in learning. We have found integration to be more complex than most other aspects of open education. In part, this is related to the longstanding dominance of a separate subject-matter curriculum organization. Teachers feel some pressures, even in the best of settings, to make certain they direct some specific energy to reading, math, and science as separate areas of learning. Social studies and the creative arts are the areas where more integrated learning tends to be organized, inasmuch as they are not *viewed as absolutely essential* to very many people.

In addition, the entire practice of standardized testing, which many schools use to respond to an array of evaluation/accountability demands, contributes to many of the pressures to work at reading, math, and science through narrow instructional means, limiting further the potential for more integrated learning. It is absolutely essential that schools get out from under the "tyranny of tests" that tends to influence instructional patterns negatively and does not contribute to the learning of children or to the capacity of teachers to improve the quality of what they do. While many educators, in particular those involved in the North Dakota Study Group on Evaluation, are attempting to provide support for alternative means of evaluation, few foresee a rapid end to the pressures of standardized testing efforts.

Graded patterns of school organization also seem to work against more integrated learning. Teachers with whom we are involved feel that they would make greater progress if they remained with a group of children over a two- or three-year period rather than being assigned a new group of children each year. They argue, correctly I believe, that integration demands that teachers know the children so well that they are familiar with their interests, can anticipate their responses and questions, know the learning extensions individuals are likely to make, and sense the materials that are most appropriate to the learning styles of particular children. In research we have conducted (Patton, 1973a) since 1971, the variable that has continued to have the greatest influence on the degree of openness in a classroom has been multi-age grouping.

In spite of the growing movement toward open classroom practice, with its emphasis on community resources, there remains a narrow use of the community. In general, it has tended to bring parents to the schools. As positive as this is, the schools remain dominant in the exchange, establishing most of the conditions. This is not an issue the classroom teacher can really be expected to contend with alone. Meeting children well in the classroom, as well as organizing to use community resources there, is an arduous task in itself, let alone arranging for the myriad of potential learnings that exist outside, *in* the community. Schools would do well to provide staff who could devote *all* of their energies to organizing/facilitating the use of resources outside the school. But it might not be enough. The community itself needs to see itself as integral to the entire process of education, not separate from it. Bringing about an intersection of the school and the community is necessary if the strengths of each are to be made a part of children's education. I am not at all optimistic that progress in this arena will be very rapid.

It should also be noted that much of the base upon which open education in the United States rests has been developed with the use of federal and private foundation dollars. Now that a base has been established and expansion is more possible than ever before, federal and foundation dollars are declining rapidly. The effects of this loss are not apparent enough yet to make any large generalization. However, if our experience at the University of North Dakota is typical, open education may well begin to level off. The staff at the Center for Teaching and Learning capable of giving support to open education practice declined by 30 percent between 1972 and 1975. Our advisory services have been reduced. We can no longer respond adequately to the large number of requests for assistance. So much energy is being devoted to meeting our present, scaled-down efforts that little is left for extending our formulations about open education and its practice. And our experience is not unique.

Another factor that may have an effect on open education practice is the well-publicized "teacher surplus." It could foster a resurgence of conservatism in educational practice, less willingness to risk the struggle that open education often demands. It surely will limit the access to teaching of large numbers of new teachers who have had good preparation, making renewal in schools more difficult.

I suspect that it would be easy enough, given the "recession" in education, to withdraw from efforts to make schools more responsive to children, to negate what is being learned in the process of educational reexamination and more open processes of education, to "go back to the basics," a growing euphemism for the conservative reaction in education that has parallels in the arenas of economics, social welfare, and civil rights. Fortunately, the commitments are larger than that. While I do not foresee a time soon when schools will be, on a massive scale, as responsive as they *could be*, decent and humane schools are increasing. The progressive hopes, revived with the advent of open education, are still alive.

CHAPTER SEVEN

Progressive Schools: A Critical Legacy in Conservative America

This talk was given at a 1982 conference hosted by the Miquon School that brought together approximately 75 schools with longstanding progressive traditions; it was subsequently published in the proceedings, entitled Reunion and Reaffirmation *(Jervis, 1983). Many of these schools were founded in the 1920s and 1930s by progressive reformers. Parts of this paper had previously been presented at the 1976 Conference at City College, New York celebrating ''The Roots of Open Education'' and were published in the proceedings (Arthur Tobier, editor). The Miquon Conference sparked the beginning of a new progressive education publication (*Pathways*) and a resurgence of interest in progressivism. The Bank Street-Columbia Teachers College Progressive Education Conference in October 1986 and the Cambridge School Progressive Education Conference in October 1987 kept interest high among increasing numbers of educators from public and private schools. While a revival of the Progressive Education Association is unlikely—and probably not desirable, given the bureaucratic formalism of its structure—national and regional gatherings of those who support progressive formulations are becoming more common.*

It is important, even when it appears that there is more interest than ever in conservative, fairly narrow educational directions, not to lose sight of an ongoing and important progressive education movement, to keep in mind that other possibilities exist. What currently passes for education in many school districts is not particularly uplifting.

This is a time, for example, when a large number of public school systems in the country view the arts as elitist, if not frivolous, inquiry as a luxury in addition to being inefficient, community studies as political and controversial, reading as decoding, and writing as mechanics. The achievement of such goals as "raising attendance by 5 percent," "increasing reading scores (on some standardized test) by 10 percent," or "reducing suspensions by 12 percent" is celebrated in many schools. Some even announce these kinds of goals to the world on billboard signs as a means of demonstrating their "purposefulness and vigor." The dominant definers of educational discourse have increasingly become embodied in such phrases as *direct instruction, time on task, basic skills, competency measures,* and *instructional systems,* to mention only a sample. These are not especially liberating or progressive formulations, even though the full-blown descriptions make use of much that was common in progressive language—such as individualization, high expectations, and focus on learning.

In light of current educational circumstances—and one could certainly find corresponding examples beyond education—it may appear anomalous to be celebrating as we are the visions of those who began the still-flowering progressive schools represented at this conference. Those who poured their lives into these schools wanted settings in which children and their growth, natural interests, curiosity, and creativity were primary, places that developed, as Grace Rotzel (1971) notes, "all of the native capacities of each child" instead of just teaching reading, writing, and the gathering of facts. Those who sacrificed to construct a base for these schools even talked unabashedly about wanting for children a world in which cooperation, human understanding, democratic practice—citizenship writ broadly—and peace were dominant themes. And they characteristically saw the schools as being central to the fulfillment of such a world. While such visions may seem on the surface a bit out of place—even contradictory—in this current manifestation of a technocratic and conservative America, they remain critical, part of the important legacy that each of us needs to keep alive, the base for a continuing and necessary progressive outline of education.

Historically, progressivism in American life, whether in education or in the larger culture, has been juxtaposed in one way or another to a number of contrary world views. At the turn of the century these progressive views were proclaimed in loud and brassy tones and appeared on the verge of becoming the dominant ideology of twentieth-century America; in the 1920s and 1930s, in the aftermath of a tragic war and in the midst of the Great Depression, progressivism became quieter, while still maintaining much of its intellectual vigor; with World War II and the Cold War years that followed, progressivism went into a significant slump; after a brief flowering in the 1960s, progressivism has become muted, its sounds barely audible. Much of the responsibility for bringing back a progressive voice, reestablishing in concrete terms a vision of what is possible—at least in regard to education—rests with many of us here.

Given the commemorative nature of this event, it seems appropriate—maybe even necessary—to provide an outline of progressive education in America, to place the schools represented at this gathering within an important historical frame. But it is also necesssary to outline a perspective aimed at assuring that the best of progressive thought continues to offer a challenge to the conservative, and simple, formulations of education that are being adopted today with such a vengeance. Neither of these tasks can be done comprehensively in a short space, causing me necessarily to address large themes at the expense of critical detail.

As a self-conscious movement, progressivism in America belongs to the turn of the current century, defined by historians as "an attempt to develop the moral will, the intellectual insight and the political and administrative agencies to remedy the accumulated negligences of a period of . . . growth" (Hofstadter, 1964, p. 4). As a philosophy, however, its roots are obviously older, going back well into the eighteenth century. And as an educational formulation in America, it is necessary to go back to at least the pre–Civil War period for a significant base. It is in this pre–Civil War period that I will begin this abbreviated discussion of progressivism. Beginning at this point educationally is not to suggest that schooling was an unimportant element in American life earlier—after all, legislation supporting public schools came as early as 1647 in Massachusetts. But it is in that period, specifically the 1840s, when a serious commitment to universal education was initiated (Cremin, 1961).

Nineteenth Century

Horace Mann in Massachusetts, Henry Barnard in Connecticut, and John D. Pierce in Michigan were the early evangelists for universal education, the establishment of schools where, to paraphrase the sentiment of the day, all of America's children could meet, where democratic life could be nurtured, strong character built, and economic and cultural growth guaranteed. While the common schools hardly became, understandably, the enlightened settings Mann,

Barnard, and Pierce envisioned, they did rather quickly become an integral part of the fabric of American society. Those of us from the West, the other side of the Appalachians, were steeped in the literature of our nineteenth-century origins—of schools and towns being built simultaneously, with the ever-present search for a suitable "school marm."

The schools grew even more rapidly than Mann could have envisioned, especially in the post–Civil War period. But not surprisingly, given such growth, pedagogical practices and teacher training tended not to keep pace. (This also occurred to some degree in the growth period of the 1950s.) As the schools enlarged in number and became incorporated into state systems, they also became increasingly more systematized and formal. America's rhetoric has always favored informality and decentralization, but our organizational practices have tended to be otherwise. The graded patterns we know so well had become the norm by 1870. Covering the material encompassed within first-, second-, and third-grade readers, for example, became a dominant theme in the schools. (There has even been in some settings a resurrection of these nineteenth-century readers in the belief that some idyllic past can be reconstructed.) Memorization took up much of a child's time. The language of the factory, rapidly becoming in the latter nineteenth century a dominant force in the American economy, became, as well, the metaphoric language of the broader culture, the schools included (Katz, 1971; Pratt, 1973).

While universalism was the stated goal, it was difficult to achieve. Fewer than 25 percent who began school in the nineteenth century, for example, completed the elementary programs. And in spite of the best hopes of such egalitarians as Mann, the common schools, especially in the East, served mostly the poor and lower middle classes (with blacks generally excluded). Those with means found other institutions for their children. Widespread public commitments to support secondary schools came only in the closing decades of the nineteenth century. There were, to cite an example, 35,000 elementary school students in North Dakota in 1890 but fewer than 500 enrolled in secondary schools (Rolfsrud, 1963).

Tending to be academic in nature, these late nineteenth-century secondary schools attracted, in contrast to the common elementary schools, few young people from working-class or newly arrived immigrant families. Only in the 1920s did the high schools begin to attract these individuals in any significant numbers. (See Curti, 1964; Greer, 1972; Krug, 1964; Rugg, 1947; Spring, 1972; Tyack, 1967;

Welter, 1962). In 1900, only 8 percent of the secondary school-age population were attending a post–eighth grade school. And we need, in fact, to go to the post–World War II period before the percentage attending secondary school gets close to anything that can truly be called universal.

This nineteenth-century beginning was fraught with difficulties not unlike those currently faced by a myriad of Third World countries. (That, by the way, is how my Third World students understand this history.) Fiscal support was inadequate, and school facilities could not be built rapidly enough to take care of the numbers of children who wished to attend. In addition, precedents for mass schooling did not exist, and the surrounding social order was in a state of rapid transition, especially in the urban areas. The urban population, for example, increased from 9.9 million in 1870 to more than 30 million by 1900. And many of our major cities doubled in population during this period of time (Hofstadter, 1968).

In spite of the acknowledged difficulties, however, there were persons willing to challenge pedagogical practices and organizational patterns in the schools, to offer alternative visions of what was possible. This is particularly important to acknowledge now, when so many have given up on any belief that much can be done in the schools or that it is possible to speak about change. To read these turn-of-the-century accounts is to gain some understanding of the intelligent, thoughtful, often courageous debates that undergirded the early twentieth-century progressive critique that led to the founding of so many of the schools represented at this commemorative conference. Narrowly, the basic challenges tended to focus on breaking the linear curriculum chain, the rote nature of teaching and learning, the formalism, and the growing centralization of schools. Broadly, the focus was on the creation of a more democratic society. Brooks Adams, a prominent historian and Boston school board member, framed the critique as well as anyone in an 1879 *Atlantic* essay when he wrote: "Knowing that you cannot teach a child everything, it is best to teach a child how to learn" (quoted in Beringause, 1955, pp. 66–67). With this, Adams proceeded to show that most practice had little connection to such a purpose.

Although the general thrust of such a critique did not represent a majority position, it was repeated, as well as elaborated upon, often enough by a sufficient number of people to encourage the beginnings of an important reform movement. Who were some of the early progressive reformers of the common school? Referred to by John Dewey as the "father of progressive education," Francis W. Parker accepted in 1873 the superintendency of the Quincy, Massachusetts, schools with a commitment to bring back enthusiasm for teaching and learning. He quickly initiated policies to bring an end to the linear, lockstep curriculum, along with the traditional readers and spellers; encouraged teacher initiative in the development of curriculum; supported the use of newspapers, magazines, and field trips into the community as a base for local history and geography; and introduced manipulative devices for teaching arithmetic. Parker was intent on large-scale reform, so much so that he aroused considerable controversy.

In response to some of his critics in the state Department of Education, who thought the Quincy schools were abandoning reading, writing, and mathematics and "experimenting with children," Parker wrote in his 1879 annual report to the school committee:

> I am simply trying to apply well established principles of teaching . . . the methods springing from them are found in the development of every child. They are used everywhere except in school. (quoted in Cremin, 1961, p. 130)

I suspect that many here have said such a thing on any number of occasions. Certainly Dewey's early efforts began with such a premise, as did those of the founders of the schools represented at this conference.

In 1882, Parker went on to the directorship of the Cook County Normal and Practice School in Chicago, where he continued to promote child-centered practices. His *Talks on Pedagogics* (1894) was particularly popular among teachers, representing in its own way an early progressive tract.

As the nineteenth century drew to a close, proposals to focus on the child rather than subject matter, on active rather than passive learning, began to come from a wide range of sources outside as well as inside the organized educational establishment. (This, by the way, was true also in the 1960s.) I remain perplexed, however, at how little the schools formally allied themselves with these external reform efforts, how separate the worlds were then and still are today.

One such important external source was the settlement house movement. The range of activities engaged in by the settlement houses was particularly broad (Davis, 1967). Their agendas included active campaigning for improved housing, child-labor laws, neighborhood recreational facilities, and provisions for medical care, including a national health insurance plan. In addition to struggling for the construction of increased numbers of elementary schools, leaders in the settlement houses called for a different kind of education, one that concerned itself with children's physical and social well-being along with their intellectual growth. Many of the settlement houses organized cooperative nurseries, conducted kindergarten programs, and provided a variety of opportunities for intergenerational learning. They tended to view education as having an integral relationship to their efforts at improving the quality of community life (Hall, 1971). Jane Addams (1902, 1910), one of the most active and forceful leaders of the settlement house movement and director of Hull House, used the phrase *socialized education* for the forms she advocated.

Another important early twentieth-century source of progressive educational thought came through the country life movement, which was given intellectual leadership by Liberty Hyde Bailey, Dean of Agriculture at Cornell. This movement grew out of an interest in revitalizing the quality of life in rural communities where population growth had plateaued or begun to decline. In relation specifically to schools, Bailey (1911) wanted to see the country schools without "screwed down seats" and children at work with tools and soils and plants and problems. In the first two decades of the twentieth century, Cornell turned out lively curriculum materials buttressed by a progressive orientation to schooling.

Another individual who provided impetus for progressivism in schools—indeed the person who is credited with first using the term *progressivism* in regard to schools—was Joseph Meyer Rice. Trained as a pediatrician, Rice became sufficiently concerned about school practice to undertake in 1892, on behalf of the *Forum*, a leading opinion journal of the day, a status study of American education. His report, which ran in eight issues of the *Forum* between October 1892 and June 1893, had an electric quality, stimulating widespread public discussion and enough self-consciousness among educational reformers to give some shape to an active progressive movement in education. Rice painted a dismal picture of schools dominated by politicians and filled with corruption and incompetence. He was particulary critical of classroom practices that were little more than sing-song drill, repetition, and disconnected knowledge. In addition to his sharp critique, however, Rice called attention to a number of examples of more child-centered, progressive practice, with Parker's practice school receiving his most enthusiastic response.

John Dewey, a product of nineteenth-century America, but one who maintained an active intellectual life to the middle of our current century, gave, more than any other person, the progressive movement in education its intellectual leadership. Through his writings, he continues to provide inspiration to many of those who seek more progressive practices in schools. (I have included in my reference list some of Dewey's writings, along with accounts that synthesize his ideas.)

In 1896, Dewey, his wife Alice, and several neighbors began a laboratory school to put into practice some of the educational theory that Dewey had been generating. The theory was formulated around education as a means for growth, activity, community building, reciprocity in teaching and learning, moral development, and democracy. Dewey talked often about the school reflecting "the larger society, and permeated throughout with the spirit of art, history, and science" (Dewey, 1899/1956, p. 29). The school opened with 16 children and 2 teachers; by 1902, it had 140 children, 23 regular teachers, and 10 assistants who were University of Chicago graduate students. While its life was relatively short, closing in 1904, it had a long enough history to help Dewey consolidate his educational theory. Unfortunately, however, what occurred—the practice—in that laboratory school did not become as accessible in the literature of the early progressive period as Dewey's more theoretical publications. This lack becomes quickly apparent as one reads *The Dewey School: The Laboratory School of the University of Chicago*, written by Katherine Camp Mayhew and Anna Camp Edwards, sisters who taught in the school, and not published until 1936. In this account, readers are told about the thinking, the actual curriculum efforts, children's and teachers' actions, and the careful reflection about practice that permeated the setting. It may well have been early progressivism, in practice, at its best. Had it been a more integral part of the early progressive literature, the movement might have been more solid and developed more successfully.

In *Schools of Tomorrow* (Dewey & Dewey, 1915/1962), Dewey presented his educational views in a fairly concrete fashion, as well as his belief that American education was characterized by a lack of democratic practice. In addition, he described, with assistance from his daughter, Evelyn, schools in many parts of the country that were attempting to implement progressive practice. Among the schools that Dewey highlighted was the School for Organic Education in Fairhope, Alabama, founded in 1907 by Marietta Johnson, who was to occupy one of the hallowed niches of progressive education. (Grace Rotzel, who in her 1971 book recounted her experiences as the first administrator of The School in Rose Valley, apprenticed at

Fairhope, as did many other founders of 1920s progressive schools.)

Marietta Johnson's educational autobiography, *Thirty Years with an Idea* (1974), describes well an educational transformation that many present here would likely identify with. She came from Minnesota and taught for several years in St. Paul. At one point she asked the St. Paul superintendent why the school programs had so little relation to children's natural development. His response—to paraphrase—was: "Isn't it disgraceful that they don't?" Shortly thereafter, Marietta Johnson decided to begin a school. A woman with deep insights into learning, she was also full of bravado, capable of convincing almost anyone that reform along progressive education lines was absolutely essential to children's well-being.

Given the intellectual ferment created in the early years of the twentieth century by some of those I have introduced briefly, and buttressed by a large social reform movement, a self-conscious progressivism began to take hold in many schools: for example, the University of Missouri Lab School in 1904; Caroline Pratt's City and Country School, the Ethical Culture Schools in New York City, the Park School in Baltimore, Bryn Mawr Elementary School, and the Edgewood School of Greenwich, Connecticut, in 1913; Margaret Naumberg's Walden School in New York City, the Shady Hill School in Cambridge, Massachusetts, the University of Iowa Elementary School, and the Oak Lane Country Day School in Philadelphia in 1915–1916; and the Lincoln School associated with Teachers College, Columbia, in 1917. In the late 1920s and early 1930s, there was another revival, including the School in Rose Valley, Miquon, and the Open Air School in Cleveland. In addition, Friends' Schools, located in a number of eastern communities, took on a progressive orientation. The Minneapolis public schools in Minnesota and the Winnetka schools in Illinois also organized self-consciously around progressive principles in the 1920s. Even in classrooms and schools where self-conscious progressivism was not pursued, there was increasing support for taking the child into account. Formalism of the sort that dominated nineteenth-century schools began to subside (Rugg & Shumaker, 1928; Winsor, 1973).

To say that nineteenth-century formalism was receding, however, ought not to suggest that progressivism in its largest sense had become the dominant practice in schools. Harold Rugg and Ann Shumaker (1928) reported in their study of child-centered schools, for example, that: "The child-centered schools as yet constitute but a corporal's guard" (p. 3). Nonetheless, there was enough occurring to keep progressivism alive and capable of influencing educational practice in general. The same could be said of the 1960s, when media attention encouraged the belief that the schools were all changing, even though more conservative orientations remained dominant throughout the decade as well.

With the growth of progressive practice, interest in communication increased. It was this motivation, as well as a desire to bring about more pressure for reform, that served as an impetus for organizing the Progressive Education Association in 1919, the prime mover of which was Stanwood Cobb, who had been introduced to progressivism by Marietta Johnson. Charles Eliot, then president of Harvard, accepted the honorary presidency. After Eliot's death in 1927, John Dewey agreed, with some reluctance because of his concerns about the "movement," to accept the honorary presidency. From a modest beginning, the association grew to almost 11,000 members at its height in 1938. It was vigorous and mission oriented, especially in its early years. Its journal, *Progressive Education*, begun in 1924, was *the* education journal of its day.

To read the literature of the late 1920s and early 1930s is in some ways to relive education in the 1960s. There are many parallels in the language and philosophic orientations. But, as in the 1960s, the quality of the analysis did not remain uniformly high over the years. With the growing popularization of progressive views, surface descriptions became dominant. The tie of the schools to the larger culture became increasingly submerged. The interplay of theory and practice got lost in discussions about teaching methods and organizational patterns. Harold Rugg (1947) wrote later in this regard that "teachers have not become students—either of society, of child needs or curriculum construction" (p. 315). Are things different now? Are teachers, even in the continuing progressive schools, the students of teaching, of society, of child needs that successful progressivism had always promised? This is a challenge that needs addressing, now and in the future.

The Great Depression undoubtedly affected progressivism in the schools. The economic collapse was so severe that the problems of the schools paled in comparison. Nonetheless, in the face of an economic collapse greater than any other in the nation's history, school boards maintained many of the programs begun with progressive impetus; namely, those in the fine and practical arts as well as in extracurricular activities such as clubs, sports, and theater. Such is not the case in today's less severe economic crisis, suggesting that progressive impulses may not now be as potent.

The Progressive Education Association, along with the economy, fell into hard times in the 1930s. Ideological issues became especially dominant, with individuals such as George Counts pushing for more attention to "social and political obligations." Such questions as those about inequality in the schools, racial segregation, testing and tracking, and social composition of school boards, about which consciousness was growing, were set aside, though they re-emerged within the 1960s movement. These kinds of concerns are arising again as we move into the 1980s, but who is speaking?

With the Second World War, the educational debates went further into eclipse. While the Progressive Education Association continued to publish, the focus of its work became less connected to practice than in its earlier years.

"Life adjustment" education, especially in relation to the secondary schools, was part of the postwar progressive ideology. Poorly defined, lacking a theoretical base (certainly far removed from Dewey's concept of community), it floundered. "Progressive education" was no longer popular. Among others, historian Arthur Bestor, a graduate of the progressive Lincoln School, led a series of attacks on postwar progressivism. His *Educational Wastelands* (1953) was a particularly harsh statement describing "life adjustment" education as a "retreat from learning." Schools were on the defensive to an almost unprecedented degree. In 1955, the Progressive Education Association went out of existence; *Progressive Education*, long past its vital period, collapsed two years later.

Lawrence Cremin (1961) closed out his important work on the progressive education movement by suggesting that "perhaps . . . [progressivism in education] only awaited the reformulation . . . that would ultimately derive from a larger resurgence of reform in American life and thought" (p. 253). This may well have been prophetic.

The 1960s brought about a major social revolution in the United States. The Civil Rights movement, which gained in momentum in the latter years of the 1950s, was a fulcrum for social and political reform in the 1960s. The inequities in American life became increasingly apparent. The failure of the education system to provide quality schooling on an equal basis to all Americans became a potent issue. Support for pluralism, long cast aside in the wake of melting-pot theory, became recognized as necessary for the creation of social democracy. Depersonalization, created in part by increasing levels of technology and bureaucratization in all phases of American life, brought a sometimes radical response. The recognition of how rapidly our natural resources were being depleted and defaced brought an increased concern for "spaceship earth." And the war in Vietnam, which proved to be more unpopular than any previous U.S. military involvement, brought protest to a high level. It was within this particular milieu that a new wave of educational reform began, building on much that was basic to earlier reform efforts. Regarding the schools, however, not enough had been learned soon enough from the earlier progressive period to make the most of this historical opportunity. This was the case, in part, because many 1960s progressives seemed to reject historical analysis; but it was also the result of insufficient description of good earlier practice being accessible for examination.

Did the progressive movement of the 1960s add anything to earlier efforts? There was certainly more supportive theory available to buttress good practice; there was a higher overall degree of conscious attention to careful documentation; the meaning of community was affirmed in a more articulate manner; and teacher education efforts became a bit more consonant with practice. But even these advances have been insufficient to keep a reform direction alive in a recessionary economy that exists at a time in which America's longstanding and dominant technological, moral, and political position in the world has come under serious challenge.

Situation at Present

Given the current circumstances, it would be easy enough to withdraw from efforts to make schools more responsive to children, to negate what has been learned from a longstanding progressive critique as well as practice, to seek shelter in the protective environments that we all know how to create. The schools represented here, legacies of an early twentieth-century progressivism, live, in many respects, within such a protected environment, free of many of the burdens of schools in the public arena, especially those in the cities. Given the particular history to which all of us here are heir, we cannot rest. Joe Segar, headmaster of Shady Hill, said it well on the occasion of Shady Hill's fiftieth anniversary: "Shady Hill has been a pioneer, but pioneers have a tendency to become settlers" (quoted in Yeomans, 1979, p. 124). Several things are important in the struggle to maintain a pioneering spirit.

To begin with, those in schools where progressivism continues to flourish—or at least maintains itself in regard to critical areas of education—need to challenge more directly the narrow, technocratic

educational formulations that have again come to dominate thinking about schools. They need to make as public as possible their beliefs that schools can be liberating institutions characterized by
challenge, a wide assortment of materials, individualization, open-
ended inquiry, analysis and synthesis, literature, art and music, and
the like. To be effective, however, such a challenge must come from
teachers, administrators, and parents associated with both private
and public schools.

In the 1960s, there was a resurgence of progressivism in the
public schools and some 1920s-style reconnections between public
and private school practitioners. But while this progressivism may
have survived in long-established private schools, it was dealt heavy
blows in the public schools during the 1970s. With the diminished
support in the public schools for more child-centered, progressive
practices and the corresponding dominance of such narrow formulations as "basic skills instruction" and "time on task," private-
public school connections seem again to have dwindled, even collapsed. Those in the public schools who wish to continue to struggle for a more uplifting, liberating view of education are especially
beleaguered, lacking in significant support. Those in the private
schools need to reach out again, to join those in the public sector to
reaffirm the most constructive elements of progressive practice, to
regain together a sufficiently potent voice to challenge current formulations of education.

To reaffirm those aspects of progressivism is, in part, to begin
again to give thoughtful attention to articulating purposes and practices, to reestablish some control over the language of good education. One means for such a reaffirmation is to give renewed attention
to careful descriptions of teaching and learning written by teachers
in classrooms that value children's interests and intentions, where
the educational encounter is viewed expansively rather than narrowly. Such descriptions are one way of challenging an increasingly
debilitating literature and correspondingly debilitating conventional wisdom that suggest diminished teacher autonomy, reduced
professionalism, and an emphasis on schooling rather than education.

To speak of challenging conventional wisdom, to reaffirm support for those older progressive visions, is also to be concerned about
the quality of persons now attracted to teaching. My interest in
careful description is related. The 1960s brought into teaching a large
number of young people who genuinely believed that within the
schools there would be support for creative attention to the social and

intellectual needs of children and young people, room for significant integration of academic and community interests, education in the broadest sense. The Peace Corps attracted similarly motivated persons during those years. Too many of these young people are gone, and too few like them are now considering teaching as a career. Teaching today is neither generally viewed nor typically described as personally enriching, challenging, and potent; in part, this is because teaching in too many schools has lost its authority, its source of individuality, and schools, especially in the public arena, have ceased to be centers of inquiry that promote teacher efficacy.

Teaching as a field needs revitalization; it needs to attract again the best and brightest, intellectually and morally. Building a literature of teaching written by those in the midst of settings where teaching continues to have potency would be a wonderful counterpoint to the descriptions of teachers as managers, passing out and collecting worksheets geared to skill deficiencies identified by scores on a host of standardized and criterion-referenced tests. We need good descriptions to counteract those suggesting that "effective teaching," especially in settings with a predominance of minority and poor children, consists of carefully sequenced curriculum, whole group instruction, drill, a narrow range of materials, little elaboration, and questions of a low cognitive nature.

I suggest that we all go back again to the descriptions of the Dewey School, to the writings of Grace Rotzel, Julia Weber Gordon, Caroline Pratt, Agnes DeLima, Ella Flagg Young, Lelia Partridge, Susan Blow, Marietta Johnson, Edward Yeomans, Katharine Taylor, Lucy Sprague Mitchell, Harriet Johnson, Elwyn Richardson, Frances Hawkins, Dorothy and John Paull, Lydia Smith, Patricia Carini, Eleanor Duckworth, among others, for some sense of what these descriptive efforts might look like.

As a historian, I view these descriptions as more than grist for challenge to contemporary formulations of education; I view them also as an important base for the long-term progressive struggle for better schools, as part of an ongoing effort to assure that what is learned is retained, as capable of informing the next generation of progressives who might be even more successful because of our efforts now when conditions appear so unsympathetic and complex.

Part III
TEACHER EDUCATION

CHAPTER EIGHT

The New School
and Some Thoughts
About Teacher Education

The New School was an extraordinary institution that existed as an experimental college at the University of North Dakota from 1968 to 1972. This particular statement was written in the fall of 1972 as the Center for Teaching and Learning was beginning its "replacement" life. It was an attempt to get some of the history together. It draws heavily from "The New School" (written with my colleague, Warren Strandberg), which appeared in the Elementary School Journal *(Vol. 71, No. 8, 1971) and was later reprinted in Ewald Nyquist and Gene Hawes,* Open Education: A Sourcebook *(Bantam, 1972). The paper is included in this collection for historical purposes but more importantly because it expresses a point of view about teacher education that has relevance for current discussion.*

Teacher education programs, as typically practiced, are narrowly based, often isolated from schools and communities. And the lack in most programs of a central, well-defined, intellectual and moral purpose has limited greatly their possibilities. While departments and schools of education are found in most colleges and universities, they are seldom highly respected; the quality of their scholarship and intellectual inquiry tends to be low, and the effectiveness and thoughtfulness of their service are typically limited by the inadequate experience level of their faculties. While the increasingly harsh critique of public education weighs heavily on elementary and secondary schools and teachers, college and university faculty involved in the preservice and inservice preparation of educational personnel must bear considerable responsibility for many of the difficulties in the schools.

Reform in teacher education has been on the social agenda for several decades. Nonetheless, few institutions have gone beyond tinkering, limiting their efforts, for the most part, to alterations of credit-hour requirements, adding a little more internship experience for the students, and utilizing some new technologies (principally television). The New School, from the outset, sought to do more.

The New School was consciously organized as a center for educational renewal—constructive change—not only for North Dakota's elementary schools and their teachers but also for the state's teacher education programs. The hope was that the New School could provide to schools *and* programs in teacher education some needed fresh perspective by organizing alternative patterns for working with teachers, schools, parents, and children. In relation to the question of a fresh perspective, John Gardner (1964) notes:

> The ever renewing organization is not one which is convinced that it enjoys eternal youth. It knows it is forever growing old and must do something about it. It knows that it is always providing dead wood and must for that reason attend to its seed beds. The seed beds are new ideas, new ways of doing things, new approaches. (p. 68)

Some of the major threads of these alternative patterns—different ways of doing things—are outlined below.

The Community and the University

Teacher education programs, even those considered most innovative, seldom have a significant impact on public education in the regions they serve. That portion of a university committed to the preparation of teachers is often removed from the societal forces that effect change in the public schools. At the same time, local school districts and the communities they represent do not make any meaningful contribution to the preparation of teachers. For the most part, the contacts between the two agencies are peripheral, limited to arrangements for placing student teachers, consulting, and conducting inservice workshops. This is much too wasteful of valuable human resources and hardly intense enough. Neither party, for example, is obligated in such an arrangement to examine the other's area of prime responsibility; the "mutual strengths of the two kinds of institutions involved" are not exploited (Goodlad, 1969, p. 5). There is virtually no challenge for renewal, for moving beyond convention. The university and local school districts can offer each other considerably more by establishing the kinds of relationships that encourage each to participate more productively in the sphere of the other, that call for a greater reciprocity, for mutual growth.

The isolation that has traditionally existed between the university and local communities was bridged to a fairly large degree in North Dakota by the establishment of cooperative relationships between the New School and participating school districts. One of the major reasons for establishing closer ties between the two was the desire to upgrade the preparation of the 60 percent of North Dakota's elementary school teachers who lacked a baccalaureate degree. This remained an important objective throughout the four years in which the New School functioned as an experimental college. But the relationships moved far beyond this, becoming more ecological— more encompassing—in relation to teacher education, schools, and communities.

In the teacher exchange program, one element in the renewal effort, a school district that formally agreed to participate in a cooperative relationship with the New School temporarily released some of its teachers who lacked baccalaureate degrees so they could complete their college education. In several instances, an entire elementary school staff returned to the university.[1] Each of these teachers was replaced by a teacher-intern enrolled in a master's level program in the New School. The teachers who participated in the exchange by returning to the university were, by and large, individuals who *wanted* to increase their effectiveness with children, were concerned about personalization, were anxious to become learners again, and were willing to assume risks. I am convinced that the voluntary quality of the teacher exchange program was one of the major reasons for its success.

One important result of the teacher exchange program was a productive collaboration between the New School and individual school districts. The New School assumed increased responsibility for the quality of instruction in classrooms staffed by New School resident interns. The cooperating school districts in turn became more active participants in the process of teacher preparation. Each enterprise began to share more in the responsibilities that had traditionally belonged to the other. Further, by accepting the New

---

1. These teachers enrolled at an appropriate academic level and continued through the completion of a baccalaureate degree. While enrolled at the university, they received a stipend equal to approximately three-fourths of their teaching salary.

School master's level interns into its schools, the local community was expressing its willingness to allow alternative patterns of thought and action to be brought into juxtaposition with its more established ways. Thus the local community had an opportunity to gain greater insight into what it was doing. Additionally, by entering into a cooperative agreement, the local school district agreed to assist the New School interns in creating more individualized and personalized modes of instruction in its classrooms. In return, the New School pledged its institutional resources in support of the interns' efforts in the classrooms. It also provided in-service assistance to other teachers in a cooperating school.

An Alternative Learning Environment for the Elementary Classroom

There would be limited value in an alternative teacher preparation program—any teacher preparation program, for that matter—and different university-community relationships if they did not lead to significant changes in teachers' practices and the learning environments provided for children. Such a view was taken seriously.

The New School was established on the assumption that a focused advocacy was necessary. That advocacy was developed around the following beliefs: Children's learning is enhanced when it is centered on their own experiences, needs, and interests and when the children participate more actively in the direction of their own learning activities; children's learning is extended constructively when their parents are active participants and the fullest resources of communities are made accessible to children and schools; and teachers are capable of becoming students of teaching, critical and thoughtful curriculum makers and decision makers about classroom practice. While the educational literature has long given support to such beliefs, most North Dakota schools, indeed most schools throughout the country, did not and still do not function on the basis of such understandings. But schools *can* be places where children, and teachers as well, are given back a sense of potency about learning. Schools *can* relate to children's experiences outside of the school; involve parents and other human resources within a community; nurture the inquiring, imaginative spirit characteristic of children as well as teachers; and maintain sufficient flexibility so that the interests, ambitions, and needs of each child can be taken into account. Creating and fostering such settings became central to the New School's work.

Structural Organization

Almost all teacher preparation programs, including those most actively engaged in change, operate within curriculum and administrative structures that separate the liberal arts from professional education. They are almost universally identified as *the two major components* of teacher education. The unique character and function of most teacher preparation programs, even those committed to change, seem to be developed within such an established framework (Silberman, 1970). But teacher education tends to suffer when institutional, epistemological, or curriculum structures necessitate that liberal and professional education be carried out in isolation from one another, always seen as different. Not only does this limit the alternatives for action, but, more importantly, it also tends to limit the ways we think about education.

Teaching can be, and ought to be, a liberalizing force in one's life, infusing it with vitality and a sense of purpose. If we are to build into the professional life of teaching an opportunity to be creative, a sense of commitment, and a willingness to challenge existing practice, then we are going to have to recast teacher preparation. In the process, teacher education will take on a more liberalizing quality. We might do as Paul Nash (1966) suggests:

> Rather than follow the traditional pattern, which often consists of tacking "liberal arts" courses upon professional courses in the hope that some alchemy within the individual will transform the ingredients into a liberating education, we should experiment with the use of the individual's professional interest as a focus from which he can move out in a liberating exploration of its wider human implications. (p. 41)

The education that prepares a person for such a liberalizing occupation as teaching ought to express within itself a sense of unity. The life of teaching cannot be compartmentalized, and neither should the education that prepares a person for that life. While the established structure of liberal and professional education may reflect the realities of our present situation, that structure does not reflect the possibilities of an educational setting that makes preparation for a future occupation an integral part of a person's total life-meaning.

The New School was created, in part, to test the validity of an alternative to the longstanding liberal arts/professional education separation. From its inception in 1968, the New School operated as one structural unit. It brought together faculty members with diverse academic and professional backgrounds in the humanities, the

social sciences, mathematics, the natural sciences, and education. All
faculty members shared equally in the shaping of the academic program. Because of this unique structural organization, the New School
was able to offer its participants all components of a teacher preparation program without the liabilities of traditional distinctions between liberal and professional education. Students did not have to
remove themselves from their focus on teaching to participate in such
areas as creative writing, history, poetry, literature, math, science,
art, and music.

The structural organization of the New School made it difficult
for faculty and students to fall back on the traditional dichotomy between liberal and professional education by establishing a setting
where a variety of educational perspectives, interests, and modes of
inquiry could intersect. Such intersection at times caused considerable tension, but it also stimulated a great deal of joint planning and
cooperative teaching across academic areas. "Developing Mathematics Concepts" was organized by a mathematician and developmental psychologist. "A Study in Sound" combined the efforts of
faculty in poetry, music, and physical science. The "Creative Arts
Classroom" brought together faculty in children's literature, language arts, mathematics, science, and philosophy. The examples of
integrated activity are just too numerous to list. The unitary structure also made it as reasonable for a faculty member in religious
studies to work with third- and fourth-grade children in a cooperating elementary school classroom as to conduct an on-campus seminar in the Old Testament. The importance of a range of faculty
experience in school settings can hardly be minimized. It has the
potential of removing the "mystery" associated with schools and
causing everyone, regardless of academic background, to ask again:
"What can I contribute to teachers and children?" If *all* faculty in a
university regularly asked such a question, we would have better
prepared teachers and more interesting and intellectually challenging schools.

Teaching-Learning Relationship

The New School was especially concerned about the quality of
the relationships between faculty and students in the design and
operation of the educational program. A commitment was made at
the outset of the program to place the student at the center of the
learning experience and to work for a shift of emphasis from teach-

ing to learning. Because we believed that elementary school teachers should foster independence in learning on the part of their pupils and take into account the students' needs, interests, and hopes, we felt that individuals preparing for teaching or involved in in-service education should have ample opportunities to experience the same independence. Because we wanted our teachers to be self-starters, to be persons who could take major responsibility for planning and initiating learning, we encouraged them to take more initiative for their own learning.

Many recent efforts at building teacher preparation models have focused on the identification of behavioral objectives to be met by prospective teachers, essentially an application of systems analysis. The emphasis on outcomes in these efforts, on teacher and pupil behavior, and on the overt operational procedures by which specific behaviors can be elicited is, to some degree, an advance. These approaches certainly reinforce the belief that the ultimate test of a teacher preparation program rests on what teachers and children do in elementary school classrooms, even though the focus is on *particular*, already-defined behaviors. One problem with this approach to teacher preparation, however, is that it assumes that the complex act of teaching can be broken down into simpler, more easily identifiable skills and techniques that can be identified by experts for *all* students. Further, it assumes that the conditions under which these skills and techniques are realized can as readily be specified. In contrast to more traditional programs, such an approach provides students preparing for teaching with a much more individually tailored program with respect to points of entry, pacing, and sequencing. Still, students remain passive. They do not give sufficient direction to their own learning and play little or no role in specifying the outcomes desired, the conditions under which these outcomes can be realized, or the competencies they need, as teachers, to provide the conditions necessary for children's learning. And the role of the faculty member toward the student remains essentially unchanged, determining what is to be learned and how that learning is to be acquired and evaluated.

I realize that some readers may ask: "So what's wrong with that? Shouldn't faculty members determine what is to be learned and how that learning is to be acquired and evaluated?" That might have full legitimacy in a static world, with static understandings of knowledge. But such conditions do not exist. They have never existed. It might also be "acceptable" in a society that values vested authority over real authority. While vested authority tends to predominate in the world, it is hardly the practice that a self-conscious community of learners ought to support.

If we are to restructure relationships between faculty and students, we have to give more attention to potential student contributions. For example, there may be different ways for a student to demonstrate a given competency or understanding. As long as we cannot specify with any degree of confidence the *exact* conditions that give rise to specific pupil behaviors, prospective teachers ought to be actively engaged in identifying conditions that they find work best for them. Students preparing for teaching ought to have opportunities to personalize their own abilities as they relate to their own unique styles of teaching and to the instructional objectives that they have had a part in formulating. Faculty were active in the New School. They expressed strong beliefs about teaching and learning issues. They challenged students all the time. But they also came to understand that students had to be decision makers, that their intentions were critical, and that these intentions always needed to be taken into account.

As noted earlier, the New School cooperated with local school districts throughout North Dakota to introduce more individualized and personalized modes of instruction into elementary schools. To be effective in contributing to that kind of change in elementary school instruction, the New School believed that its college-level program had to become consonant with the kind of environment it was promoting in elementary schools. Operating on the assumption that teachers teach, in large measure, as they have been taught, faculty members continually looked for ways to personalize and individualize the college-level program, encouraging students to assume greater independence and initiative for their own learning. Success at this task, however, did not come easily. Many students preferred a more traditional setting, where the requirements for learning were prescribed by the faculty. And it was particularly tempting, at least early in the program, for faculty to respond quickly to this student preference. Moreover, it was difficult for some faculty, particularly at the outset, to restrain themselves from prescribing what they felt was necessary for the preparation of each student. The unitary structure of the New School was particularly helpful in coping with these problems. Faculty members brought a variety of perspectives about what was valuable and thus created an environment where the thinking of students became vital.

During the time the New School existed as an experimental college, we learned that to get students to participate in decisions about their own, learning the academic program had to have openness built into it. There had to be a variety of alternatives and a valuing of diverse patterns of learning. And we felt it essential that a spirit of inquiry and capacity for discovery be nurtured in the college academic program—even to the point of giving students the opportunity to formulate and operate on many of their own beliefs about what is essential for teaching. Faculty increasingly were willing to approach students in a more flexible manner. Instructional objectives were never so firmly set that students contributed little or nothing to conceptions of a good teacher or to the determination of the tasks to be undertaken in preparation for that role. In the abstract, the foregoing may appear rife with risks. In practice, by keeping the program open, possibilities soared and the quality of student learning expanded.

Academic Program

The total New School effort—including undergraduate, master's, and doctoral levels—had two basic but interrelated directions. One was concerned with the education of teachers and the other with the education of teacher educators. The maximum number of participants at any time for the three phases was set at 200 undergraduate, 100 master's, and 15 doctoral students.[2]

The undergraduate program, which began in the third undergraduate year, was a preparation and retraining program for prospective and experienced elementary school teachers. Upon successful completion of the undergraduate phase of the program, these students received a baccalaureate degree and full teacher certification. Many of the graduating seniors, along with other teachers from cooperating districts who held baccalaureate degrees, proceeded to the master's-level program, which had as its core a year-long resident internship in one of the cooperating school districts. The master's degree program served in a dual capacity—to prepare master teachers and to prepare teachers of teachers. In some school districts, the New School master's-level teachers began to serve as teachers of other prospective and practicing elementary school teachers by the example they set in their own classrooms and

---

2. During the fourth year the undergraduate portion of the program reached 250, primarily because of the enlarged Future Indian Teacher Program. In addition, ten postdoctoral fellows, mostly from liberal arts fields, were added during the fourth year.

through their cooperative teaching efforts involving colleagues at all levels.

The doctoral program was designed principally to prepare individuals for positions in the state colleges and in local school districts as teachers of teachers. Some doctoral graduates returned to their former colleges as teacher educators and, in many cases, to assume positions of leadership in that role. Others went to local educational agencies, where they provided leadership in improving the quality of instruction in the elementary schools of that district. Still others went to positions in state education agencies that involved curriculum development and teacher training responsibilities.

Throughout the four-year period that the New School was in operation, faculty and students had the opportunity to experiment with many alternative patterns of instruction. It was the third year before some well-defined directions in program emerged. One significant direction was the establishment of functional advisor-advisee relationships. To strengthen and broaden this relationship, students and advisors were given the responsibility for planning and evaluating each student's entire academic program.[3] Under this arrangement, several possibilities emerged for students. Faculty members designed activities that they felt would contribute to the personal or professional development of teachers. Some activities were organized jointly with other faculty. Students, planning with their advisors, could choose to become involved in a number of the faculty-organized options. Or the students could choose to initiate activities that were conducted independently of the more formally organized activities. These independent studies were undertaken with the advisor or in association with some faculty member in whose area of specialty the student wished to study. Again, the determination of what students were involved in and the way in which they were involved became joint decisions of the faculty advisor and the individual student. It was through this intense advisor-advisee relationship that the faculty of the New School attempted to facilitate greater involvement of the students in defining and evaluating their own learning.

As this relationship developed, both the advisor and advisee

---

3. The New School moved away from traditional grading at the outset, believing that the evaluation process had to be consistent with its educational philosophy. Grades were recorded as "credit received" (CR) and "credit deferred" (CD). While the evaluation process underwent change, the philosophy supporting the process remained intact.

struggled in an authentic way with the question of what the student should do to prepare for teaching. Because the advisor-advisee relationship was so basic to the program, it was the focus of considerable discussion. While it never reached what many of us considered to be an optimal stage of development, progress was made. Faculty and students alike began to focus on its strengths. And each gained increasing levels of confidence with evaluation and planning.

It is difficult to define with any specificity the precise content and the organization of the undergraduate program.[4] Students came with diverse backgrounds; some were practicing teachers with many years of experience but without a baccalaureate degree, while others were prospective teachers with little understanding of the complex process of teaching. Academic backgrounds also varied widely. Even within a single area of inquiry, student activities were not uniform, simply because student needs differed. What was sought was a higher degree of interaction among a diverse faculty as they interacted with students. Also sought was closer personal contact between students and faculty in order to create an academic program that was more responsive to the needs of individual students as they prepared for teaching.

The undergraduate program was interwoven with field experiences involving elementary-school children and parents. Every attempt was made to tie what was learned in the college classroom to practical experience gained in working directly with children. Given the flexibility of the academic program, students could move freely from the campus setting to an elementary classroom. Students and their learning, rather than a formal schedule, came first. Juniors and seniors typically gained their field experience in classrooms of fifth-year interns, where they were involved almost immediately with children. We stressed that the relationship between the undergraduate and the resident intern be one of collegiality, not the more traditional supervisor–student teacher relationship. Undergraduates were urged to engage in joint planning and cooperative teaching with the intern. Although the intern teacher was ultimately responsible for the classroom, both the intern teacher and the undergraduate were students, and as students each had to be willing to be open to the ideas of the other. In this way, each could contribute to

---

4. "Creative Expression," "Modes of Communication," "Quantitative Reasoning," "Nature and Conditions of Learning," and "Human Responses to the Environment" served as the umbrella areas in which students registered.

the education of the other. Any supervision that was necessary in this situation was given by the clinical professor, advisors, or co-operating principal.

Those students involved in the master's degree program participated in a year-long resident internship. As a member of an instructional staff, each intern had full responsibility for teaching in a cooperating elementary school. This internship was designed to permit the students to investigate the general hypotheses that emerged from their study, observations, and earlier involvement with children. The internship afforded them the opportunity to refine their skills and practical insights into the nature of learning and to reinforce their commitment to the individualization and personalization of learning through their own teaching.

Besides serving a resident internship, master's degree candidates devoted two consecutive summers to academic study. The summer session immediately prior to the internship was spent preparing for that experience. Upon completion of the internship, the students returned to campus to study in areas where they identified their needs to be greatest. In addition, all master's-level students engaged in an individual classroom-based research activity, culminating in an independent project. During the internship period the students also participated in a continuing seminar in which educational problems unique to their own elementary-school classrooms were explored in depth.

The success of the total New School program depended, in large measure, on the ability of the master's-level interns to introduce new modes of instruction into cooperating school districts. For our program to have any lasting impact, our interns had to relate differently to children, and this change in relationship had to be productive in terms of powerful educational objectives.

In the doctoral program, students' schedules of activities were planned around their academic and professional backgrounds and future plans as educators of teachers. In association with graduate faculty advisors, students planned individual programs of study tailored to their needs, strengths, and previous education. The individual programs that were developed tended to reflect the interdisciplinary quality of elementary education and the contribution of many areas of knowledge and understanding to teaching in the elementary school. All activities were conducted in close relationship with what was occurring in elementary school classrooms. This linkage between college study and elementary schools pervaded all phases of the program, including course study, research, and clinical experience. A related prerequisite of every doctoral student's program of study was internal consistency, or unity, among these major program elements.

All three parts of the New School program—undergraduate, master's, and doctoral—were interrelated, each contributing to the strength of the other. Most doctoral students, for example, gained their clinical experience by working in the undergraduate program and by joining the master's interns in the field to work directly with children. The research carried on by the doctoral students was closely tied to activities of these other two groups of students. In turn, the undergraduates and the master's-level students drew on the doctoral candidates as resource persons. The master's-level students contributed to the undergraduate program by opening their classrooms for undergraduate field experiences. Similarly, the undergraduates, by actively participating in intern classrooms, contributed to the intern's efforts to change the nature of elementary school instruction. As a consequence of these interrelationships, each level of the program made a significant contribution to the education of teachers and to the education of teacher educators.

Related Programs

In addition to the programs described above, the New School also carried out a program to prepare Native Americans to become teachers and coordinated several Follow Through Projects sponsored by the U.S. Office of Education (USOE). The Future Indian Teacher (FIT) Program, initially supported through the Trainers of Teacher Trainers Program and later funded principally by the Career Opportunities Program (both USOE programs), enrolled Native American men and women from North Dakota's four reservation communities in a work-study effort. The students spent part of their time working as teacher aides (generally under Title I) in their home-community schools and part at the university for intense academic study. In 1972 there were 75 students enrolled in this program at the freshman, sophomore, junior, and senior levels. Considering the fact that there are only a handful of Native American teachers in the state now (the Native American population is roughly 18,000), the FIT Program will have considerable impact as the students are graduated and assume teaching positions in their home communities.

The Follow Through Program is a federal effort to continue work with "less advantaged" children previously enrolled in Head Start programs. Follow Through operates in kindergarten through third grade in selected school districts around the country. Each school district approved for a Follow Through Project selects a "program sponsor" to help implement an effective instructional program for "less advantaged" children. The program also must provide for improved nutritional, recreational, psychological, and social care services as well as community participation. The New School was among about 20 sponsors enlisted by the USOE and was selected to implement a program of informal education by school districts at Fort Yates, North Dakota; Zuni, New Mexico; Great Falls, Montana; and Burlington-Edison, Ferndale, and Sedro Woolley, Washington. We provided assistance to the sites, including on-campus and inservice training for teachers, aides, and parents.

It should be pointed out that the Follow Through and FIT Programs did not operate in isolation from the "regular" teacher preparation program. The programs overlapped in many ways both on and off campus. For example, at Fort Yates a master's degree candidate served her internship in a Follow Through classroom and had an FIT student as a teacher aide. And, of course, faculty and doctoral students conducted workshops and classes for participants in all the programs. Also, when they became juniors, FIT students joined the regular undergraduate program while on campus.

An Overview of Governance

As mentioned earlier, there were no departments or divisions in the New School. An organizational chart would show a dean, a program coordinator, faculty, and students. Decision making at first took place through a "committee of the whole" involving all faculty and students. Parent councils served as a voice for local communities, along with local boards of education. In an effort to broaden and formalize the decision-making apparatus, a new body was created and implemented during the 1971–1972 school year. This committee, or "monthly meeting" as it was called, consisted of *elected* representatives of faculty, students, alumni, parents, school administrators, Native American community members, and personnel of the state Department of Public Instruction. The 44-member group met once a month on the campus to make policy and operational decisions regarding the New School. The dean, who also sat with the group and provided considerable educational leadership, was especially responsible for making sure its decisions fell within the various requirements of the university, the state Board of Higher Education, and the Department of Public Instruction. Several standing committees, whose members also represented the various constituencies, did much of the detail work for the main group.

The chief reason for establishing such a decision-making body was to bring together representatives of the various parties having a stake in education. It was one of the ways the New School hoped to operate a program in conjunction with, rather than in isolation from, the constituencies it intended to serve.

A Postscript

The New School program—the community it established, the strong commitments it engendered, the educational activities it fostered—was unique in a myriad of ways. There was a constant flow of philosophical and pragmatic questions about teaching, learning, and schools that kept the environment rich. The various questions were debated *not* just in the first year but throughout the four years, generally at increasingly higher levels. I believe these intense and ongoing discussions moved the University of North Dakota forward as an institution interested in teachers and schools. Some of the most debated questions were:

- What are the limits of freedom?
- What is the meaning of authority?
- What is important to know?
- What are the boundaries of legitimate inquiry about teaching, learning, and schools?
- What are appropriate modes of evaluation?
- What is the role of the liberal arts in teacher preparation?
- What kinds of student-faculty relationships are most productive of social, psychological, and intellectual growth?
- What is an appropriate means of governance?
- Is advocacy a legitimate role for a university program?
- How can the New School lend support to educational reform?
- What are the most appropriate mechanisms for involving parents in teacher education and in schools?
- How can the New School organize to support the interests of North Dakota's Native American communities?
- What, if any, are the limits of diversity among students and faculty?

- How can multiculturalism be assured more than rhetorically?
- How can a community of learners be firmly established?
- What are the best ways to support teachers who are actively attempting to change their classrooms and their approaches to children and parents?
- What are the most appropriate ways to extend children's learning?
- What are the critical characteristics of informal education?

In closing this discussion on the New School, its role as an important national catalyst for reexamining teacher education and giving impetus to school reform should be acknowledged. During the four years, close to 2,000 individuals—parents, school board members, legislators, teachers, school administrators, and college faculty—came from 42 states, 9 Canadian provinces, and 13 other countries to North Dakota to participate in New School programs. They remained anywhere from a day to several months. In addition to the many visitors, the New School received and responded to close to 2,500 requests each year for information. While much of this level of interest receded with the formation of the Center for Teaching and Learning—the institutionalization of the New School and an existing college of education—and the generally more conservative educational climate in the United States, the center committed itself to maintain this important demonstration/dissemination role and to continue providing local, regional, and national leadership to teacher education.

CHAPTER NINE

A Perspective on the Center for Teaching and Learning

The Center for Teaching and Learning had a history of taking "time-outs" for communitywide conversations. This paper was prepared for a November 6, 1978, "time-out" focused on "the quality of education within CTL" and was intended to provide a stimulus for discussion. The questions I raised reflected my observations of life in the Center. I include the paper in this collection because it presents a personal perspective about teacher education that may be useful to readers. It also says something about my belief in the power of collective thought.

Alfred North Whitehead criticized education institutions for fostering "second-hand learning" and focusing on "inert ideas," essentially the ingredients of mediocrity and limited cultural development (1929, pp. 3–7). I would like to connect the foregoing to Saul Bellow's Nobel lecture (1977), in which he spoke of a society filled with "private disorder and public bewilderment . . . visions of ruin" (p. 320) and the enlarged need for every person to remain able "to think, discriminate and feel" (p. 321).

What are we doing in our teaching to help preservice and inservice teachers and administrators enlarge their capacity "to think, discriminate and feel?" Have we helped them to become critical observers of children and young people, of materials and instructional procedures, of organizational patterns? Have we provided them with appropriate opportunities to document, reflect on, and explicate their observations, their learning? Have we encouraged *writing* as a means of communicating and clarifying thought and *sharing* as a means of extending thought?

Ultimately, the knowledge that is meaningful, that is the basis for thought and feeling, is that which is personally owned. Second-hand knowledge may be useful, but first-hand knowledge—that which comes from a personal investment, reflection, observation,

119

experience—is what gives an individual power. Teachers and administrators who have developed a personal construct about learning, who own knowledge and are able to articulate that knowledge, can attend to the important issues confronting education because they will be less intimidated by external educational models. They will be decision makers rather than captives.

What does this suggest for faculty? How *thoughtful* are we in our interactions with students? How *intense*? Do we *demonstrate* our own capacity for *learning*? How *much* of that fresh learning do we *share*? Are we, in any ongoing process, *examining critically* educational issues of importance, materials, methods, theoretical constructs? Further, are students being *prepared* to perpetuate the schools as they are, or are we providing for and with them a vision of what the schools might become? What their educational lives might become? Are we helping students to make commitments to the largest possibilities that can be imagined? Questions such as these often bring the response that "we have to be realistic—we ought not to build expectations that are too large." Such a response might be acceptable in a setting where teacher education is viewed as a technical process, a vocational activity in the narrowest sense. My view of the center, however, is larger, having a strong intellectual and moral base and being rooted in the traditional outlook of the liberal arts, where the language—the vision of possibilities or the potential for reconstruction—tends always to outstrip the practice. Where the language meets *only* the existing practice, the practice itself tends to decline in its quality.

I am aware that tensions exist in the center about whether technical or liberal considerations should dominate the stage. Technical considerations are seen as the sole *raison d'être* for most schools of education, which may explain, in part, the current malaise surrounding schools and schooling. Technical considerations *are* important. Persons going through the Center for Teaching and Learning (CTL) *should* possess skills relating to how to organize a reading program, how to use simulation activities, how to approach phonics instruction, how to introduce cursive writing, how to use a basal series, how to develop a science program, a personnel records' system, and the like. More importantly, however, they need to be readers and writers, to be learners and decision makers, to possess a personal view of what it means to teach, to have a capacity to think, discriminate, and feel. CTL, in my view, can only remain a special place, an extraordinary school of education, if it holds out against the temptations—more compelling now than ever—to let its liberalizing commitments decline. In what ways do faculty, program areas, and students manifest the values just expressed? What is the intellectual quality of our courses and programs? How coherent are our programs? How integrative are our commitments? How much reading do students and faculty engage in? How intense is that reading? Do they talk about it together? Are students being introduced to the best and the most challenging of the current literature in education? Are they being provided with an appropriate historical perspective? Are they expected to understand the ethical issues that confront schools in American society?

The foregoing section of this discussion paper has a philosophical orientation. I wish now to raise a number of very practical issues.

In order to build intensity into the learning situation, faculty need to be organized—to have *thought* about their purposes. They need also to be *available* to students, willing to respond to individual concerns, questions, and interests. How thoughtfully have we organized for our teaching? How available are we to students?

Do students know what kinds of opportunities/options exist for them within the center? Is the knowledge uniformly available or available only through chance encounters, accessible to the few?

I tend to define *evaluation* as a process for promoting growth. It is a process that calls for clarity of purpose on the part of faculty, commitment on the part of students, and provision for appropriate response from both. What is the quality of our evaluation efforts? Are students responded to? Are their papers read carefully, commented upon thoughtfully? Are students assisted in the process of establishing learning goals and personal philosophies about teaching, learning, children, families, and communities? Are they encouraged to develop self-evaluation skills?

Integration of learning—connecting what is learned in one area to learning in another area, using what is learned in one area to extend learning in another—promotes intensity. To what degree do we make efforts to establish connections, to build on the previous experience and understandings of students? How much do individual faculty members know about what other faculty consider to be important in their teaching? How much sharing occurs? Is there an ongoing basis for collective thought?

How thoughtful is our admissions process at the undergraduate and graduate levels? Are we looking closely at the quality of each applicant's experience? How personal is the process?

How responsive are our programs? Are we addressing, through our program directions and course offerings, the concerns of students as they struggle to become learners of consequence, professional educators, students of teaching in a Deweyan sense? Are we addressing the needs of schools and communities?

Many of my questions are addressed to faculty. They could almost as easily have been addressed to students. Teaching and learning, after all, are reciprocal constructs that relate to faculty and students alike. My choice of questions gives *some* sense of what is important to me as I look broadly at the center. How would I respond to the questions? Mixed! We have intellectual stimulation of a high order and some occasional pedestrian irrelevance. We have high, as well as low, levels of personal interest and commitment. We have persons who are active learners and individuals whose learning plateaued years ago. We have students who are eager to learn—who have made enormous personal commitments to teaching—and we have students who assume limited responsibility for *their own* education.

My hope is that this center Forum discussion will provide some renewed sense of purpose for each of us—that we will highlight together areas in which we might *all* make some renewed efforts to assure that what we do as individuals or in programs is of *high quality* and has important potential for improving the quality of schools as well as our personal and collective lives.

CHAPTER TEN

Teacher Education and Progressivism: A Historical Perspective

This paper, in a more extensive form, was prepared for presentation at the October 1986 Progressive Education Conference organized by Teachers College (Columbia University) and the Bank Street College of Education. The larger paper was published in the proceedings of the Cambridge School Progressive Education Conference, Fall 1988. Portions of the current form were also presented in talks at Michigan State University, the University of North Carolina at Greensboro, and Harvard. In light of the current efforts to bring reform to teacher education I thought it might be useful to review some aspects of the history.

Much that is central to current teacher education reform proposals has been the subject of earlier debate. Yet historical perspective seems to be missing. It is another example of our continuing reluctance to examine carefully other reform periods, to place before us a larger number of possibilities, additional ways of thinking about reform. My purpose in this paper is to bring elements of the history to the surface, principally by reviewing some of the progressive vision about teachers and their preparation.

Normal Schools

In the mid-nineteenth century there was considerable division about whether teacher education should occur in the colleges or in specialized institutions such as normal schools. The normal schools won out, in part because Horace Mann and others did not believe that the existing colleges, with their particular social- and economic-class orientations, would produce persons with any willingness to teach in the schools, persons who would have the necessary technical interests and skills or sufficient enthusiasm for working with children (see Borrowman, 1965; Cremin, 1961; Mann, 1891; Messarli, 1971). In their earliest years, the normal schools were technical academies for elementary school graduates, tied closely to the schools themselves. They were not academies for scholars, because scholars were not seen as necessary or necessarily attractive. Even as late as 1866, the Massachusetts Board of Education placed strict prohibitions against offering secondary school subjects in the normal schools (Borrowman, 1965, p. 23).

In the years after the Civil War, as America's common school movement began to take hold, the normal schools expanded in numbers and influence, building around them a distinctive ideology. Richard Edwards, the president of Illinois Normal University, made the ideology clear in his presentation to the National Teacher's Association in 1865:

> The whole animus of both teacher and pupil [in the normal school] is the idea of future teaching. Every plan is made to conform to it. There is no other aim or purpose to claim any share of the mental energy of either. It is the Alpha and Omega of all schemes of study and modes of thought. (quoted in Borrowman, 1965, pp. 77–78)

Another element of the ideology was the religious or spiritual calling that the normal schools routinely promoted in their convocations and course work. Teachers were "called" to be the missionaries of moral health and democracy. Some of that missionary spirit continues even today.

The normal schools used such ideological arguments in their own defense at the turn of the century as they tried to fend off the inroads of the universities. Giving over teacher education to the universities would, the argument went, surely mean fewer teachers with the requisite calling and technical skills. Variations on this theme have reappeared recently—this time coming from the education schools—in response to suggestions that the liberal arts colleges assume more responsibility for teacher education.

In fairness, there were individuals even in the early normal schools who believed that greater emphasis should be given to liberal considerations, and by the end of the nineteenth century studies in history, literature, natural philosophy, and child study (a focus on "the teacher as naturalist") had become commonplace. But given the shortness of programs (from six weeks to two years) and the generally limited educational backgrounds that students brought to the normal schools, technical considerations were always dominant.

Rather than let the normal school pass too quickly from mind, and as a way of understanding better its characteristics, I would like to take a fast-paced excursion into its interior at the end of the nineteenth century. Our guide will be Hannah Knudsen, a 104-year-old woman in Westhope, North Dakota, who shared with me her Iowa State Normal School classnotes and papers (Perrone, 1986). While continuing to be exclusively a teacher-training institution, the Iowa State Normal School at Cedar Rapids had become, by the time Hannah entered in 1899, a two-year college that claimed to bring together the liberal and practical arts.

Like many of her classmates, Hannah had already taught for a few years before entering the normal school, in the year between her eleventh grade and the completion of high school and the year after high school graduation. She noted about those years that she was thankful for the daily guides produced by the Iowa Department of Education.

Hannah received at the Iowa State Normal School an interesting history of education, beginning with nature study and science "as practiced in ancient Egypt"; art and philosophy as "contributions from Greece"; law and government as "gifts from Rome"; and moral and religious life as "an endowment from Israel." Regarding morals, Hannah's notes make clear that "the primary teacher cannot escape teaching morals, although she may not and should not teach sectarianism. Teaching morals is important as the nonreligious spirit has warped the minds of many." (Some things just never change.) The two quarters of coursework in this historical area, which went on to address important intellectual thought of the seventeenth and eighteenth centuries, represented an imaginative attempt, even though strained at many points, to integrate the history of Western Civilization with the function of schools and school content.

Important philosophers and social and educational reformers, such as Francis Bacon, John Locke, and Horace Mann, were studied in what I found to be surprising detail. Rousseau, interestingly enough, was missing. In her notebook, Hannah had outlined carefully each individual's dominant educational thought—labeled as principles—and discussed how such thought could be translated into educational practice.

One could argue, of course, that this background in history, philosophy, and political thought represented a meager liberal education, but at the time it was considered a fairly extensive effort.

Another strong thread in Hannah's program related to school organization—relationships with the superintendent, other teachers, the community, and the like. With regard to the superintendent, it is clear from Hannah's notes that *he* is to be respected and feared: "The superintendent may be blunt, gruff, and outspoken but he is usually the sincere and true-hearted man. . . . He can be likened to the father in a home." In relations with other teachers, "unless you can say something good say nothing at all about your fellow teachers . . . be helpful and friendly but most especially to new teachers." And when it comes to the community, "be interested . . . do not criticize the town and its people . . . avoid gossip." Expectations for a teacher were large and also value-laden: "The teacher is expected to have a sincere desire to serve her children . . . as a teacher, you must not isolate your work from that of all other grades." And with regard to her conduct, "the teacher should be a fit example outside of school. . . . You must measure up to the best."

In addition to formal coursework in child development, there was a great deal of attention on how to teach phonics, reading, mathematics, and nature study as well as an introduction to a variety of games designed to foster interest. There was also a course in children's literature and the admonition "to read to children every day." In regard to child development, Hannah noted carefully: "Parents and teachers should always keep in mind that the child is a serious researcher for knowledge and strive to lead him in the right channels of thought. . . . Thoughtful children seek always to put meaning into communications about the unseen world." Now *that* is pretty progressive.

But the activity that was most personal and systematic for Hannah was her course in child study, which had become by the 1880s the real mainstay of the normal schools. Hannah observed carefully a nine-year-old, an only child, in the home where she boarded as a normal school student. She also did a child study rooted in a classroom. Her daily observations of the two children she studied were enormously interesting (and, I might add, very well written). They were full of detailed descriptions and were fairly free of normative judgments. Her completed child studies were well-crafted statements organized around a variety of themes from physical gestures to language use and interests.

As a teacher, Hannah followed closely county and state course-of-study guides and stayed within the confines of the textbooks and their directions. She offered, as best I can ascertain, a good basic education to children, especially in the area of language arts. Though only five feet tall and weighing less than 100 pounds, she described herself as a strict disciplinarian. Discipline has been through the years a constant theme, it seems, for teachers.

Like others such as herself—and this was the history of much of the nineteenth and early twentieth centuries—Hannah did not teach many years. Marriage, at least until the 1920s, usually meant a departure from the classroom. Turnover, the lack of a strong professional corps of teachers, was a serious nineteenth- and early twentieth-century problem. For example, in his report for the years 1904–1906, the Superintendent of Public Instruction in North Dakota noted that "an almost entire change in the personnel of the teaching force takes place about every three years" (*Biennial Report*, 1910, p. 19). And as most of us know, it takes that long in a supportive environment to begin the process of becoming a real student of teaching.

With the arrival of the twentieth century, teacher education became a part of the expanding state university systems. And by 1930 the two-year normal schools had, for the most part, either closed or become state colleges offering baccalaureate degrees. In the period of transition, however, normal school advocates fought for the survival of their institutions, arguing vigorously for the benefits of a single purpose, reviving many of the old 1840s shibboleths. Those in the four-year colleges and universities argued that the benefits of a broad liberal education in a setting where scholarship was viewed as important greatly outweighed any gains that existed in the single-purpose normal schools. The middle ground that emerged, the schools of education within the universities, has not really been able to satisfy well either side of the argument. That they have struggled for academic credibility is not surprising.

The clearest generalization I can make about the history of teacher education is that the quality of teachers and schools was always uneven. How could it have been otherwise? Putting 17- to 20-year-olds into classrooms without much assistance, often without significant opportunities for interaction, and with a limited range of materials (and in some settings, expectations) virtually guaranteed such mixed results. We have criticisms of teachers today, but they seem mild beside the criticisms registered at the turn of the century.

John Dewey and the Education of Teachers

John Dewey, of course, occupies a special place in any discussion of progressivism in relation to education in the schools and in the education of teachers. And while many contemporary reform-minded people hesitate to draw heavily on Dewey for fear of being seen as romantic or soft or, worse yet, a liberal, I continue to recommend him. I make an annual ritual of rereading *The Dewey School* (Mayhew & Edwards, 1936/1966)—that wonderfully rich account of the laboratory school founded by John Dewey and his wife, Alice, in 1896—each time finding something fresh to think about. I also reread often *The School and Society* (1899/1956), Dewey's classic set of lectures to parents.

Dewey believed the schools were foundering because they had lost their connection to a society undergoing rapid social, economic, and cultural change. In his view, the schools were still encumbered by an outlook of America as a small town with tree-lined streets and lovely single-family homes, with an economy fueled by agriculture and sustained by common religious beliefs and cultural backgrounds, holding a singular vision of the nation—at a time when the population of our metropolitan centers was exploding and high-density apartment dwellings were expanding, differences were becoming more pronounced, and wage labor, rooted in the impersonality of factories, was the economic reality (Handlin, 1959b).

The laboratory school was for Dewey a setting concerned with community building, cooperation, and democratic life. He talked of the school as community-centered, not child-centered, and of activities as the means for evoking from children stimulating questions. What should be taught, he would argue, "would justify itself because it answered questions the student himself asked" (quoted in Handlin, 1959b, p. 42). Lucy Sprague Mitchell (1928) makes that point especially well in her discussion of the teaching of geography. To hear the questions, Dewey insisted, called for careful listening and skilled observation. In this he shared a common theme with much of the critical thought that informed progressivism prior to his work in Chicago and long after it—namely, its grounding in close observation of children in natural settings or in a literature that grew out of close observation, that had a quality of immersion about it, an eye for detailed description, a passion, a belief in children as persons with real interests and capable of gaining a personal and well-understood control over the basic mechanism and modes of thought necessary for sustained learning. This teacher-as-naturalist theme was particularly strong. Preparing and sustaining that teacher-naturalist ought today to occupy a larger share of our attention. This is a liberal and liberating direction that is likely far more important than the current preoccupation with defining particular academic majors. It may, in fact, be beyond majors, closer to an older definition of a liberal and liberalizing education.

Dewey was critical of teacher education in general for its lack of connections to scholarship and questions of what to teach, that real struggle about what is basic to an understanding of science and history and literature, how language should be formulated, and the like. I suspect he would wonder a good deal about many of the contemporary reform regulations that mandate particular courses as if such mandates answer the question of what ought to be taught. Further, Dewey believed that schools—be they primary schools or universities—needed to be staffed by scholars, not technicians. True scholars, he wrote, are "so full of the spirit of inquiry, so sensitive to every sign of its presence and absence, that no matter what they do, or how they do it, they succeed in awakening and inspiring like ardent and intense mental activity in those with whom they come in contact" (quoted in Mayhew & Edwards, 1936/1966, p. 265).

For Dewey, change—of view, of understanding, of related practice—was a close correlate of scholarship. Dewey's understanding of teacher education institutions was that they did not conceive of themselves as preparing scholars "to change the conception of what constitutes education," scholars who viewed themselves as "investigators" (Dewey, 1976, p. 263).

For the most part, he was correct. How much has changed since Dewey's day?

One of the things that attracts me over and over again to the various accounts of the Dewey School is my interest in what persons *not* intentionally prepared as teachers in traditional school terms—the physicists, chemists, historians, geographers, philosophers, and artisans—did with children. They did not, as some might have expected, teach physics and history and philosophy as subjects or fields of study. Rather, they put out interesting materials and observed children's use and understanding of them. In addition, they posed engaging questions about the materials and took children into the community to observe the connections between their studies and the world. Essentially, they used their backgrounds to go beyond their subject specializations.

The walks through the University of Chicago's heating plant and the United States Steel rolling mills were directly related to some of the explorations of those physicists and chemists, and the walks through the Back of the Yards neighborhood on Chicago's West Side and visits to the settlement houses were well connected to many of the explorations of historians and geographers.[1] Accounts such as these, tied closely to Dewey's belief in collective thought, which I will comment on shortly, might provide a useful way to think about the questions that contemporary reform supporters get often: "Do you really want a chemistry or history or sociology major teaching in the primary grades?"

Before leaving Dewey and that University of Chicago lab school, it might be useful to share some of what he learned that is worth further reflection, especially in light of the current teacher education proposals. Dewey was particularly conscious of the power of social relationships, believing firmly that the development of intelligence and knowledge, whether for an individual or a culture, grew from cooperative exchange. The Dewey School prospered from the strength of its almost daily discussions about teaching and learning, an intellectual approach to practice. In relation to this concern for interchange he wrote:

> Cooperation must . . . have a marked intellectual quality in the exchange of experience and ideas. Many of our early failures were due to the fact that our exchanges were too practical, too much given to matters of immediate import, and not sufficiently intellectual in content. (quoted in Mayhew & Edwards, 1936/1966, p. 371)

Groups with which I have worked over the years have done far better when they did not quickly get too practical; when they did not feel compelled to finish discussing a book or an idea too quickly; when they chose really to understand issues deeply, uncovering rather than covering content; when they came to understand with Tolstoy that "only that which demands interpretation and imagination and provokes thought is easy" (1967, p. 289), and, I would add, productive and liberating.

Dewey firmly believed that teachers could and should learn from each other. Such a view caused him to see the ideal school as one with a very diverse staff, made up of people with a variety of inter-

---

1. In relation to this, I listened to the late Jerrold Zacharias, a distinguished physicist at MIT who devoted much of his later life to education in the schools, describe what he believed would be the best physics course possible in a secondary school. It would be, he said, "one where the teacher brought in a large gas combustion engine and spent the year working on it. There would be a prohibition of discussion about principles and technical terminology until students had made their own observations, invented their own language, and understood what made the engine and its parts work." Eleanor Duckworth (1986) demonstrates this mode of scientific exploration well in *Inventing Density*.

ests, skills, and aptitudes, a situation he believed could encourage ongoing learning for everyone, teachers and students alike. Persons might have formal preparation in mathematics or history or sculpting; but in a healthy cooperative environment, they would grow in their understanding of many other fields, ultimately enriching their own fields of inquiry as well as those of others. I believe that to be true and would hope that we would not reform ourselves into more rigidities than we now possess.

Dewey also believed that the schools could never be as productive as was possible until teachers were provided the freedom to act on their closely observed and collectively nourished understandings. That vision is becoming a firmer part of the current teacher reform literature. Too often, however, it is connected to—and limited by—a *quid pro quo* revolving around some kind of test, a particular accountability model, the use of a particular set of books, and the like. This was not quite what Dewey had in mind. Dewey wrote, in this regard, that the schools would not be vastly improved until primary teachers had "the same power, the same freedom that now goes to university teachers" (quoted in Mayhew & Edwards, 1936/1966, p. 372). And when criticized for leaving too much decision making to teachers acting "in association and exchange," he wrote that it was vastly better "to err in the direction of placing the responsibility on teachers for [educational] directions and content. . . . Whatever . . . was lost, vitality and constant growth were gained" (quoted in Mayhew & Edwards, 1936/1966, p. 373).

Closely connected to this view of teachers as collaborators, naturalists, and scholars is Dewey's conception of teachers needing to be "students of teaching," individuals not dependent on decisions made externally by persons far removed from the reality of a particular setting. To be a student of teaching in his terms was to establish and maintain a reflective capacity and to become clear and articulate about one's intentions. The beginnings of that reflective capacity, I would argue, develop in the preservice years as part of that broad liberalizing education that is so necessary. Dewey might ask a teacher, for example: Why do you organize that way as opposed to another? Why that array of materials and not another? What are you leading toward and why? What are these particular experiences leading toward? How does a learning activity in one area make a connection to learning activities in another? How do your provisioning decisions promote community building as they support individual growth? How are the different inclinations of each student in the room being supported? How do you know growth is occurring?

Students of teaching would, of course, be able to respond thoughtfully and articulately to such questions. They would be persons in control of their craft intellectually, aesthetically, and practically.

Teacher as Artist

Having now shared Dewey's outlook on the teacher as scholar, the teacher as naturalist, and the teacher as student of teaching, particular directions that some teacher education programs by the end of the nineteenth century attempted quite consciously to foster through their child study programs, I now want to comment on another popular progressive formulation, namely, the teacher as artist. It, too, ought to be considered in contemporary reform discussions relating to a liberalizing education.

Herman Horne, writing in 1917, described the teacher-artist as one "who keeps her students open-eyed" (p. x). While noting that a teacher-artist may not always have the tidiest workshop, Horne informs his readers that "her job is the neatest in the end," because students come to deep understandings and complete work they can honor (p. xi). Horne continues that while "her methods are round about (and slow moving) what she gives to her pupils more than compensates for the length of the route taken" (p. xi). In this regard, it is quite instructive to examine some of the photographed work of children in many of the early progressive schools—the landscapes and portraits, the constructions, the writing. And there are also wonderful examples from contemporary progressive schools, public and private, where work of all kinds is extraordinary because it has had the benefit of the artist's time for development and is honored.

I like the discussion of many of the progressives about the need for time and patience, the commitment to deep understandings and intense engagement. What a difference from the world of time on task, which does not have anything to do with roundaboutness or time for sitting and thinking and engaging in intense inquiry. It is, rather, a view associated unmistakably with the values of the technician, not those of the artist.

The artist as described in those early twentieth-century days was also *involved* in the world. Horne would argue that an artist, unlike a technician, would permit "the world to sweep through the classroom" (1917, p. 51). The artist was also viewed as maintaining an expansive view of possibilities, seeing great potential in uncertainties and ambiguities.

Harold Rugg and Ann Shumaker, in their 1928 study, *The Child-Centered School: An Appraisal of the New Education*, offered a wonderful account of the difference between the artist-teacher, who they felt was needed, and the artisan-teacher, who they thought was in plentiful supply.

> The artist . . . is a student of both the child and the society . . . understands the psychology of growth and also has a rich mastery of . . . interrelationships, movements, and fundamental ideas in the broad sectors of life with which she is dealing . . . [In contrast] . . . the artisan has her eyes on the answers to the arithmetic problems. (pp. 321–23)

Rugg and Shumaker noted further that the artist-teacher is also a student of both the child and the society who "knows when to abandon technique and fall back on the more human method of 'humbly and lovingly muddling along' with children" (p. 323).

Marietta Johnson, a giant among progressives, extended the conceptualization of the teacher as artist to creative experience—a reconnection to personal learning. She wrote in her *Thirty Years with an Idea* (1974) that "all teachers in training should have experience in nature study, arts and crafts, folk dancing, dramatics, woodworking, and storytelling" (p. 124). That was her way of opening up learning—to bring adults back in touch with themselves as learners. Eleanor Duckworth (1987), a faculty member at the Harvard Graduate School of Education, pursues a similar route through her seminar on "moon watching," which pushes students to understand again, in very personal terms, what it means to learn and to know. Will that kind of focus on personal learning—certainly as liberal a learning activity as one could pursue—be encouraged within current formulations of teacher education? Johnson believed that prospective teachers need experience in observing children closely, experience that allows them to understand "when a child is thriving and when languishing" (1937, p. 216). This did not mean for Johnson any kind of clinical framework or interpretation.

Another formulation that Johnson shared with most other progressives was a belief that teachers should "understand and recognize the value of social relationships . . . not [be] afraid to face, understand, and cooperate with efforts toward building a better social order" (1974, p. 122).

Johnson's Fairhope was, over the years, a setting where many progressive teachers received their training, mostly at the postnormal school or liberal arts baccalaureate levels. Quite apart from a university environment, it was an intellectual setting of great power rooted in reflective practice. Can the professional schools envisioned by those leading current teacher education reform groups be as intense intellectually and as focused on the theory-practice nexus? That, of course, will be a very large challenge with which schools of education have only limited experience.

One of the persons who did her teacher training with Marietta Johnson was Grace Rotzel, the first director and founder, with parents, of the School in Rose Valley. Her book by that title (1971) is enormously interesting, a wonderful "student of teaching document." Of her five years at Fairhope, Rotzel wrote, "I gained the confidence to work toward change in education" (p. ix).

The teachers who were brought to the School in Rose Valley came from a variety of settings across the country and had very diverse experience as teachers. Regardless of their background, however, they all had to learn together, as Rotzel noted, "what learning from children meant" (1971, p. 7). They grew as progressive teachers through their shared inquiry and their shared reading. Among the books they read together in the 1930s were Herbert Read's *Education Through Art* (1943/1970) and Whitehead's *Aims of Education* (1929). They were also introduced to the writings of Tolstoy. Two of the teachers, Lee Stephens and Ann Rawson, became so involved in Tolstoy's writing on education they produced a book on the subject (Rotzel, 1971). The ongoing teacher seminars were equal to the best that a liberal arts college could offer in any field and would likely not be matched often in many of the education schools. Such intellectually oriented schools need to be available as our demonstration schools.

Teachers as Researchers and Inquirers

The quintessential embodiment of a progressive response to the preparation of teachers has to have been Lucy Sprague Mitchell and her associates in the Bureau of Educational Experiments, that precursor to Bank Street. (For those who have not read *Our Children and Our Schools* [1950] for a long time, I recommend a rereading, especially as teacher education reform is on the agenda. It is quite surprising to me that so few people I meet in schools of education know this important work.) Beginning with the Cooperative Nursery School and the City and Country School, the bureau began a teacher-as-researcher effort that has likely not been duplicated since. It served as an important base for the Bank Street teacher education effort.

Mitchell saw most teacher education efforts failing both because they did not attract persons who wanted to experiment, who viewed themselves as serious learners and inquirers and, relatedly, because the interests of those they attracted were so narrow. The ideal teacher, she believed, was one with broad Renaissance-like interests, who had a rich life beyond the classroom but enjoyed living with children. She, like so many other progressives, also saw teachers as persons who needed a vision of a social order better than that which existed and who were deeply involved in creating that world. That they would display an attitude of openness and a willingness to question everything was taken for granted in her schema. How do we assure such teachers? And is that truly the teacher that is desired in our schools?

In her workshops with experienced as well as prospective teachers, Mitchell stressed that the study of children's development should neither be a theoretical subject nor be about children in general. That focus on specificity, the individual child, is a particularly important point that we need to consider in our movement toward reform. Mitchell also noted that the bulk of the source material for children's learning was "in the functioning world outside the classroom." Further, she believed that all teachers needed first-hand experience with the arts, to be painters and writers along with the children.

I want to provide one of Lucy Mitchell's (1931) overarching statements about aims that was directed to prospective teachers in the Bureau of Experiments' Cooperative Student Teaching Program, an effort that involved colleges in the New York City area and beyond:

> Our aim is to turn out teachers whose attitude toward their work and toward life is scientific. To us, this means an attitude of eager, alert observation; a constant questioning of old procedure in the light of new observations; a use of the world, as well as of books, as source material; an experimental open-mindedness; and an effort to keep as reliable records as the situation permits, in order to base the future upon accurate knowledge of what has been done. Our aim is equally to turn out students whose attitude towards their work and towards life is that of the artist. To us, this means an attitude of relish, of emotional drive, a genuine participation in some creative phase of work, and a sense that joy and beauty are legitimate possessions of all human beings, young and old. If we can produce teachers with an experimental, critical, and

ardent approach to their work, we are ready to leave the future of education to them. (pp. 251–252).

In addition to getting children into the world, Bank Street also organized systematic excursions into the world for teachers and prospective teachers as a means of encouraging them to become more observant of "the geographic, cultural and social-economic world" they lived in. Accounts of trips to the Fulton Fish Market as well as the TVA fill the memories of large numbers of Bank Street graduates. Charlotte Winsor described the "long trip" as follows:

> The "long trip" became a high spot in the experience of Bank Street students in the 30's and 40's. The choice of places to visit reflected the teaching purposes of the trip—a mining town, a steel mill, war industry towns like Waterbury, Connecticut, the TVA. Such areas were investigated from their geological beginnings to their socio-economic characteristics. School programs as a reflection of the community visited were always part of such study . . . on an adult level, Bank Street students were having similar experiences to those they were asked to provide for children. They were being helped to use their environment as *a tool for learning*. (quoted in Cazden, 1983, p. 1)

Courtney Cazden, a Harvard linguist, shared, in a talk honoring Charlotte Winsor, highlights of her 1948 "long trip" to a segregated black school in the rural south, the TVA, and the Highlander School, where she and the others were taught a local hymn that became in the 1960s the anthem of the Civil Rights movement—"We Shall Overcome." She described the trip as a journey to "a world not made up and not subject to our control . . . a world of very real other people" (1983, p. 4).
We may want to think about what this might mean today.

As envisioned by earlier progressives, teacher education was intended to encourage a personal intensity about learning, a propensity for inquiry and invention, a commitment to change, a powerful social vision, and broad experience. This is ultimately what a liberal education is about. It is what our contemporary discussions about teacher education should be about.

Part IV

SCHOOL TESTING

CHAPTER ELEVEN

Testing, Testing, and More Testing

This paper was prepared for the November/December 1981 issue of Childhood Education, *which was devoted to "Pressures on Children." It draws on several presentations I made to parent and teacher groups in North Dakota, Minnesota, and Washington, D.C. Unfortunately, testing has escalated greatly over the past decade, taking on in the schools a "high stakes" quality. Even kindergartners are now being retained because of scores on tests.*

In 1976 the Association for Childhood Education International and the National Association of Elementary School Principals called for a moratorium on the use of standardized tests in schools. This position grew out of their belief that tests were being used indiscriminately and were having deleterious effects on children and programs (Perrone, 1976). While recognizing that they were making, at best, a moral statement, the ACEI and NAESP hoped that such action would encourage a serious reexamination of test use.

Though a vigorous debate has ensued, the pressures to test children remain high. Many educators, school board members, and state legislators prefer, it seems, to be on the side of too much rather than too little testing. In part this reflects their continuing belief in the power of science. It is also, however, a reaction to a persistent decline of confidence in the schools.

In light of our current circumstances, it might be useful to explore the kinds of testing children experience in the schools, the consequences of such testing, and possible alternatives. Test-scoring mechanisms will also be discussed as a way of bringing greater understanding to procedures that have often been regarded as mysterious.

Children and Tests

Many children now undergo a variety of preschool screening assessments, some related to physical development (can the child skip or stand on one foot for 20 seconds?), others to cognitive development (can the child retell a story in its proper sequence?), and still others to social and environmental experience (can the child count to 10, recognize colors and shapes, manipulate a crayon or a pencil?). Often the results of these screening activities are used as a basis for cautioning parents to "wait another year before starting your child in kindergarten." They are also used as a means of "early identification" of individuals (essentially, labeling) "who might be expected to have difficulty in school, might need special assistance." Even in this kind of non-paper-and-pencil testing, those usually identified as "most in need" are either poor or from minority backgrounds. Although there is scant evidence that such early screening is beneficial for either children or schools, it is, nonetheless, increasing.

In kindergarten, children typically receive their first paper-and-pencil test, which ostensibly gauges "reading readiness." Those who score in the bottom quartile are often encouraged to spend another year in kindergarten or are placed in a K–1 transitional setting, which often leads to later retention. The underlying rationale is that the child benefits from the knowledge teachers gain from this kind of testing. Yet teachers gain little, if any, important knowledge from such tests. When there is so little evidence that reading readiness scores correlate with reading success, or any other kind of school success, their use appears unwarranted. To retain children on the basis of such tests is a scandal.

Beginning in first grade and continuing through the remaining elementary grades, children in most schools receive at a minimum (and it is important to know that many children receive many more) an annual achievement test battery such as the Metropolitan Reading Test, Metropolitan Achievement Test, California Test of Basic Skills, Stanford Achievement Test, or Iowa Test of Basic Skills. Until the past few years, most children also received two or three group IQ tests, essentially instruments purporting to measure intelligence or aptitude, during elementary school. But group IQ tests have not fared well in the courts as placement tools, and as meaningful educational instruments they have been criticized severely. As a result, they are increasingly being withdrawn from many school testing programs. This is a small victory.

When achievement tests are used solely to monitor children's "growth" from year to year, they can be relatively benign; however, the tests acquire a considerably different, and less benign, meaning as their purposes expand. School officials increasingly tend to find multiple uses for achievement tests as a means of justifying the cost and time involved in their administration. For example, in many school districts, how well individual children score determines whether they will be placed in a gifted-and-talented program or become eligible for special tutoring. The results of annual achievement testing also determine eligibility for a variety of enrichment programs, special classes, foreign language instruction, and so forth.

Stratification (tracking) by achievement scores also occurs as an outgrowth of such testing, reflecting the belief that homogeneous achievement groups facilitate more efficient teaching. That such grouping on the basis of a test leads mostly to inequity seems not to be sufficiently considered. And in recent years, test results are being used to determine whether a child should advance from one grade to another. This represents a new dimension.

All in all, increased testing results in increased pressure on teachers and children. If, for example, tests play a significant role in grade advancement, teachers feel compelled to spend considerable time preparing children to take the tests. In such settings the tests increasingly become the school curriculum. This is hardly a salutary development. Further, results on a standardized test battery can hardly represent a particular child very well, making problematic any attempt to attach critical importance to the results. The early years of schooling represent for most children a time of uneven growth, marked by plateaus and spurts. Because they are still developing many of the skills needed for school success, the potential loss of a child's self-esteem, which is only one possible result of the testing, should lead us to great caution in the use of tests.

An educator's principal purpose, as we know, is to enhance the growth of *every* child. But if children are labeled "unready" or "slow learners" as an outgrowth of standardized test results, their educational opportunities generally become narrow, uninteresting, and unchallenging. One-dimensional tasks, such as skill sheets, workbooks, and various drills, figure prominently in their education.

Why should we be so cautious about test results? Tests used in grades 1 and 2 are, of course, different from those used in grades 3 through 6. The early tests are picture and vocabulary dependent, while the later ones place greater stress on content. Consequently, high scores in the early testing may not carry over to the later testing. Because tests include diverse subject areas, they may or may not relate directly to what children have been taught or evoke from particular children any intrinsic interest. In addition, the multiple-choice format of standardized tests confuses many children because they are not accustomed to recording their understandings in that manner.

Recognizing spelling errors in a reading passage, for example, does not mean that the same child can actually write correctly spelled words or write a letter or descriptive statement. For a host of reasons having little to do with their ability to read, children who read very well may select "wrong" answers from among the limited choices available. Peculiarities of testing abound: Children who have been routinely encouraged to be cooperative learners are forbidden to talk during testing; children taught to work problems out slowly are told speed is essential. The message is clear: "Don't take your time—guess if necessary." Such conditions cause many children undue anxiety, even if the ultimate consequences of test-taking are not devastating.

Scoring Mechanisms

Understanding the scoring mechanisms associated with the tests also helps explain why teachers and parents should apply test results cautiously to individual children.

Test results are most often reported as percentile scores, stanine scores, or grade-level equivalency scores. Forty-three correct answers (the raw score) out of 80 items on the language section of a very popular achievement test taken at the end of the seventh grade are, for example, converted to a percentile score of 52. This indicates that 52 percent of those who took the test as part of the norm population scored 43 or less and 48 percent scored higher than 43.

Stanine scores, unlike percentile scores and grade-level equivalency scores, are suggestive of a range. (For this reason test publishers are increasingly encouraging their use.) A stanine score is developed by organizing percentile scores into nine groups. A stanine score of 5, encompassing 20 percent of the percentile scores, is considered average; 40 percent of the scores will then fall above this average and 40 percent below. On the test cited above, the percentile score of 52 falls within the fifth stanine, along with *all* percentile scores between 40 and 60.

The grade-level equivalency score is derived essentially by assigning to the median raw score of a seventh-grade norm population a grade-level equivalency of 7.0. Scores above and below the median are assigned grade-level equivalencies above and below 7.0. These assigned grade-level equivalency scores represent an estimation, nothing more. The score of 43 on the language section of the test under discussion (taken at the end of the seventh grade), which converted to a percentile score of 52 and a stanine score of 5, produces a grade-level equivalency score of 8.3 (eighth grade, third month).

The publisher of the test from which the foregoing derivations are taken lists a standard error for the language section of 3.9. This standard error indicates that two-thirds of the time one could expect a raw score fluctuation of 3.9 for a given student. The true score, then, for a student with a raw score of 43 could be said to fall between 39 and 47. This is between the 44th and 60th percentiles, or stanine 5; the grade-level equivalency range, on the other hand, is 7.2 to 8.9. Because these scores are very imprecise, one has to be very careful about attaching too much importance to them. Grade-level equivalency scores are especially misleading, and although most test publishers discourage their use, they remain very popular in the schools.

Another Direction

Teachers and parents should insist that standardized test scores resulting from their district's testing programs never be the major source of any decision making about a particular child. Alternatively, an evaluation process of consequence should be developed to counteract growing reliance on standardized testing programs.

Educators must communicate effectively with parents and their respective communities. They need to state clearly their aims regarding the basic skills and expressive arts, how they propose to achieve those aims—what procedures they plan using to assure children's acquisition and growth in basic skills and expressive arts areas—and how they will report to parents. The failure to communicate the foregoing successfully has undoubtedly been one of the reasons testing programs have become so prominent.

Teachers may directly gauge a child's progress through a systematic program of informal assessment, observation, and record keeping. This should be a teacher's basic mechanism for keeping in touch with children's learning and responding to the related evaluation issues.

In schools that keep consistently careful records, teachers can learn a great deal about the status and pace of their children's growth in the basic skills and expressive arts from previous teachers' reports (ongoing portfolios of learning). For each child these reports might include: lists of books read, samples of writing over time, themes explored in various media, examples of mathematical concepts and applications that are understood, results of reading inventories conducted on an individual basis, and summary evaluation statements about the various skill areas. These kinds of records should provide teachers with some important insights into individual children's learning levels, giving them a broader and more realistic array of starting points in relation to curriculum. (The standardized tests provide little that gives direction to curriculum development.)

To understand their pupils personally as well as establish baseline data for the year, teachers might administer a variety of informal assessment exercises. In the area of reading, for example, teachers might use a published informal reading inventory (McCracken, 1973; Silvaroli, 1973) or one that they themselves might develop (using a passage from a popular trade book enjoyed by children at the relevant grade level) to determine how well a child reads and the kinds of difficulties experienced. These kinds of assessment activities typically ask a child to read a passage silently, describe orally what the passage is about, read the passage aloud to the teacher, and then add orally to their earlier description (Engel, 1975). The published forms have a scoring mechanism, based upon the frequency of errors, which permits the teacher to categorize the child's reading level. Parents can replicate this activity; consequently, they may experience the same insights as the teacher. Reading might also be examined by using the Miscue Analysis (Goodman & Burke, 1972), a linguistically based assessment activity that focuses on comprehension and gives teachers some direction in relation to instruction. This assessment process provides teachers with excellent information about the reading strategies that a child brings to print material.

In the areas of mathematics and writing, a variety of assessment activities can be developed easily by teachers, constructed around the curriculum materials and content related to the particular grade levels of the children. In mathematics, these might include a sampling of math symbols, computational exercises, and problem-solving activities completed in a conference setting with the teacher. In writing, children might be asked to engage in several different writing activities, permitting the teacher to learn about the child's use of language, range of expression, and so forth. Brenda Engel's *Handbook on Documentation* (1975) and *Informal Evaluation* (1977) provide numerous examples of informal assessment in all curriculum areas, as does Clara Pederson's *Informal Evaluation and Record-keeping* (1977).

Having established some baseline information about children's skills, interests, and learning styles, teachers need to establish a record-keeping system and regularly note individual children's development during the course of the year. Included would be periodic assessment activities of the type described above; projects in writing, mathematics, and art; lists of books read and understood; and audiotapes that focus on children's reading or language use. These would all address concerns about growth over the course of an entire year. In addition, these kinds of records should assist teachers in their instructional planning. They can use the information to determine focused grouping patterns or enrichment needs. Aiding the learners, after all, is the principal reason for maintaining careful records. These records can also serve as the basis for periodic conferences with and written reports for parents. The record-keeping process might additionally illustrate for parents a way that they, too, might follow their children's progress more closely.

In addition to the benefits discussed above in relation to systematic record keeping, experience reveals that teachers who have begun to document children's learning through carefully organized records tend also to become more knowledgeable about children and learning. They become the "students of teaching" that schools need and parents desire. Teachers able to describe children's learning in great detail are teachers who are trusted and are capable of helping reestablish parental confidence in the schools.

The above focuses on individual teachers and classrooms. The school, as a whole, also needs to address some of the same evaluation issues. The school might distribute annual reports summarizing a variety of classroom data for its parents and community. For example, how many books on the average were read by children at various grade levels? What percentage of children at each of the grade levels mastered grade-level learning objectives in mathematics, reading, and writing? What approaches were used to help children who were having difficulty meeting the learning objectives? How did parents respond to their children's overall experience in school and, specifically, in the basic skills and expressive arts (possibly derived from parent interviews)?

While such information could be useful to the community, it

would be particularly useful to a school staff, providing a base for reexamining their collective efforts. If the staff note areas of particular difficulty for children, they have a basis upon which to act. By reviewing common data systematically, they can be assured that their judgments are empirically sound.

If such informal assessment and record keeping occur systematically, the standardized tests would be clearly unnecessary. If it were, however, deemed politically important to engage in some minimal level of standardized testing, the results of such testing could be viewed as merely another means of evaluation and would not assume the kind of significance that intimidates and distorts the educational process.

Conclusion

This paper stresses the continuing potency of standardized testing in school programs, especially the schools' use of test results for increasing purposes. It argues that teachers and parents should oppose using test results for making any important judgment about a child. Alternatively, teachers and schools are presented with a means of entering the assessment arena systematically and beneficially, guaranteeing a greater understanding of the growth of individual children—possibly the only method of reducing the importance of testing programs.

CHAPTER TWELVE

Competency Testing: A Social and Historical Perspective

Accountability as an educational formulation flourished in the 1970s. Following the lead of Florida, states rushed to establish testing programs to determine grade promotion and graduation. In North Dakota, a competency testing bill was defeated in the 1977 legislative session but was replaced by legislation authorizing a Basic Skills Committee to study the feasibility and desirability of implementing competency testing. I produced this paper for the Committee, on which I also served, in October 1978. It was later published in Educational Horizons *(July 1979). The North Dakota Basic Skills Committee, in its report back to the legislature, recommended against statewide competency testing. I include the paper in this collection because competency testing remains a national issue.*

The kinds of testing that have come to dominate discussions of educational standards in our schools grow out of a twentieth-century belief that language, intelligence, and achievement are subject to assessment through a series of relatively simple multiple-choice, paper-and-pencil exercises. While doubts about these testing practices—their underlying assumptions and validity—are escalating rapidly among educators, students, and parents, their use is nonetheless increasing.

The current debate over testing in the United States is beginning to focus on the minimal-competency movement and a range of related procedures governing grade promotion and high school graduation. This has not occurred because other testing practices in the schools are benign. It is more that competency-testing programs have become very popular among members of state legislatures and departments of education and are being advocated as vehicles for bringing about a "return to standards," for achieving an overall improvement in the quality of the schools. In order to make a discussion of this latest effort more intelligent, I will place it within a larger historical perspective as well as raise some of the related measurement problems and educational dilemmas that need more thorough examination.

Current Context for Competency Testing

What is the basis upon which 35 states, either through legislative mandates or state education agency regulations, have instituted competency testing? Winsor Lott (1977), chief of the Bureau of Elementary and Secondary Education Testing, New York State Department of Education, provides a straightforward response that epitomizes the related national literature:

There are probably two reasons for the current interest in basic Competency Testing throughout the nation. First, there is concern that schools are awarding high school diplomas to individuals who lack some of the basic skills, who can't read and write, for example. In addition, because of the cost of education, there is a continuing interest in accountability. Here it seems [that] various state legislatures . . . are demanding proof that the schools are doing a good job and that taxpayers are getting something of value for their investment. (p. 84)

The foregoing relates to the erosion of confidence in the schools that has characterized the 1970s, particularly as it has been expressed in debates over accountability for test score results and educational costs. H. D. Shalock (1976), a serious student of the competency-based education movement, suggests that "technological" advances have also contributed to the current level of interest. He writes:

Another condition that has contributed [to competency testing] is the remarkable progress that has been made over the past decade in the technology of instruction, assessment and information management. The emergence of the performance or goal based instruction movement, the concept of mastery learning, and the development of [criterion] tested instructional materials are cases in point. . . . The information storage and retrieval capabilities now available through computer technology, and the evaluation strategies for data management and utilization in decision making, make it possible to apply effectively the instruction and assessment capabilities previously unavailable to schools. (pp. 1–2)

The "current context" is outlined above in high relief, but clearly, the context is larger, more subtle and complex. Readers should, however, keep this high relief in mind as I turn now to an historical review.

Historical Perspective

Before directing this discussion to efforts to use tests to certify whether individual students have succeeded with various levels of education or to determine basic educational standards that exist in schools, it is important to comment on the historical perspective in general. Public education in the United States has a history almost as long as the republic itself, yet we lack extensive historical accounts of schools and their interaction with the culture at large. In large measure this is because educators have not seen historical perspective as critical to the improvement of schools. If we had, for example, better descriptions of school curricula, organizational patterns, and instructional processes, as well as the political, economic, and social factors that influenced them, we might have a better grasp of what educational reform demands. Lacking historical perspective, we often enter into what are viewed as new directions for reform without a sufficient base or inclination for examining earlier, but similar, efforts and their contexts. Competency testing is among a number of contemporary examples and the one that I will use to illustrate the point.

The Boston schools, in 1845, instituted a common secondary education certifying examination, and the New York legislature, in 1877, established a system of examinations "to furnish a suitable standard of secondary school graduation." By the turn of the century, most states had testing programs affecting promotion and graduation. To be sure, these early examinations were not of the multiple choice variety—that technology developed most notably in the post-1910 period—but their effects were not dissimilar. What were the consequences of this early testing?

The certifying examination had, for the most part, negative consequences for minorities—at least those who were in schools—and the poor. Their failure rates tended to be high, and few entered the secondary schools. At the turn of the century, such a circumstance was not viewed adversely by educators, politicians, or societal leaders. A wide range of social, cultural, and racial inequalities were tolerated, and testing was accepted as a legitimate means for selecting students into and out of educational opportunities. Equality of educational opportunity as a matter of public policy is, after all, a post–World War II development.

Was it disastrous at the turn of the century for an individual not to complete high school? While the completion of secondary school clearly opened up many opportunities inaccessible to those without a high school diploma, the lack of a high school diploma did not prevent the majority of individuals from gaining an economic livelihood or place them in a radically different social position from most of those around them. After all, less than 10 percent of those who began school in 1900 completed secondary education. As educational attainment increased after World War I, not having the high school diploma became a larger burden, but it was not until almost 1950 that it became a catastrophe. In 1950, 52 percent, for the first time a majority, of the 18- and 19-year-old population completed high school. This attainment figure peaked nationally in 1967 at 76 percent. But throughout the twentieth century, the poor and minorities have carried most of the burden of limited schooling.

It should be noted that this overall increase in high school completion took place as statewide examination systems, which related to promotion and retention, began to decline in number. By 1950, they had virtually disappeared. Accompanying the increased levels of educational attainment—and the growing commitment in America to expanding educational opportunities for all Americans—school programs became more diverse. A natural consequence of this diversity was that high school diplomas lost whatever common meaning they had. Surprisingly, this consequence went unnoticed, to be interpreted in the 1970s as a sudden decline in standards.

What effect did the certifying tests have on curriculum? The evidence is that the tests influenced significantly what was taught. The diaries of early twentieth-century teachers were filled with accounts of the long periods in which they prepared students for the state examinations, giving up learning activities they considered to be more engaging for the students. *High School and Life: The Regents Inquiry into the Character and Costs of Public Education in the State of New York* (Spaulding, 1958) reported that the Regents Examination had, in effect, become the curriculum. What did not appear on the examination was not taken seriously by teachers or students. The broad goals of locally established curricula were given little attention. George

Madaus and Peter Airasian (1978), who have examined the history of certifying examinations in the United States as well as in Australia and Europe, comment:

> Faced with a choice between one set of objectives which are explicit in the course outline and a different set which are explicit in past certifying examinations, students and teachers generally choose to focus on the latter. This finding holds true over different countries and over many decades. . . . Most studies have found that the proportion of instructional time spent on various objectives was seldom higher than the predicted likelihood of their occurrence on the external examination. (p. 3)

And what can one say for the interest in "technological advances" that H. D. Shalock (1976) suggests is a basis for the interest in competency testing. Such technological advances as systems analysis, instruction by objectives, objectives-referenced testing, and mastery learning have earlier antecedents, if no greater theoretical support. They are part of a long-term fascination in the twentieth century with applying science to education. One has only to read Raymond Callahan's classic *Education and the Cult of Efficiency* (1962) to gain some historical perspective about how little such efforts have contributed to the improvement of schools. An understanding of how this "curriculum science" influenced schools can also be found in the classic debate between Franklin Bobbit (1924), who described the curriculum maker as a "great engineer," and Boyd Bode (1937), who saw in all of this an anti-intellectualism and a limitation on learning.

Have we not had other periods when the schools and their standards were under attack? The nineteenth century produced a number of examples, which generally resulted in greater centralization of schools and increased levels of uniformity of school practice. The work of Michael Katz (1971) is particularly helpful in understanding this. Testing was a related phenomenon.

Within the past half-century, we have experienced two major debates about the quality of schools. Interestingly, each has touched off different responses. The first was precipitated by the Russian launching of Sputnik I in 1957 and continued through much of the 1960s. While there were some who argued for the reestablishment of state testing programs and instructional uniformity, the prevailing response was to put resources into improving the quality of teacher education and instituting a wide range of curriculum development programs considered to be more challenging. At a time when

governance of schools was understood as local in nature, teacher education (preservice and in-service) and curriculum development were
natural responses. In contrast, the response to the 1970s debates over
the quality of schools is testing. Why the shift in focus? In large
measure this has occurred because the nature of educational governance is changing. It is clearly more complex now, with considerably more authority resting at the state and federal levels, than has
ever before been the case. Removed as state and federal legislators
and bureaucrats are from the complexity of classrooms and the social consequences of school programs, testing has a simple appeal.
Being far away always seems to simplify difficulties.

What does the new wave of testing emanating from state legislatures and state departments of education look like in relation to
previous efforts? Walter Haney and Kabiru Kinyanjui (1979) note that
minimal-competency testing programs are "not aimed at improving
the quality of education for all students but instead [are] aimed at
those toward the bottom of the educational heap." And who is at the
bottom? These same authors cite figures from a Congressional Budget
Office study in which it was reported that among high school seniors in 1972, "21 percent of the white students and 60 percent of the
black students were in the lowest quartile [based upon grades, test
scores, and so forth]" (Haney & Kinyanjui, 1979, p. 2). Minority
students are more often retained than nonminority students, tend
as a result to be older in the secondary schools, and are more often
in nonacademic programs. In Florida, for example, 30–40 percent
more blacks are in nonacademic high school programs than whites,
and 50 percent more blacks than whites failed the Florida Functional Literacy Test. There is sufficient evidence already on record
to demonstrate that the new wave of testing for purposes of promotion and graduation is having its most negative effect on minorities and lower socioeconomic populations. In a major publication,
Testing . . . Grouping: The New Segregation in Southern Schools (Bryan
& Mills, 1979), the Southern Regional Council presents its concerns
about the growing interest in competency testing among the southern states, citing its potential for resegregating the schools.

Judging from the results of 1970s competency testing efforts, little appears to have changed since 1900. The only difference is that
in 1900 public policy had not yet coalesced around such directions
as equality of educational opportunity. Does this new wave of state
testing suggest that the more recent public policy commitments to
equity are faltering? It has that appearance to me!

Are "teaching to the tests" and "a narrowing of curriculum" consequences of the new wave of state testing programs? Ralph Tyler (1979) reports, on the basis of his inquiry in Florida, that

> We were told that many teachers interpreted the emphasis on basic skills to mean that they must devote most of their attention to routine drill. This usually results in a decrease in the student's interest in schooling and it diminishes the time that should be devoted to the meaning and application of those skills. (p. 30)

During the recent Florida court case (decided against the state of Florida) in which the Functional Literacy Test and the withholding of diplomas was under question, considerable testimony indicated that remediation programs established for those not succeeding on the examinations were geared almost entirely toward items that were on the examinations. Preparation for the tests had become for many students the curriculum of the schools.

In a major review, which colleagues and I conducted of how teachers functioned in a Michigan school district where test scores carried major significance (Patton, French, & Perrone, 1976), it was clear that the curriculum had been narrowed, teaching to the tests being the principal curricular activity. Teacher after teacher noted that test scores were going up while the overall quality of education in the district was declining.

Schaffarzick and Walker (1974), in summarizing the data over the past 20 years on curriculum and testing for the *Review of Educational Research*, note that it has been consistently the case that test scores reflected the degrees of emphasis placed upon the specific information asked for in the tests. *Different curricula*, as they report, *bring about different patterns of achievement*. To follow the major research is to understand that the drive toward minimal-competency testing is a drive toward less diversity of curriculum at a time when no significant consensus exists about what curricular patterns ought to exist in schools.

In 1900 the victim was the student, and we see similar consequences today. Improving education in 1900 was viewed by those supporting a growing "scientific" movement as a technical question. The nature of existing competency programs suggests that improvement is still viewed as a technical question. That we have not learned from our experience is disheartening. To the degree that states expend their energies and resources toward testing programs under the veil of accountability or minimal-competency testing, they are engaged in an effort with limited educational potential and one that will most likely do little to reestablish broad public confidence in and understanding of schools and schooling. The same can be said for most other technical efforts that tend to reduce the diversity of educational practices and programs.

Educational Dilemmas and Competency Testing

In order to provide greater understanding of the complexity of competency testing, I pose in this closing section a number of questions that are important to keep raising.

How valid are the tests? Testing programs that depend on a multiple-choice, norm- or criterion-referenced format are relatively new in American society. While they often purport to measure one's ability to read, for example, it must be clear to most educators that they cannot represent reading as reading is commonly understood; they are at best weak indicators of reading. Persons who read very well may select "wrong" answers from among the limited choices available for a host of reasons that may have little to do with their ability to read. The literature is full of descriptions of the drawbacks that multiple-choice formats possess, such as single correct responses, ambiguity, and cultural and linguistic bias.

Is competency in writing, as another example, knowing rules of grammar and spelling, or is it the ability to make oneself clear in a written statement? In most of the tests that exist, grammar and spelling dominate. The problems multiply when efforts are made to use our existing technology to make judgments about functional literacy, life-skill competency, and the like.

How are cutoff scores to be determined? If tests are used to determine promotion or high school graduation, how are cutoff scores to be determined? There is, as yet, no empirically based process for determining cutoff scores. Those that now exist are largely arbitrary.

At this point, cutoff scores are being established on a political basis; for example, how many students can be held back, not given a diploma, without a serious public response? Another concern that needs to be raised in connection with the establishment of minimal standards is *whether the minimal standards become maximum standards.*

What effect are external standards likely to have on teachers and students? Will teachers' roles in schools be reduced even further, leaving them as technicians? If teachers are not free to respond to children, to particular occasions, to enter into significant inquiry into learning *with* children, are they likely to remain enthusiastic about their work? All of the evidence indicates that teachers in technician roles lose their commitment to intensive learning. Teaching becomes "merely a job." If we have learned nothing else over the years, we have learned that the teacher is the critical factor in what happens for children in classrooms.

And what can be said about a related concern—student intentions? Stuart Hampshire (1960) framed it well when he wrote: "A man becomes more and more a free and responsible agent the more he at all times knows what he is doing, in every sense of this phrase, and the more he acts with a definite and clearly formed intention" (p. 91). William Spady and Douglas Mitchell (1977) introduce a similar concern, arguing that

> It is not enough for state legislatures, school boards, administrators or even teachers to have clearly specified goals—students will only achieve a higher level of devotion to their learning goals if they themselves have identified this as important and as an appropriate basis for channeling their energies and actions . . . narrow and constraining performance demands destroy vital student motivation. (p. 18)

How narrow are the external standards to become? Because of our limited conception of human behavior and our similarly limited ability to measure it, external standards, when established with mandates for quantitative measurement, quickly turn to those things most easily conceived and measured. Broader, more diffuse goals dealing with human action are difficult to translate into specific behaviors. And even when the translation is accomplished, the inferential leap from behaviors to objectives tends to be great and, in the process, the intentional quality of human action is lost.

So many more questions and concerns could be raised. In spite of the questions and concerns, however, the movement propels itself forward, not yet having to face a substantial challenge. Lawrence Cremin (1978), in *Public Education*, writes that

> Good theory . . . should convey a sense of the richness and complexity of the phenomenon it seeks to illumine. And it is precisely a sense of

richness and complexity that has been missing from the educational discussions of recent years. (p. x)

Nowhere is the validity of Cremin's concern more evident than in the competency-education movement as it now is unfolding. My hope is that the complexity will be realized and will become a source of critical debate before we are all led further down a trail filled with frustration and bitterness and with little potential for educational improvement.

Part V
CURRICULUM

CHAPTER THIRTEEN

Science Education:
From Sputnik to the Toyota

This paper was first presented at the North Dakota Academy of Sciences meeting on April 26, 1983. Portions of it were used in October 1983 in an MIT-Wheelock Conference on Science Education entitled "This Side of the Rainbow." It was later published in Insights *(April 1984). Because science education has been in recent decades the lightning rod for school reform, I attempted to provide some historical context for a discussion of science education. Reflecting on science education today, I am pleased to see the movement toward greater experimentation, a fuller understanding that science is more a cultural than a technical subject, and a large commitment to inquiry as a mode of learning. But many of the problems I noted in the paper continue to stand, not yet made much a part of the fuller discourse.*

Being principally a historian, and finding as I do that historical perspective is generally neglected in discussions of contemporary issues, I feel compelled to make some general comments about schooling in the United States before I get to science education specifically. My hope is that these historical remarks will provide a useful context.

Historical Background

Our nation's commitments to elementary and secondary schools have for much of the past 100 years had something of a boom-bust quality. Fiscal support as well as expectations have been very uneven. Schools were once expected to provide the rudimentary skills of reading, writing, and ciphering to the majority and higher-level skills and broad cultural knowledge to the few. For the former who went beyond the elementary school, and their numbers were small, vocational training was added in the early twentieth century. For the latter, who came principally from the middle and upper classes, were white, and were not of recent immigrant status, the basic liberal arts–oriented curriculum expanded at the turn of the century to take into account the rapid advances in science and technology. While there was in 1900 a growing and potent rhetoric about universalism and equality of opportunity, along with a recognition that society's educational needs had enlarged greatly, it would be a number of years before the practice began to correspond.

By 1940, universalism was well on the road to realization for whites in America—the majority were completing high school programs by this time. But the high schools were also different in 1940 from what they had been in 1900. They were more comprehensive, with fewer requirements in what were once core academic courses. The study of foreign languages, for example, peaked in 1916 and declined each year from that point on. A high school education began to be something different for different students.

As this universalism became increasingly the practice, expectations for the schools also enlarged greatly. There is considerable talk today about the expansion of courses and programs in the 1960s. We hear, for example, a great deal about "proliferation." But the program expansion in the 1920s was significantly larger: In addition to their usual fare, schools were becoming centers for personal counseling, nutrition education, moral development, consumer training, and co-op education.

In the 1950s, universalist conceptions finally began to take into account minority populations. And the numbers of young people staying in high school through graduation began to escalate more rapidly than in any other period in our history. From the 52 percent of the total age cohort completing high school in 1950, the percentage rose by 1967 to 76 percent, a figure considered remarkable by many at that time. It was reached in part through a continuing differentiation of standards and expectations along with the acceptance of an increasing array of social obligations by the schools—drug and alcohol counseling, safety and driver education, family-planning education, career exploration, and job-placement programs.

In this "reform period" of the 1980s—though the percentage of students completing high school has declined from the 1967 peak—there is a great deal of talk about needing to redress the equity-quality balance in favor of quality, essentially a belief that we have somehow paid a price for so much attention to universalism or equity. That is not a particularly uplifting or refreshing pattern of thought. And in light of where we are with regard to educating *all* students well, it is an argument that deflects us from serious, long-lasting reform.

Without question, we need to concentrate our energies and resources on both equity and quality. We cannot be satisfied with our level of universalism because it is not adequate. It has already fallen behind that in France, West Germany, the Soviet Union, and Japan. And we clearly cannot be satisfied with the differentiation of quality for those who persevere in the system. At the upper levels, our students may well receive an education equal to the best in any country. But at the lower levels, it is far poorer than a modern, technology-oriented, democratic society ought to accept. Not all of those Soviet 17- and 18-year-olds in calculus, for example, succeed in the fullest sense of what is meant by the word *succeed*—but they do clearly gain from the experience and the surrounding commitments to support them at the level of their understanding. They are not sent off to do elementary arithmetic in their last years of secondary school. This is not a plea for universal calculus study in American schools. It does suggest, however, some rethinking of the kinds of alternatives we have tended to encourage for those seen as a bit less able academically. The kind of tracking we now do—and tracking is reaching unprecedented levels in the schools—is neither constructive nor conscionable.

Though the recent report of the National Commission on Excellence in Education (1983)— *A Nation at Risk*—does not express the point very well, today more than ever we need a coherent statement of purposes and expectations for schools buttressed by the will to support the related implications. Our discussions about purposes tend now to be couched almost exclusively in technical and economic terms and move us away from serious attention to critical issues of curriculum, teaching, and learning. Further, the kinds of regulatory legislation now being proposed for improvement, devoid as they are of much philosophical content, may well make things worse.

Post-Sputnik Reform Era

Science education in the schools has once again become, as it was after October 1957 when the Soviet Union put their silver ball into orbit, a topic of widespread popular discussion. In 1957, there was concern that America's technological superiority *might* be in jeopardy if math and science teaching did not better reflect the post–World War II advances in scientific knowledge, especially with regard to the physical sciences, and if interest in math and science did not enlarge.

The drive for reform in science education in the post-Sputnik era was led by university scholars and supported by a healthy infusion of federal dollars through the nascent National Science Foundation. Many of those giving leadership to the reform—Joseph Schwab and Charles Wolcott in biology; Philip Morrison and Jerrold Zacharias in physics; David Hawkins and George Hein in elementary science; William Hull and David Page in mathematics; and Jerome Bruner in psychology, among others—produced wonderful materials and spoke eloquently for the need to encourage a scientific mode of thought. Math and science were not conceived by these reformers as being organized around immutable facts or laws, as linear subject matters. Inquiry as a model of discourse was reaffirmed— questioning, maintaining a healthy skepticism, developing hypotheses, experimenting, examining a range of information, confirming and disconfirming, arriving at a variety of possible explanations. An open-endedness characterized the discussion. The active use of materials and ideas growing out of careful observation over time became the critical ingredients. There was talk of the need to "uncover a subject" rather than "cover a subject." A great deal was made out of the distinction.

I quote below from an introductory guide to the NSF-supported Elementary Science Study, one of the most imaginative of the various science curriculum reform efforts, and a model of what science at its best ought to be about.

> It is apparent that children are scientists by disposition: They ask questions and use their senses as well as their reasoning powers to explore their physical environments; they derive great satisfaction from finding out what makes things tick; they like solving problems; they are challenged by new materials or by new ways of using familiar materials. It is this natural curiosity of children and their freedom from preconceptions of difficulty that ESS tries to cultivate and direct into *deeper* channels. It is our intention to enrich *every* child's understandings . . . we want children to be at home with modern technology, not be intimidated by it. We have tried to incorporate both the spirit and the substance of science into our program in such a way that the child's own rich world of exploration becomes more disciplined, more manageable and more satisfying. (*Guide to the Elementary Science Study*, 1967, pp. 1–2)

In regard to teaching strategy, the ESS guide relates:

> In the course of developing our units we have found it worthwhile to abandon a great many conventional ideas about teaching. We want students not only to recognize scientific authority but also to develop both the confidence and the skills to question it intelligently. For this reason we feel it is necessary for the student to confront the real world and its physical materials directly, rather than through intermediaries such as textbooks. (p. 2)

And further: "We caution teachers against explaining things prematurely and against overdirecting student exploration" (p. 2). Are the values inherent in the foregoing philosophical and pedagogical orientation—skepticism, questioning, challenging, openness, seeking alternative possibilities—the values that permeate the schools? or the society as a whole? One does not have to be a student of American society to know that such values have long struggled for acceptance. Answers, rather than questions, have dominated the social and intellectual discourse. And the schools have always been mirrors of the society. How could they be otherwise?

The teacher-training institutes that flowered and indeed provided for many teachers a revitalization, a significant increase in math and science knowledge and understanding, and a fresh, even a liberating, way of thinking about teaching, insured that some of the reform would find its way into the schools. But only a minority of teachers received the benefit of the institutes. By 1969, though, the science and math reform boom had already begun to wane. Stung by a strong political backlash against "Man, A Course of Study" (MACOS), an imaginative program with strong evolutionary themes, NSF curriculum efforts ended.

Evaluation of Reform Efforts

Two years ago I listened with great fascination to Peter Dow, who directed the MACOS project, describe his first public hearing on the content of the program, organized by a congressional delegation in Arizona. He presented, as he said, "in the best academic form possible," the theory that guided the development of the program as well as scholarly and pedagogical rationales for the particular selections of topics and materials, only to be asked "Dr. Dow, is this a hand [the questioner's hand was held up] or a fin?" At that first hearing, Peter Dow suggested he did not understand the question's connection to MACOS or his presentation. But the question was repeated—not only there but in public hearing after public hearing. Dow ultimately came to understand the question too well! One could argue that the entire NSF curriculum development effort should not have been forced to bear the burden of the public controversy surrounding MACOS and thus brought to an end, but NSF learned, as did others in education, that public policy can take many contradictory directions, can be influenced by the most improbable events.

The NSF-commissioned study conducted by Robert Stake and Jack Easley (1978) confirmed what observers had already noted—that few remnants of the science reform movement existed. Fewer than 10 percent of American students were using materials spawned in that period. Inquiry-oriented programs existed in such schools as the Bronx High School of Science and in the best of America's private schools but were virtually absent in most public school settings. The NSF-sponsored curriculum materials had gone into storage or been discarded. Textbooks and workbooks, the bane that the scientists found in 1957, had again become the backbone of teaching practice. And in relation to the textbooks, the threat of censorship had become more potent than ever. We have come, in many respects, to see aspects of the *Scopes* trial resurface.

What went wrong? What ought we to think about as we prepare for what *may* become a new interest in math and science education?

When Joseph Schwab was asked this question, he stated that the reform efforts did not early enough involve the thoughtful teachers who existed, persons who could have helped guide the process in directions more consonant with actual classroom conditions. He also noted that funding dropped off at the most critical juncture—when the important revisions needed to be made. Unfortunately, we have very little careful description of the excellent practice that existed in the schools during the period when math and science reform was on the public's mind. As a result, we do not have much information on the conditions that contributed to successful practice, the kinds of questions raised by teachers and students in the process of successful practice, the reflections of teachers about their classroom efforts and the diverse uses made of the materials.

Further, what the reformers sought was apparently counter to the experiences of many of those responsible for governing and administering schools. It was also counter to the experience of many of the parents who had children in schools. The power of prior experience, as most people in and around schools know, is great. Additionally, what the reform efforts called for demanded more time and energy, the higher level of intensity that inquiry-oriented teaching demands. Reformers found that school schedules were difficult to modify. At the secondary school level they advocated a teaching load of 3–4 hours a day, with flexible time schedules desirable. And they viewed teaching loads of 75–100 students as maximum. To expect a larger teaching load, as Morrison, Zacharias, and Hawkins often noted in their public discussions, was to assure that teaching practice would return to textbooks, workbooks, and didactic instruction—whereby inquiry would not likely be sustained. But the loads continued to include 150–175 students and 5–6 hours per day of teaching. The conditions of teaching were not then particularly favorable and they remain problematic today.

Jerrold Zacharias spoke of the lingering effects of "testing mechanisms" and "covering material" as being too powerful—always in the way, pulling teachers back to textbooks and workbooks and away from science as scientists understand and practice it. William Hull noted that the skepticism math and science most needed as a response was not desired in the schools or in the society. Rather than the exploration of alternative possibilities, certainty, he believed, was the preferred outcome.

In this retrospective vein, I commend an essay by David Hawkins (1978) on "Critical Barriers to Science Learning," prepared originally for the Division of Research and Development of NSF. He offers, with regard to science, an alternative view about the difficulties of instituting major reform. Rather than affirming fully that the schools and the society are encumbered with attitudes antithetical to science at its best, Hawkins suggests that those who sought reform "failed to extend that very spirit of investigation [they were encouraging] far enough to become radically troubled about the dimensions of the task at hand" (p. 19). In this regard he noted John Dewey's telling comment that science is in need of a reconstruction aimed at "increasing its permeability by the common understanding—the design of a working ambience for students which initiates them to begin to practice the ways of thought which science has evolved" (quoted in Hawkins, 1978, p. 19). Hawkins describes in the essay the elementary scientific understandings that were centuries in the making but remain counter to casual observations—observations that are not discarded with the provision of counterinformation and are "critical barriers" to productive science learning. As an example of scientific counterintuitiveness as well as understanding, Hawkins provides a description of the growth of plants.

For thousands of years farmers have farmed well in the belief that their crops are earth-earthy, pushing up from the maternal soil and somehow composed of it. Water and the heat of the sun were necessary but the stuff of life came from below. That view, like some Jungian ancestral memory, still dominates the thought processes of most of us. It is only a few generations since there was a scientific realization that trees are essentially shaped from air and water, that sunlight drives their circulatory systems, that they grow from the outside in. A large majority of our adult students will tend to believe the opposite: that plants—grasses or trees—push up out of the ground, their blades or branches slowing rising, their newest growth in the center, and all this despite a forgotten course in biology. (Apelman, Hawkins, & Morrison, 1985, p. 9)

"Size and scale" is another example that is illuminating. Maja Apelman (1978), a master teacher and teacher-educator who worked with David Hawkins for two weeks on the effects of size and scale, describes some of the issues:

One afternoon a group of teachers and I went outside to try to estimate the leaf area of a large maple tree by using the tree's shadow. We never got past measuring the shadow. Here we were, five teachers and an advisor, all totally absorbed for a good hour trying to calculate its area.

First we measured the length and width of the shadow, approximately twenty-five by forty feet. Then we multiplied these two figures—we all remembered that lesson from school. The result was one thousand square feet. Nobody would believe that; it sounded far too big for what we saw. We remeasured and recalculated and got the same figure. J. said she wished there was a ruler that would measure square feet. We tried to invent one: for each foot in length a corresponding square area would flip out—one linear foot, one square foot, two linear feet, four square feet, etc. Since we didn't have such a ruler we improvised. I had a pad of 8½ by 11 paper, and we figured that each sheet could represent a square foot if we left some space between the sheets. (There was no problem going from one linear foot to one square foot.) We started to cover the shadow area with our yellow sheets. We soon realized that we might well need a thousand sheets to cover the whole shadow area. We were amazed. Then J. remembered buying carpeting for her two bedrooms. She was sure that her bedrooms were at least as large as the shadow area of the tree but she was also sure that she didn't order a thousand square feet of carpeting. "What are the dimensions of one of your bedrooms?" we asked her. She didn't know. "How much furniture is in your bedroom?" we continued. "A double bed"—two of us promptly lay down on the grass—"and a chest of drawers"—another class member lay down to represent the chest. Now J. realized how small her bedroom really was, compared to the maple tree's shadow.

We all marvelled at our lack of experience with square feet. Our intuition was completely wrong yet we were so sure we were right that we refused to believe the figures we calculated until we had built up a good part of the thousand square feet one square foot at a time! Later on I tried to analyze our difficulty. We were all comfortable with linear measurements and could probably have estimated the length and width of the shadow fairly accurately. But when we multiplied twenty-five by forty (as we had been taught to do to get area—the sort of thing that is rarely questioned when you first learn it in school) we got a very large figure: one thousand. One thousand what? Again we did what we had been taught and tacked on "square feet." But our minds were still on linear dimensions and we could not see how an area *enclosed* (even that word may connote smallness) by twenty-five and forty feet respectively could suddenly measure one thousand. That number seemed far too big since we had so little experience switching from linear to area dimensions. (pp. 24–25)

I realize that I took a good deal of time with this point, but I agree with Hawkins and Apelman that reform is more than more courses and more information. We need to provide much more experience *with* math and science, and this takes a lot of time and considerable teacher understanding. Schools appear not to want to spare the time on understanding. Knowing something, however, does not necessarily correspond with understanding something.

Current Reforms in Science

If in 1957 there was a fear that American technological superiority *might* be in jeopardy, in 1983, the "year of the Toyota," there is a belief and a good deal of corroborating evidence that American technological superiority indeed no longer exists. There is, however, in contrast to 1957, another educational fact that might make a resurgence of reform difficult. The teaching profession is in the midst of a decline in quality and spirit. A large number of America's teachers have indicated in surveys that if they could live their lives over, they would not consider teaching. Many came to the schools because they believed in the ideas expressed in the 1960s science reform, but they now feel that such beliefs are not valued. They planned to teach chemistry but found that much of their day was spent with general science or that they were asked, because they had taken 12 hours of biology and 12 hours of physics in college, to teach those courses as well. They also found that they had little say in the selection of instructional materials or time schedules. Further, the numbers of well-prepared science and math teachers have declined; not enough are being prepared nationally to fill the positions being left vacant by retirements and departures for fields outside education.

Legislative bills aimed at encouraging more individuals to pursue science teaching careers and incentives for business and industry to give some of their employees time to teach part-time in the schools are worthwhile. The need for higher salaries is also long overdue, though higher salaries are necessary for *all* teachers, not just those in math and science. Reports encouraging states and local school districts to increase high school requirements in math and science are likewise useful. But problems still exist. They relate in large measure to the kinds of issues that emerged in the early post-Sputnik period as well. But there are also others. What is to be taught? Is our concern the understanding of "size and scale" (one of the critical barriers both Hawkins and Apelman note), helping children and young people develop their own systems for solving problems, or is it arithmetic and scientific facts—basic skills instruction? It is not the ability to multiply and add and to learn a few science facts that students struggle with today. The standardized test data make this clear enough. It is in the application of mathematics and science to solve complex problems that students falter. Filling workbook page after workbook page has clearly not produced understanding, or application, or interest. Indeed, interest in math and science is lower today than in 1957.

How will university scientists reenter this arena of education after their earlier and not particularly encouraging experience? To talk of making science and math more prominent, to extend it, to bring inquiry back is to support a fairly broad reform agenda. It means much more than increasing the numbers of math and science teachers or increasing math and science requirements in the schools. For reform to touch math and science in significant ways, it needs to touch the curriculum far beyond math and science as well. If inquiry, skepticism, and open-endedness are not part of the curriculum in history and English, for example, such qualities and dispositions will not in the long run survive in math and science programs either. This, among other things, was learned earlier. Unfortunately, this broad view is not yet a part of the contemporary discourse.

In regard to teachers, we need desperately to get into the faculties of our schools our most able and committed young people, even if they remain for only a few years. My experience is, however, that math and science faculties in our colleges and universities have tended for a long time *not* to recommend that their best and brightest students consider teaching. Until they do, limitations in what can be done in school math and science programs are likely to remain.

A concern discussed often in the 1960s was related to the nature of collegiate coursework in science. The changes being proposed for the schools left unaffected much that went on in the colleges. Schwab (1963) noted that science teaching at the university level tended to remain—in spite of the reform being fostered in elementary and secondary schools—didactic, linear, not particularly exploratory or problematic, nonconsonant with the most promising theory and practice. Is it different today? My sense is that it may be less open-ended, less focused than ever, and that a premium is still being placed on coverage and memorization, rather than on *doing* science.

We need to give more attention to math and science in the schools *and* in our colleges and universities. But to really make a qualitative difference in the outcomes, we need a fiscal and moral investment far greater than we have made in a long time. We need more continuity of effort from college and university faculty in math, science, other liberal arts fields, and education over a *long* time. I remain unconvinced that we have many people willing to make the necessary long-term commitments.

We have today begun to recapture public interest, but reform is more than rhetoric. We have to begin again, but we also ought to know we have traveled some of the paths before and experienced some of the difficulties. As a consequence, we should prepare ourselves for growth that may not move the mountains as quickly as we would like. Nonetheless, better to chip away than do nothing.

CHAPTER FOURTEEN

Reflections on Computers and Schools

This paper was written for a special issue of The Journal of Computer Education *(Spring 1984), edited by my University of North Dakota colleague, Steven Harlow. I originally suggested to Steven that I would rather not make a contribution. At his insistence, I sat down and wrote rather quickly this reflection, believing my first response would likely be my best response. It was later enlarged in a talk given at an interdisciplinary faculty seminar at the University of North Dakota. Some five years later, my views remain pretty much the same. Computers have proliferated even more but their uses have not expanded greatly in classrooms.*

Computers these days are the "talk of the town," part of the infrastructure of what is being labeled the high-tech revolution. While poorly defined as an educational construct, "computer literacy" is, nonetheless, being promoted as a new basic skill, the equal of the longstanding basic skills of reading, writing, and arithmetic. Not to be computer literate, according to many school-computer enthusiasts, is to take a risk on the future. A school without computers has, overnight it seems, become a rarity. The popular press cannot seem to write enough about computers in the schools. Even new educational journals supporting this computer "revolution" have emerged. Within this fury of discussion and action, I have attempted to step back a bit for some reflection, using as a base my experience in schools, my concerns about teaching and learning, and my related historical understandings.

It needs noting early that even as passion abounds in the overall discourse, I have been unable to arouse very much passion when thinking about computers. A local newspaper education writer, knowing well my personal commitment to the humanities and arts, called me recently, certain that I would express at least moderate objections to the increasing use of computers in the local schools. He was surprised at my response—essentially that I was not particularly troubled by the introduction of computers into each of the elementary schools, the required course in computer awareness at the junior high level, or the large computer laboratories in the high schools. In fact, I suggested that these were probably positive developments with many useful possibilities for enlarging students' learning.

I know many who view the computer as revolutionary, a tool for constructively restructuring teacher-student interactions, teaching and learning, even the schools themselves. While there is potential for some restructuring of educational encounters and the related classroom environments, such grand views can hardly be taken too seriously. Disappointment will too likely be the outcome. On the other hand, others view the computer as a serious threat to a number of longstanding educational values, especially those related to the humanities and arts. There are some concerns of this sort to be addressed, but, in general, such a perspective is also largely overstated. These contrasting perspectives are, of course, even with their passion, rather conventional, part of the rhetoric that has accompanied many other technologies at other times. I rather think that my ambivalence stems in large measure from the conventionality of the computer-related discourse.

Schools should certainly have computers. They should also have an abundance of books, magazines, films, science laboratories, arts and crafts centers, videoplayers, audioplayers, and the like. Because schools are designed principally as intentional learning environments with a capacity for fostering, as well, a myriad of unintentional but important learnings, the richer, more diverse they are in resources, the greater their potential.

To speak of the desirability of a broad range of resources that call for a variety of possible intellectual and physical responses is to acknowledge at some level the need to ensure more possibilities for success among students. The computer, for example, might well provide for some young people success where there had previously been little. It might provide for some students an entry to learning that had been more problematic through encounters with other resources. Even after such acknowledgments, however, I am still left with a number of dilemmas. At the present time schools tend to be relatively impoverished in the more traditional tools of learning, most of which I continue to view as important. Science laboratories are wretched in too many schools, and centers for the support of the arts often nonexistent. Easels for painting, for example, are no longer present in classrooms much beyond kindergarten, if there. Vocational facilities are present in most secondary schools, but the equipment often appears decades behind the state-of-the-practice outside the schools. While textbooks and workbooks are pervasive, almost universal, they are often outdated, and tradebooks and libraries of consequence, the sources of real literature, are limited.

Few, of course, would really argue that computers should be purchased to the neglect of other resources or that the purchase of computers necessarily means that other resources will not be enlarged. My experience, however, suggests that thoughtfulness does not characterize the ways schools manage teaching and learning environments and resources. Schools tend to want what is "hot." I have observed settings in which books, science, and arts materials are being sacrificed for computers, where decisions are made to seek a person with a computer background rather than a person with a background in art or dance. When I have inquired about such a decision, I have been told: "Computers are the future. How can we be seen as a serious school without a computer teacher and computers?" I am dismayed with all the talk about the critical nature of computers and computer-prepared teachers and how little parallel discourse exists about all of the other needs that abound in the schools and are certainly as critical, if not more critical.

In relation to the practice, the actual use of computers in the schools, I tend toward caution, principally because we are still in a fairly early stage of development. What we see today in the schools may not be the practice tomorrow. As the experience of teachers enlarges, they will likely become more creative about computer usage than they tend to be now. Such has to be the hope.

I agree with Seymour Papert (1980) that the computer at its best offers a myriad of possibilities for creative learning encounters, for the development of higher-level thinking skills. The word-processing technology has, it seems, added many fresh possibilities for assisting students with writing. Further, the technology related to graphics has enlarged, increasing in the process the potential for students actually to construct models to match concepts and develop a variety of visual designs. For Papert's conceptualizations, as well as the full power of word processing and graphics, to be realized, however, classrooms would need to be quite different from what they tend now to be; for example, time and related schedules would have to be more flexible, textbooks and workbooks and skill sheets less dominant. Further, powerful ideas, rich content, greater student initiative, and personalization would have to be paramount. Moreover, the purposes and related curricula would have to take some different directions. Enthusiasts might suggest that all of this will happen—and it will in a limited number of settings. But I cannot envision in the near future such a large-scale revolution that challenging computer uses and other active learning possibilities will become more universally accepted.

I am impressed when I hear from highly skilled people, usually at the university, occasionally at technology fairs, about all that computers can do. I have seen few of these wonders in the schools. The standard fare is drill and practice, workbooks on the screen, with some occasional simple programming activity. For excitement, there are some games reminiscent of the video arcade. This is hardly noteworthy.

Further, students tend not to be in control of many aspects of this technology, a serious limitation given its possibilities. (One could argue, of course, that students control little of their learning beyond the computer either. That is also true, and it limits children and learning.)

Part of the reason for the ways computers tend to be used in the schools is that the software is being prepared by the same enterprises that produce so much of the print material that has long existed in the schools. That the software is the same simple response material in a different medium ought not to be surprising. Another reason for the current condition is that schools have tended to jump into the computer revolution without having thought much about purpose, the ways computers might actually enlarge their overall educational mission. In this regard, I agree with Ernest Boyer, in *High School* (1983), that more caution would be desirable, that we need much more than mere computer literacy or the knowledge of how to put into a personal computer a simple-minded, workbook-like, program. The caution of the Japanese, who have chosen not to use computers in the elementary schools, is, I believe, understandable. While I do not view the Japanese as providing educational models for us, their caution might at least cause us to wonder a bit about our efforts.

To raise the issue of purposes raises another dilemma. Computers are, like so much of our technology, fast. They encourage the view that information comes in tiny chunks, is authoritative in quality, and is almost instantly available to anyone who knows how to retrieve it. They are part of an economy—even a culture—that is increasingly characterized by "fast-food." Further, much is now possible because of the computer, but all that is possible is not necessarily desirable. One ought not, I suspect, make a jump from the schools' use of computers to the use of computers in the vast array of weapons systems and other human-control mechanisms and the possibilities of human judgment yielding to the sensor data that triggers a computer output. But I cannot help doing so. This is, after all, 1984—not only our calendar year, but George Orwell's metaphor of life under the shadow of Big Brother, a portrait of human loss in a nightmarish scientific and technological age. Novelists, of course, can never be held to any final truths—their portraits and webs are, at their best, only approximations of reality. Yet there is often something left at the core of the novelist's work to wonder about, that causes some internal stirring. Such is the case with Orwell's *1984*. Human judgment, human sensibilities, the capacity to reject simple solutions, and understandings of the fragilities of human culture need cultivation. When everything is fast, when too many steps of human contemplation give way to technology, such cultivation is threatened. This is not an argument against computers in the schools; it is an argument to consider purposes more thoughtfully than seems now the case.

Having raised Orwell's *1984,* I cannot help but mention Orwellian-like language that has accompanied the growth of computers. To endow this machine with language and the capacity to act, to link it metaphorically to the human brain and human interaction is to risk the dehumanization that many fear. Language distortions need to be addressed. Where there is consciousness about language, the language surrounding computers can be attended to constructively—challenged, controlled, and understood. But language consciousness seems in this technological age to be slipping.

When pushed, I also worry some about the issue of access. In our society, with its vast economic disparities, those with out-of-school, home access to computers appear to become even more advantaged as school programs develop. This, of course, is not an isolated phenomenon. It exists in other areas as well. While the schools certainly cannot be held responsible for these kinds of inequities, they should take care that they do not exacerbate the disadvantages in the computer field as they have in some other areas of school learning. Another equity issue that deserves some comment relates to the male-female disparity. Somehow, computers have become dominated by males. Teachers report that boys tend to push harder for time on the computers than girls. The nature of many of the programs in use likely contributes to this. The games, for example, tend to be aggressive, with some form of conflict dominating. Boys appear much more attracted to such activities. In addition, because many of the educational programs are remedial and skills-oriented in nature, they are assigned more frequently to boys, who, in the elementary grades, tend to have more difficulty than girls with reading and math. The fact that they are machines also tends, in our culture, to make them male things. We cannot afford to continue to support these kinds of inequities. Girls as well as boys need special encouragement. This concern, of course, speaks once more to a consciousness about purposes when considering introducing computers into the schools. It also relates to the number of computers available. If we reached Papert's hopes of a computer for every child, some of the access issues would be less dominating. But we are decades away from such a circumstance.

In my more cautious moments, I also tend to think about the quality of human interaction in the schools as, and if, the computer revolution takes hold firmly. The specter of children facing keyboards and screens many hours a day, together but silent and isolated, is one of the bad dreams that emerges. Many enthusiasts have suggested that teachers and kids can communicate through the computers in interesting ways, that instant feedback is now possible. They obviously can, but the possible communication losses need to be understood. Language is the most basic of the school's purposes. Where the computer can contribute to language development writ large, it should be used. But this large language issue should not be put aside, made ever to appear less critical.

I began this reflection with a statement about dispassion. As I commenced writing, I began, interestingly, to feel some passion. I have a particular view about teaching and learning, growth and development. This view causes me to be cautious about any technology that moves very far beyond an individual's absolute control and capacity for understanding. It also causes me to want a clarity about purposes when introducing any new technology, some sense that what is vital does not become distorted for the sake of change. The computer does have considerable potential for constructive change, for the qualitative improvement of teaching and learning in schools. It is a tool whose overall benefits are potentially large and are far from being exhausted. But our beginnings seem very limited, not particularly thoughtful, and isolated from the broad and persistent issues of teaching and learning in schools.

CHAPTER FIFTEEN

Peace Studies and Schools

This paper was presented as the introduction to a larger work-shop on "Peace Studies" organized for members of the North Dakota Council for the Social Studies, October 1985. It followed closely a large national debate about the Strategic Defense Initiative and Crisis Relocation Planning and discussions I had been having with elementary, secondary school, and college students about war themes. While the current détente with the Soviet Union and recent agreements on the reduction of nuclear arms have altered public discussion, the responsibility for teachers to continue to engage in ongoing discussions of the interrelationships of nations, groups, and individuals remains large. "Peace Studies and Schools" was published in Insights *in February 1986.*

Before I get very far into this discussion, I wish to establish several critical points. To begin with, while social studies goals at the elementary and secondary levels have similarities, there are important differences as well. There are aspects of peace studies—for example, a "reverence for life," in Albert Schweitzer's terms; or *ashima,* the nonviolence against any form of life so eloquently expressed by Mahatma Gandhi; or conflict resolution; or learning about diverse cultures and world views—that can be addressed in similar ways across the various grade levels. On the other hand, issues of active citizenship will assume some different directions, and one would hardly face very young children with all of the dilemmas of nuclear arms. They certainly should be spared all of the possible views of Hiroshima and Nagasaki. In the area of peace studies, as with all other curricula, regardless of their perceived political or social content, the teacher needs to bring a powerful understanding of child development as well as good judgment.

By implication, I have already suggested that peace studies is more than a study of nuclear arms or of war. But inasmuch as peace studies is often defined in this narrow manner, its appropriateness has become a matter of debate. A number of politically conservative

176

organizations have registered opposition to curricula that focus attention on nuclear arms and nuclear war, viewing such studies as value-laden and political. They are, of course, essentially correct (though I believe the analyses they make are questionable). To examine closely the history of the current arms race—including the failed efforts to establish reasonable controls, the redundancy in the numbers of missiles and warheads, and the search for superiority through yet *another* technological breakthrough—and the dangers that surround us is to bring into the classroom an overload of political and moral dilemmas. But given my view that the schools should be intentional citizenship-forming institutions, settings that encourage the active participation of students in their communities and in the social, political, and economic life around them, places that encourage a deep understanding of the issues that give shape to public discourse, I would, of course, support the inclusion of the arms race, with all of its political, economic, and moral dilemmas, in a peace studies program in the schools.

In contrast to this interest on behalf of active citizenship, some argue that the schools should be neutral, to as large a degree as possible value-free. Yet we know that the schools can never be neutral in any absolute sense, and they cannot be value-free. By what they do and do not do as institutions in their stated curricula and procedures; by what teachers do and do not do, stress and do not stress; and by the ways in which teachers live out their lives, the commitments they make as citizens, important *values* are constantly being expressed.

At our 1984 University of North Dakota Peace Studies Symposium, Brian Petkau, a Canadian teacher, presented *A Prairie Puzzle* (1982), a powerful personal statement about the presence of nuclear missiles across the North Dakota landscape and what these weapons represent in terms of danger to human life. Several young North Dakota students who were in the audience expressed considerable anger about how little they knew. They asked why they had not learned more about the missile fields, the kinds of weapons that existed and something about their control mechanisms, the cost of these weapons, and, they stressed, their potential as targets. In not making the nuclear arms in North Dakota or in the country or in the world a matter of serious study in the schools these students attended, what kinds of values were being expressed? Were students being prepared for active citizenship?

Whether we like it or not, there exists a specter of fear among young people that may well be unparalleled in history—a sense that the future is not at all secure. This comes out in many ways—in the silence, in the denial, in the expressions of confusion. I sat with a group of eighth and ninth graders a year ago who shared with me their constant sense of fear. One said, "every time I hear about more weapons, I think the war is getting closer." Another said, "I'm glad to be living in Grand Forks because I know I'll be killed immediately and won't have to go through weeks or months of suffering and agony."

Two years ago, we asked all of our incoming freshmen—essentially two months removed from high school—to read *Nuclear War: What's in It for You* (Ground Zero, 1982). Those who came to the discussions—about 200 of the 1,500 incoming freshmen—expressed almost universally surprise about how many weapons existed as well as the magnitude of their destructive capabilities. They were also dismayed about their personal levels of ignorance, their sense of despair. We spent a good deal of time stressing the major theme of the book: namely, that the critical issues surrounding nuclear weaponry and nuclear policy are absolutely understandable by common persons—even students—and that nuclear policy can be influenced by what individuals do or do not do. They tended not to believe this; their sense of impotence was particularly powerful. In this regard, conservative columnist James Kilpatrick recently suggested that the so-called keepers of the wisdom of nuclear arms have brought us closer to catastrophe than security and that the understandings of so-called nonexperts—the citizens—need to become paramount or there is little chance of a reversal in the arms race. It was the first time in years I found myself in agreement with him. That, of course, was President Dwight Eisenhower's point as well when he spoke of the need for citizens to reassert control over the "military-industrial complex."

I need to make one more comment about that group of freshman students. In the 1950s and 1960s, one met few high school graduates who had not read John Hersey's *Hiroshima* (1946/1975). Among these particular freshmen, only a handful had read it. It is a classic that needs to be read by every generation of students. It is, as Robert Lifton suggests, "our text," the work that puts us in touch with the past and the present and possibly the future.

I asked a group of 25 high school juniors and seniors a few months ago to rate their understanding of nuclear arms. On a 1–10 scale, with 10 being high, every response fell at 4 or below. When I asked what they believed their understandings should be, everyone checked 8, 9 or 10. In response to the question, "Is it possible for you to know as much about nuclear arms as the president of the United

States?" No response was above 5. In response to whether the school should offer a strong instructional unit on nuclear arms issues, every response was above 8. With regard to a question about whether individuals can influence public policy, no one responded above 3. I also asked how likely it would be for them to attend a public hearing on "nuclear war crisis relocation." Twenty-two responded "not at all likely." Most had never attended a major public hearing on any subject. Needless to say, I believe we have a lot of work to do.

To address the subject of peace studies, we need to work our way through war as a topic of inquiry, but we cannot stop there. Historically, war has long carried with it an imagery of the heroic. (In this regard, if I were in a high school today, I would work *Rambo* into a major inquiry study.) My early schooling provided the usual detached, matter-of-fact accounts of war. And the Saturday afternoon movies were a constant stream of stirring western victories over the "savage Indians." My early memories of World War II, in most respects a war fought for understandable, even righteous, purposes, revolved around glamorous men—soldiers-at-arms. As the war was coming to an end, however, by then being a bit older, I had experienced the changes in my mother with the loss of my brother, killed in the skies over Frankfurt, Germany. The accumulating gold stars in the windows in our neighborhood, symbols of young men killed in the war, changed many of my understandings. I had also begun to learn about the numbers of children, women, and old people killed in the fire bombings of Hamburg and Dresden, in the atomic furnaces of Hiroshima and Nagasaki, in the Holocaust of which Dachau was but one symbol and reality, and in the siege of Leningrad. And increasingly I could identify with them all. Witnessing the streams of refugees in all parts of the globe seeking new, possibly secure, homes was also a transforming experience. By the time I finished high school, I had come to realize, as did many others, I suspect, that war means far more than soldiers and heroic combat—it means even more the devastation of children, their principal nurturers, and their nurturant communities. Such an understanding has increasingly become the conventional wisdom in these last three decades as we have come to witness numerous tragedies—the deaths of millions of men, women, and children in Korea, Vietnam, Cambodia, the Middle East, Nigeria, Afghanistan, Central America, South Africa, and elsewhere.

To what degree does war—its motivations, its heroic dimensions—dominate our social studies programs? Our children learn a great deal in school about the glorified violence in the lives of Caesar, Napoleon, Grant, and Patton, but very little about those who opposed militarism. How much reading do students do about our recent peacemakers—Martin Luther King, Dorothy Day, Mother Teresa, Adolpho Perez Esquival of Argentina, Helder Camara of Brazil, Desmond Tutu of South Africa? How much is known about Mahatma Gandhi or the long history of nonviolence? How much of what is offered as text opens up fresh ways of thinking about war or the alternatives to war. What do we know about the current struggle between the Soviet Union and the United States? How is it different from or similar to the struggle between Sparta and Athens in the Peloponnesian Wars, between Rome and Carthage in the Punic Wars, between France and Germany in the late nineteenth and early twentieth centuries? Students learn about the standardly expressed causes of war—there were five for the Civil War, four for World War I, and six for World War II—but do any of them carry much real logic? Are they convincing? Or are they filled mostly with ironies? Even when they are all neatly listed on a paper, do they really add up to the death and destruction that followed? I was deeply moved as a high school student by Remarque's *All Quiet on the Western Front*, by Mark Twain's *War Prayer*, and by Dostoevski's "Grand Inquisitor." More recently I found enormously moving the scene in Kurt Vonnegut's (1971) *Slaughterhouse Five* where Billy Pilgrim watches an old World War II film, grows weary as the night progresses, and then begins to see the movie running backward. I want to share a bit of that:

> American planes, full of holes and wounded men and corpses took off backwards from an airfield in England. Over France, a few German fighter planes flew at them backwards, sucked bullets and shell fragments from some of the planes and crewmen. They did the same for wrecked American bombers on the ground, and those planes flew up backwards to join the formation.
>
> The formation flew backwards over a German city that was in flames. The bombers opened their bomb bay doors, exerted a miraculous magnetism which shrunk the fires, gathered them into cylindrical steel containers, and lifted the containers into the bellies of the planes. The containers were stored neatly in racks. The Germans below had miraculous devices of their own, which were long steel tubes. They used them to suck more fragments from the crewmen and planes. But there were still a few wounded Americans, though, and some of the bombers were in bad repair. Over France, though, German fighters came up again, made everything and everybody as good as new.
>
> When the bombers got back to their base, the steel cylinders were taken from the racks and shipped back to the United States of America, where factories were operating day and night, dismantling the cylin-

ders, separating the dangerous contents into minerals. Touchingly, it was mainly women who did the work. The minerals were then shipped to specialists in remote areas. It was their business to put them into the ground, to hide them cleverly, so they would never hurt anybody ever again. (pp. 63–64)

War clearly needs to be painted with a much broader brush than we have used. But more than on war, a peace studies effort ought really to focus greater attention on peace. Is peace merely the absence of war? Or is it the absence of violence? And is violence only direct killing, or is it violence when persons are treated badly, not provided adequate food or shelter, educational and employment opportunities, or political liberty?

Some of the most interesting attempts I have seen in the schools to focus on peace have worked around the following themes. What is peace? What is peacemaking? How can problems be addressed nonviolently? How can students be involved in peacemaking? The possibilities around these themes are, I believe, endless—in the elementary as well as the secondary school. What makes the themes interesting is that teachers and students can enter them as co-inquirers, persons who together attempt to create a vision of peace and identify and practice the skills that make for peacemaking.

I have only touched the surface. I have not mentioned foreign-language study; cross-cultural studies, sister-city and sister-school projects in relation to the Soviet Union or China or Mexico or Nicaragua or Argentina or Kenya; an examination of the language of the atomic age from missiles as *peacemakers* to the possible destruction of cities as *demographic targeting;* or the importance of teachers as models of optimism through work as activists on behalf of peace. These, too, are related to a program of peace studies. A social studies program that does not address peacemaking; that does not help students understand more fully the critical public discourse of the day, which is in many respects the preview of the future; that does not give far more attention to the world community, the problems of resource use and distribution, the possibilities for greater sharing and cooperation, the potential of greater respect for and understanding of difference—that kind of social studies program is not adequate in this difficult age.

Part VI
EDUCATION AND POLICY

CHAPTER SIXTEEN

Parents and Schools

This paper was originally prepared for the New School's Follow Through Program in 1971 and later published in Primary School Potpourri *(Association for Childhood Education, 1976). Support for parents has suffered enormously since this paper was originally written. In part this is related to the increasing number of mothers in the workplace. But it is also related to a reluctance in the schools to rethink their schedules, priorities, and commitments. Parents need to be active partners if children are to be well served in the schools. I believe this as strongly now as ever before.*

Schools desiring the fullest possible social and intellectual growth of children must actively encourage parent participation. They must accept parents as valuable teachers, nurture increased levels of teacher-parent interaction, and support the legitimate rights of parents to be involved in school decisions that affect their children.

Large numbers of schools and teachers claim to support such a value orientation. Yet there are few successful parent participation/partnership programs. The high degree of professionalization and curriculum specialization characteristic of so many contemporary schools may be one significant barrier. The enormous time and energy commitments that are demanded of teachers as well as parents to keep home-school connections vital also contribute. And, to be sure, some communities have a history of school-community hostility.

Helping teachers move beyond such inhibiting factors and become more comfortable in actually implementing closer ties to parents is a major purpose of this paper. Since parent participation takes on its greatest meaning for the child, teacher, and parent at the level of the classroom, I will focus most of my attention there rather than on the school as a whole.

An Overview

First, let me suggest some activities that parents can handle adequately in the elementary classroom. The list is not intended to be all-inclusive. And as will become clear, the suggestions do not include clerical tasks, which ought not to be assigned to a parent volunteer. Involvement with children's learning brings commitment; running off stencils in a back room or correcting worksheets does not. Appropriate activities might include:

- Reading to children
- Listening to children read
- Assisting children in such activities as sewing, cooking, knitting, auto mechanics, woodworking, art, music and dance, and so forth
- Presenting slides and films of trips to interesting places
- Taking small groups of children on field trips associated with their various interests
- Assuming responsibility for particular interest and activity centers
- Sharing interests, hobbies, and unique cultural backgrounds and experiences with children
- Preparing instructional materials
- Assisting children in the use of audiovisual devices and other technologies
- Assisting teachers in program evaluation

Such activities bring children into contact with adults, other than the teacher, who can share a potentially broad range of interests, occupations, and lifestyles. Not only can this be an enriching experience for children in general (how many adults, other than their parents and teachers, do most children talk to in depth?); it may also help provide increased opportunities for individualization, thus increasing the possibility of children's working closer to their potential rather than just getting along. Another outcome is an enlarged possibility for parents to relate their home life to school and the school more directly to home, thus strengthening the parents' sense of involvement with the education of their children. And, of course, it has the potential of helping teachers gain added perspective from parents about the larger community in which the school exists. In settings where teachers increasingly live outside the neighborhoods and communities in which they teach, this is particularly important.

In addition, such parent participation has the potential of increasing public understanding of and support for the schools. Teachers and school administrators often argue that positive change is impossible in their schools because "parents will not support change." Our experience at the University of North Dakota might be instructive. We have, for the past eight years, been actively involved in helping teachers and schools move toward more open and active learning environments. In many settings, classrooms have undergone enormous change. Yet parents have tended to be very supportive, in large measure because teachers have actively sought to involve them (not "sell" them). The more time parents have spent in the classrooms, interacting with children and discussing education with teachers, the more supportive they have been (Patton, 1973b). Parents, like teachers, need to experience larger possibilities. They need to understand that schools can be different from what they experienced as children. And they need confidence in the teacher.

Some Ways to Begin

Teachers need to communicate, as early as possible, their desire to have parents participate in the life of the classroom. Sending a formal note home to parents inviting them to "visit some time" is not the way. (Have you ever received that kind of invitation? How seriously did *you* take it?) *Organizing* for active participation and making parents feel they *can* contribute is essential. For this, teachers need to make *personal* contacts with parents. Informal coffees, home visits, and telephone conversations have all been useful in establishing an early rapport. Through such informal interactions, teachers can begin to share some of their hopes for the children and gain a corresponding perspective from parents. Discussions about such matters as goals and purposes, classroom organization, materials, evaluation processes, and ways for parents to participate can be addressed by the teacher. Parents, in turn, can share important perspectives on their children as well as be encouraged to relate any personal interests that might be useful to the teachers and helpful to the children. Relationships formed in these early interactions will help both the teacher and the parents focus on assisting the children.

In the early meetings, a checklist can be given to parents with positive suggestions of classroom activities in which they might participate; their responses can become the base for a classroom resource file. Using the file, the teacher can begin to organize parents to participate in classroom or classroom-related activities. It is also possible to have a parent committee assume the responsibility for organizing volunteers.

It is usually a major step for a parent to volunteer to assist in a classroom. One way teachers can assure that the early experiences for a parent are successful is by keeping the initial classroom activities quite specific. Many parents will feel more comfortable knowing that they are coming to the classroom at 10:00 A.M. *this* Tuesday and Thursday to teach knitting to five children for a half an hour; or that they will assist a small group of children in preparing pancakes at 9:00 A.M. on Friday; or read stories to children at 11:00 A.M. on Monday and Wednesday; or take four children to the supermarket at 11:00 A.M. *this* Thursday. Providing such precise definitions may well be the pattern for most of the parents throughout the year. Others, however, may feel comfortable enough to come at a specific time each week—for example, each Tuesday afternoon—to assist in whatever manner seems appropriate at that time.

In our work in schools, we have also found that parent participation generally increases in classrooms that are moving in more open directions, becoming more decentralized. Parents can enter such settings more easily; there are so many more entry points. In highly structured classrooms, where most teaching is carried on in a whole-group manner, the entry of a parent tends to be "disruptive" (everything seems to stop and everyone looks). We have found also that when parents are encouraged to devote time to highly structured classroom settings, specialized training is generally demanded, thus reducing in many communities the number who can participate.

Before proceeding, I should add a caution. Teachers need to avoid making negative judgments about parents who do not participate in the classroom itself. In many communities, single-parent families are common and the parent works. There may be preschool children at home, transportation may not be available, the parents' language might be other than English, and so forth. All of the foregoing might make participation in the classroom setting difficult, if not impossible. Teachers and the schools where they work should consider ways of supporting parents who may have special problems with participation. Babysitting services might be provided for preschool children of parents who are assisting in classrooms or taking a field trip with small groups of children. Carpools can be established to provide transportation between home and school. Written communications can be in the language of parents (Spanish, for example). Ways can be found for parents to engage in activities at home that are useful to the classroom, such as developing activity cards, making reading and social studies games, and saving scrap items useful in arts and crafts. Or a few children can be permitted to go to a particular parent's home for a learning activity; for example, bookbinding, conversational Spanish, or the preparation of an ethnic dish. Occasional weekends also afford unique opportunities. And the telephone can certainly be used to put children in a classroom in touch with a parent for purposes of gaining information.

Maintaining Communication

To sustain an active parent participation program, teachers must work at ways of maintaining communication. I commented earlier about informal coffees. There is no reason not to organize such activities several times each year. Indeed, some schools invite a small group of parents each week to have coffee with the teacher. Administrators may act as facilitators by assisting with the classroom at that particular time or arranging to do so with a special teacher—music, physical education, and so forth. (Substitute teachers might also be used.) In other settings, some parents are invited each Friday afternoon for tea and cookies, and the children assist in hosting the activity. Informal meetings may also occur in parents' homes on a rotating basis.

A classroom newsletter is another helpful way to keep parents informed. It can take on many forms. Many teachers we work with send home a newsletter with the children every day, thereby providing children an excellent opportunity at the end of each day to evaluate what they have been doing. Just as important, the newsletters keep parents sufficiently informed to carry on meaningful discussions with their children as well as the teachers.

Parent-teacher conferences, which schools tend to schedule several times a year, can also be a means of maintaining effective communication and building a partnership (especially if they are not overformalized). If possible, the conferences should be scheduled for a minimum of half an hour. Although this might necessitate scheduling them over a two- to three-week period, the results can be more satisfactory than the typical 10-minute conferences jammed into one or two days. A particularly significant parent-teacher discussion cannot occur in a 10-minute period. As many parents have told me—

and as I have also felt as a parent—"I always know that someone is waiting to come in so I'd better hurry." Teachers also find the format too rushed and, as a result, rather perfunctory.

Teachers should make the conference setting as comfortable as possible—again a sign that the school is friendly and open to the parent. If the conference must be carried out in the classroom, better to move away from the teacher's desk. The reading corner might be a pleasant place. (And there ought to be chairs adults can sit in comfortably.) It is also helpful for teachers to be sensitive to their language. The jargon that people in education often use gets in the way of effective communication with parents. And teachers need to be good listeners at conferences. If given the opportunity, parents can provide teachers with many useful insights about their children.

Parent-teacher workshops are also useful. I have participated in large numbers of active workshops, which have focused on such areas as reading, mathematics, science, and social studies. *At an adult level* parents were introduced to elements of the style of their children's education as well as many of the important classroom materials. Not only did parents gain more knowledge about education and educational materials (making attribute blocks, for example, is a good way to gain a sense of what they are and how they are used), but they also produced, along with the teachers, fresh materials for the classroom. Parents have occasionally discovered in such settings that many teachers, like themselves, struggle with some materials and their use. And parents learn as well that they are more able in some areas than many of the teachers, thus helping to reduce the gap that often exists between themselves and teachers. I believe this "leveling" is helpful, making parents less anxious about participation because they can feel more confident that their contributions will be respected.

Some schools—typically those with relatively mature parent programs—have established *parent centers* containing books, periodicals, films, and ideas for classroom activities to assist parents in continuing their learning and enlarging their capacity for ongoing participation. As elementary school enrollment declines, space for parent centers may be easier to organize.

Granted, all of the foregoing can take a great deal of time. Additional planning is necessary. Occasionally the schedule needs to be altered to accommodate the times that parents can be there. And the increased openness does provide *some* parents enlarged opportunities for criticism of teachers and the school. But the participation of parents is so critical that no problems or risks ought to stand in the way.

I have made little mention of principals to this point. But, clearly, principals are important. Their support can make a critical difference. Principals can assist teachers in maintaining effective communication with parents and ensure the school's openness to parents. They, too, need to make parents feel welcome. Effective leadership for parent participation should be one of the principal's major responsibilities.

Participant Councils

Implicit in much of what has been outlined thus far is a range of informal decision-making processes relating to particular classrooms. But much may depend on individual teachers and a particularly supportive principal. What happens if they leave? How can parents be assured that similarly motivated professional staff with similar commitments will be appointed? In some communities—though far too few—participant councils, consisting of constituent parents and teachers, are being organized in association with each school (or with segments of a school, such as the ungraded primary unit). These councils interpret the school to the larger community, represent it in its relations with the board of education, and keep the principal and staff informed of community needs and concerns. Such councils also help organize parents and others in the community who wish to contribute to the life of the schools. Further, many councils play an important role in the selection of new teachers and principals and take part in schoolwide evaluations. Such councils are in evolutionary stages, and the full range of their responsibilities is not yet clear. But they do represent another major effort to secure a meaningful parent role. They should be supported.

This paper has clearly not covered the full range of possibilities for parents and schools to engage in a larger partnership on behalf of children. But I trust that some constructive directions have been established, and the need for and the possibilities in such a partnership given fuller meaning.

CHAPTER SEVENTEEN

Making Connections: School and College Collaboration

This paper was presented at a school-college collaborative planning meeting at the University of Michigan in the fall of 1983. At the time, school-college collaborations were being discussed again, with some interesting programs underway. In many respects, these collaborations were ahead of the 1983 educational reform reports that encouraged such efforts. While my references to the University of Michigan fit the particular occasion, I believe they are related to the historical experience of many other universities. I wish it were possible to report that school-college collaborations were flourishing, growing in intensity and scale as we near the decade of the 1990s. They are not, even as the need for such collaborative activities is large.

I have asked on several occasions over the past decade or so a number of questions about school-college connections; for example, why are so few high school students enrolled in academic course work in the colleges and universities? Why is there not more formal connection between the way writing is taught in the high schools and in the colleges and universities? Why do the purposes for historical, scientific, and literary studies differ so greatly across levels? Why is there so little conversation between high school and college/university teachers about materials and pedagogy? The disconnectedness between schools and colleges—the isolation, lack of mutuality, differing expectations and discourse—is and has been enormously wasteful. Fortunately, however, in this new era of school reform, there is a growing interest in school-college collaboration. Fresh opportunities for closer relationships and greater flexibility seem possible on a large scale.

Before considering the possibilities and potential pitfalls, it might be useful to gain some historical perspective—to engage in an examination of the larger landscape. Our contemporary disconnectedness has not always defined the relationship.

Historical Background

In nineteenth-century America, there was a blurring of the lines between secondary schools and colleges and universities, in large measure because of the formative nature of these latter institutions. The University of North Dakota, my home institution, is fairly representative in this regard. Founded in 1883, at a time when there were virtually no secondary schools in the Dakota Territory, the university was forced to provide for its first 12 students a two-year preparatory program. It was not until 1904 that the preparatory school, which generally enrolled more students than the collegiate programs, was closed. The same faculty taught across the two levels. Shared purpose and curriculum continuity existed. Students went from Greek and Latin programs in the preparatory school directly to more advanced Greek and Latin programs in the college. The same was true in other academic areas.

In addition to having this direct campus and curricular linkage, the university also became the center of an emerging system of secondary schools across the state, developing curriculum materials, informing public policy, and preparing teachers—activities in which the University of North Dakota has chosen during the past decade and a half to reimmerse itself. Not surprisingly, Webster Merrifield, an early president of the University of North Dakota, was honored at his retirement in 1912 as the "father of secondary schools" in North Dakota. The linkages were indeed real.

The University of North Dakota was organized first, and then a wide range of relationships were established with schools; but the reverse direction of development frequently occurred elsewhere. For example, the latter 19th-century normal schools were essentially secondary schools whose purposes gradually expanded, ultimately becoming the state colleges and universities of our nation, establishing, in this sense, another path toward connectedness.

In many ways the University of Michigan's nineteenth-century history is particularly interesting, causing me to believe that if ever there was a place where connections across educational settings should occur, this ought to be it. The original conception of the University of Michigan was rooted in Judge Augustus Woodward's

System of Universal Science, calling for the university to be a complete, territorywide system of education that would include "colleges, academies, schools, libraries, museums, atheneums, botanical gardens, laboratories, and other useful literary and scientific institutions" (quoted in Dunbar, 1965, p. 281). How much more inclusive could one get? Even as I admit to some of the problems inherent in Woodward's formulation, I am attracted to his basic understandings of the interconnectedness of knowledge and the importance of diversity in the sources for learning, as well as his acknowledgment that learning needs to be conceptualized as a lifetime, not a momentary, experience. While Woodward's grand conception was abandoned by 1827 as impractical, the university was still viewed, for decades afterward, as the critical base out of which a cohesive state system of public education could be constructed.

In 1837, under the leadership of John D. Pierce, Michigan's first Superintendent for Public Instruction, a state system of education was carefully articulated. The University of Michigan was not only viewed as the capstone of this system; it was expected, in addition, to assume a connecting role to elementary and secondary schools by establishing mediating branches—essentially multipurpose secondary academies—throughout the state. Pierce wrote in this regard that each of the proposed branches would occupy

> the middle ground, being connected on the one hand with the primary schools by the establishment of a department . . . for the education of teachers and on the other, with the University itself, by the establishment . . . of a preparatory course . . . thus being equally designed for the benefit of the University and [local communities]. (quoted in Dunbar, 1965, p. 401)

Not all of Pierce's hopes materialized, but the roots—as well as the intentions—of mutuality were clear enough.

In 1879 the University of Michigan reaffirmed, this time internally, its commitment to interact with the schools by establishing a pioneering chair in the science and art of teaching. In announcing the chair and its importance to the university, President James B. Angell made clear the university's intent to cooperate with the schools of Michigan. From this modest beginning—a step later emulated by other major American universities—emerged a fully elaborated school of education, an experimental university high school, and a system of school accreditation and field services.

Much in the University of Michigan's history finds a counterpart in the histories of Harvard, Wisconsin, and Illinois, to mention only a few institutions. My overall point in this brief account, which used the University of North Dakota and the University of Michigan as principal exemplars, is not to suggest uniqueness but to establish that interactions between colleges/universities and schools were once relatively common and consciously pursued.

Much of what I want to convey here emerges from a continued historical review of the University of Michigan. For John Dewey spent a formative—as far as education is concerned—decade in Ann Arbor before going on to the University of Chicago, where he established a university-school collaboration of extraordinary quality.

Shortly after reaching Chicago, Dewey began putting some of his educational thought into action in a school that he and his wife, Alice, organized. Several things resulted—a body of powerful literature produced by Dewey that was influential in his day and continues to possess considerable meaning for us; literature produced by others in the school, such as Ella Flagg Young, Katherine Camp Mayhew, and Anna Camp Edwards, that has for many years influenced school practice constructively; and practical experience in university-school collaboration that provided excellent examples of how to integrate university faculty, especially in more traditional arts and science fields, into the life of a school. The Dewey School also furnished constructive models of inquiring into questions of curriculum, teaching, and learning. What emerges for me—and I commend in relation to this aspect of Dewey's work a rereading of *The Child and the Curriculum* (1902/1956), *School and Society* (1899/1956), and *The Dewey School* (Mayhew & Edwards, 1936/1966) in particular—is the validity and importance of educational settings in which university scholars and classroom teachers can consider together a range of theoretical and practical formulations about teaching and learning.

Dewey's efforts at Chicago, as well as much of the work that characterized the related progressive movement in American education, contributed to what I have come to label as an important "reciprocity of authority," an essential aspect of school-university collaboration that is critical if our interests in connectedness are to be realized at the highest levels possible. For example, progressive philosophy encouraged teachers to become close observers of children and young people, materials and their uses, and instructional practices. Many teachers became enormously articulate about education matters, easily the equals of the pedagogical scholars in the colleges and universities. The school-college collaborations that resulted had a quality of reciprocity that made for equality. The agendas, the purposes, the conditions were mutually derived. I am convinced that some of the projects that pass for educational research these days, emanating principally from the universities and often entangling teachers in the name of collaboration, would have been rejected as simple-minded and wasteful by these powerful school people.

While there is a large historical literature that could be examined as a way of understanding issues of reciprocity, a particular reference I often suggest to those who wish to think more about university-school collaboration is Lucy Sprague Mitchell's *Our Children and Our Schools* (1950). Essentially the record of a very large effort linking the Bank Street College of Education, then a group of teachers who believed in the need for a "give and take between research and practice" and the New York public schools, it documents well the collaborative experience. It gives important attention to the relationships that were built—a binding together of those within and outside of school classrooms, of the practitioner-researcher and the external scholar-researcher.

Why go through this additional historical journey? Quite simply, I wanted to make as clear as possible the belief that collaboration, however conceptualized, should, at its best, lead to greater empowerment of those in the schools, enabling them, among other things, to be more equal partners in the struggle for high-quality educational programs, in the writing of critical educational literature, in decision making about what kinds of educational research are necessary in relation to teaching practice, and in the determination of what kinds of collaboration would be most useful.

Teacher-as-Researcher Collaborations

What kinds of collaboration lead in such directions? I will comment here only on those activities that are increasingly being encompassed by the teacher-as-researcher formulation. These kinds of efforts have been aimed at assisting elementary and secondary teachers in developing means of documenting, recording, and reflecting on their efforts as well as encouraging them to begin to write and publish as a way of sharing their educational insights. Much of this particular formulation is predicated on the belief that our understandings of teaching and learning, growth and development, and curriculum are limited because there is so little good description rooted in classroom-school settings and because the reflections of thoughtful teachers tend not to be sufficiently accessible.

Historically, the child-study movement, active from the turn of the century through the early 1940s, was built around this formulation. John Dewey's belief that teachers need to be students of teaching, persons capable of reflection on their practice, independent in thought and confident as decision makers was carefully nurtured in the pre–World War II period. It is also a conceptualization that those of us at the University of North Dakota have tried to make basic to much of our work with teachers in the schools. The Institute for Research on Teaching at Michigan State University has for several years organized its work around teachers as research collaborators. And such an outlook has also been critical to much of the work fostered by David Hawkins, a distinguished professor of physics and philosophy of science at the Mountainview Center, University of Colorado. Hawkins's recent collaborative research on critical barriers to the learning of science (Apelman, Hawkins, & Morrison, 1985) is particularly provocative, encouraging a more uplifting discourse about science teaching and learning, not only in the schools but in universities. Other examples of this teacher-as-researcher direction, this belief in the need to empower those in the schools, are Lillian Weber's integrative curriculum work at City College in New York, the inquiry-oriented/community history activities of Ann Cook and Herb Mack at Queens College, the Massachusetts Institute of Technology program on the "Function of Teacher's Knowledge" organized by Eleanor Duckworth, and the Ford Teaching Project led by Lawrence Stanhouse, John Elliott, David Hamilton, and Clem Adelman at the University of East Anglia in Norwich, England, which focused on humanities and science. Another exemplary source comes through the work of Patricia Carini at the Prospect School, North Bennington, Vermont. Classroom teachers and university scholars who have gone through Carini's intensive seminars have tended to enlarge their reflective, documenting, and descriptive skills and understandings so much that they move rapidly toward the kind of empowerment I have mentioned. They are capable of collaboration at the highest levels.

All of this may seem an overelaborate way of making a relatively small—even if salient—point. But it is to me so important and so neglected in the discourse of school-university collaboration that I feel compelled to establish it even at the expense of more standard descriptions of contemporary collaborative activities, a discussion I will now enter.

Collaborative Activities

To speak of collaboration, bridges between the schools and colleges-universities, is to acknowledge that large numbers of interrelationships now exist. There are, for example, a multitude of fairly standard programs in which high school students take a portion of their academic or technical coursework in postsecondary institutions such as community colleges and universities. For the most part, however, these efforts do not result in very much communication among teachers across the two levels, generally being narrowly defined as programs aimed at benefiting students exclusively. There are also programs, such as Simon Rock (Bard College), where high school students begin full-time, college-level work in what would normally be their tenth or eleventh grades of high school. Simon Rock has attempted to share with secondary schools the ways students respond to academic coursework, the approaches faculty there are taking to curriculum, skill development, and the like, but the impact seems not to be high, the reports remote from the discourse of most secondary school educators. This is unfortunate, because the Simon Rock experiment has much to offer secondary schools in regard to the broad issues surrounding expectations.

There are also a number of minority recruitment and support programs related to the health fields at the University of Alabama, the City University of New York, and the University of North Dakota in which certain ninth-grade students are selected to receive a variety of college experiences aimed at encouraging their interests in science, mathematics, and study skills. While these efforts have engendered important insights about student transitions across the upper levels of schooling, they do not seem to generate much fresh discussion about teaching, learning, or curriculum in the schools themselves.

The Boston desegregation experience of the mid-1970s included an element of school-college collaboration, with each college and university in the Boston area being assigned by the court a school, or set of schools, to work with. The expectation was that these collaborations would result in better schools. With just a few exceptions, however, these efforts struggled for the initial five years, in part because of the postdesegregation confusion that existed in Boston but also because most of the colleges had so little experience with any long-term relationship with a school. For example, after five years, one of the more prestigious institutions, when describing its accomplishments, could only point to the development of an elaborate remedial reading program in its paired high school, which most teachers did not understand or value; the provision of resources to the school counseling staff to assist with college admissions activities during February and March of each year; and the printing three times a year of the school's newspaper. Few faculty from that institution of higher education ever spent time in the high school. Those in the school felt as isolated as ever. The fact that there were some successful collaborations in Boston, however, is instructive. In these more successful examples, teachers began to meet frequently with their higher-education colleagues to share materials and insights about teaching. The isolation that is so endemic and so demoralizing was partially breached, lifting the spirits of many teachers and reinvigorating their teaching.

One of the longest-standing collaborations—now in its thirteenth year—exists in New Haven, Connecticut, between Yale and the King School. This large-scale interrelationship, covering all aspects of school life, is described with considerable passion by James Comer, associate dean of the Yale Medical School and director of the project, in his book *School Power* (1980). In many ways, this project led the way for a number of productive interactions between Yale faculty, especially in the arts college, with teachers in New Haven area secondary schools. It is an approach that all universities could easily emulate.

There are also some teacher exchange programs in existence—essentially visiting teachers and scholars. By having university faculty teaching on occasion in the schools and teachers from the schools teaching in the colleges and universities, more commonalities of understanding are possible, thus establishing a base for constructive discourse. These kinds of exchange activities were more common in the 1960s and early 1970s than in the past decade, but the possibilities are great and need to be reformulated. In my recent semester as a visiting high school teacher, I found, among many other things, that the majority of students can certainly write, especially if provided assistance and careful evaluation, causing me to ask a different set of questions of my university colleagues, who often overgeneralize—even despair—about the "poor writing skills of incoming freshmen." I also became, through the experience in the high school and my latest teaching of freshmen students at the university, more conscious of the fact that the difference between the freshman and the high school seniors is only *three months*—a reason, in itself, for closer connections.

A writing collaboration that has had a good deal of success over a number of years is the Bay Area Writing Project associated with the University of California at Berkeley. Virtually every state has one or more higher-education institutions engaged in the promotion of this particular approach to writing. What has impressed me about the effort is that the transitions tend to be conceived broadly, encompassing the elementary-secondary connection as well as the secondary-university connection.

Also in the writing area, the University of Michigan's English Composition Board (ECB) has developed an excellent connection to a large number of schools and teachers, becoming a source of fresh thought about entering and introducing the various discourse systems that encompass our diverse disciplines (or, as I heard recently, our "academic dialects"). Writing across the curriculum—which we need badly—is being furthered through the work of the ECB.

At the University of North Dakota, we are completing our third year of a systematic "academic skills" collaboration with nine school districts from which we receive a significant number of students. The program involves interactions between secondary teachers and university faculty across a variety of disciplines; however, the areas of mathematics, science, and English dominate the effort. In the area of writing there is extensive discussion about purpose and approaches, but, as has happened here at the University of Michigan, there is often considerable conversation about motivation as well as discourse shifts related to particular disciplines. Two particularly successful activities that have emerged from the project during the last two years have been the opening workshop for our English composition faculty, conducted by a team of high school teachers, and a common math assessment and counseling project, which brings our math faculty into the schools, into contact with secondary school students and teachers.

Another activity at our institution that has a relationship to this academic skills project is our Foreign Language Task Force. Teachers in the schools helped initiate this activity by suggesting to university language faculty that they needed more opportunities to engage in serious conversation. Being the only Spanish or French or German teacher in a school, and teaching mostly introductory courses, they felt that their particular language skills were declining from the limited classroom use. Secondary teachers of foreign language now meet on a regular basis with our university faculty, conversing entirely in their respective foreign languages, regaining some of their oral proficiency. In the process they have begun working together closely to promote foreign-language instruction in the elementary schools as well as to assure universal access of junior high students to some foreign-language orientation.

Similar developments are occurring among university and school science teachers in our area. I was responsible for organizing one of the summer symposiums involving university faculty in geology, chemistry, biology, and physics and their counterparts in the secondary schools. The most interesting outcome, one that will continue to be a topic of interchange, was the mutual acknowledgment that the issues that perplex the secondary teachers are also difficulties for university faculty in introductory courses—namely, motivation, reading within the unique language and symbol systems of the science disciplines, and problem solving through connections to new situations. A major outgrowth was a lab-oriented summer program conducted by three of our finest science scholars with science teachers and junior students from the schools.

The teacher-center movement across the country has also served as an excellent vehicle for promoting school-university collaboration. The Institute for Teaching and Learning at the University of Massachusetts at Boston has served this teacher-center function, drawing broadly and heavily on university resources in such areas as multicultural and bilingual education as well as "writing across the curriculum." In North Dakota, there are now nine regional teacher centers, with the University of North Dakota serving as the coordinating-collaborative agent, providing a large array of human and curriculum resources. Each of the state's public colleges and universities is connected to at least one of the centers.

There is also a long tradition of curriculum development activity with potent school-university connections. The major curriculum efforts of the 1960s—Elementary Science Study (ESS), Physical Science Curriculum Study (PSCS), Biological Science Curriculum Study (BSCS), and Project Social Studies, among others—had their origins in these linkages. And the current computer activities associated with LOGO, Seymour Papert's work described so well in *Mindstorms* (1980), grew out of several MIT-school collaborations.

To speak of relationships is also to acknowledge that the public schools need some advocacy support from higher education. While higher education is indeed struggling fiscally in most of our states, the fiscal problems and related needs in the public schools tend often to be greater. The decline in support over the past 15 years in relation to GNP is close to 22 percent nationally. Higher-education institutions need to be advocates for enlarged support for *all* of public education. There needs to be some advocacy also to assist those in the schools from being overwhelmed by every technological formulation around. The mandates seem to grow, almost unabated and occasionally with college-university encouragement. Having talked with friends in Michigan about current educational directions, I am compelled to ask who in Michigan is arguing the cause of public libraries and against the serious cuts in social services, all critical to the success of the educational systems across all levels. The need for collaborative advocacy is high.

Issues in Collaboration

Before closing, I should comment briefly on some of what I have learned over many years of working closely with university-school collaborations—issues that must be considered.

At the university level, there has to be an institutional commitment to such a direction, one that provides time, accepts a broader than usual view of scholarship, comes to value conversation and inquiry-related teaching *and* learning, acknowledges the importance of interdisciplinary collaboration, understands the necessity of long-term involvements, and affirms mutuality, a parity of authority. At the school level, similar commitments are needed. Time is more difficult to control in the schools, but it needs to be considered. Greater teacher autonomy is also necessary, as is support from principals. An openness to dialogue, alternative structures, and greater diversity of materials and schedules are also needed to sustain a collaboration over time that is empowering for teachers and students alike.

Collaborations that focus on the technical aspects of education—teaching grammar, introducing computer programming, developing SAT preparation courses—are not very interesting or productive over the long run. Those that make connections to critical social and intellectual issues have more potential—for example, considering ways of assuring higher levels of communication skills, literacy writ large, for minority and low-income students; bringing a schoolwide focus to writing; linking school curriculum with community resources more effectively; trying to understand how various students enter the world of reading or come to understand the logic of mathematics; or assisting teachers in documenting growth, reflecting on pedagogy, materials, and curriculum content, or identifying critical barriers to learning.

Although I have covered a vast terrain, my major point is simple and straightforward: Our separateness is in many ways a scandal, a serious waste of human, fiscal, and capital resources. But we are capable of doing better. History has some high moments capable of inspiring us.

CHAPTER EIGHTEEN

Education in the 1980s: A National Agenda

This paper was prepared in November 1979 for the U.S. Senate Subcommittee on Elementary, Secondary and Vocational Education of the Committee on Education and Labor in response to the committee's request for "thoughts about a national agenda for education in the 1980s." It was later published in the National Elementary Principal *(Spring 1980) and reprinted in* The Journal of Teaching and Learning *(Fall 1980). The issues raised remain current as we enter the decade of the 1990s.*

Public confidence in the schools has declined steadily over the course of the current decade, now reaching what may be its lowest level in the twentieth century. The optimism of the 1960s, a period during which educational reform and equality of educational opportunity were central features of public policy, has given way to a variety of debilitating and demoralizing responses tending to immobilize schools, teachers, and students and encourage considerable divisiveness in public education. Bilingual-bicultural education programs, for example, are under siege; commitments to schools that are integrated across racial, social, and ethnic lines no longer appear central to public policy; tracking (whether a result of programs for the gifted, special education, vocational education, or competency testing for purposes of promotion and graduation) has become acceptable again.

One might argue that the current negative conditions of education are related to the nation's general economic slump, "which won't last," or that public education is merely in a down cycle, a period of reassessment. Embedded within such a view is the belief that the more progressive tendencies of twentieth-century public education will emerge again in the years ahead. I believe that may indeed be the case, but I am also greatly concerned about the relative uniqueness of our changing demographic patterns and how they might affect educational practices.

Public Education and Its Clientele

The big baby-boom years are behind us, and our school age population has entered a decline that is expected to continue over at least the next decade. While it will most likely begin to increase again by the end of the decade, it will also include larger numbers of minority and poor students. This demographic trend was predictable. But what was less predictable has been the ever-growing withdrawal of support for public education from those white and middle-class families that have traditionally provided schools their political and fiscal base. The public schools are becoming, especially in urban communities, schools almost exclusively for the poor and for minorities.

Poor and minority children have always provided a challenge to educators—not because they lack intelligence or motivation, but because the schools are organized, by and large, around the interests and experiences of middle-class, mainstream children. While the schools have succeeded with large numbers of young people from minority and poor families, their failures have been far larger. And the negative results are becoming ever more visible in the social deterioration of our large cities.

The parents of this changing urban public school population tend, unfortunately, to lack sufficient political power to influence public policy even as the needs of their children are large and largely being neglected. At a time when the needs in the public schools may be greater than ever, the pressures *against* supporting public education are intensifying. Those who vote in local communities and state legislatures to restrict curriculum to "basic skills education," or demand that students pass particular tests for grade promotion and graduation, or permit class sizes to increase, or limit expenditures for materials are imposing on the public school population—especially those most in need—penalties that are not imposed on those who can afford to go to private schools. No private school student in Florida, for example, faces the specter of being labeled a "functional illiterate," because private school students do not have to take the state's mandated Functional Literacy Test.

What can Congress do? First, it must recognize the changing demography—in numbers and in socioeconomic, racial, and ethnic composition—and be prepared, in conjunction with states, to offer the fiscal support that may be increasingly more difficult to acquire at the local level. We cannot afford the continuing inequities in school finance. Why should Detroit, which serves predominantly minority and poor children, for example, have so little to spend as compared with its wealthy suburban neighbors? Why should class sizes be 30–35 in Detroit and 20 in many of the school districts surrounding that city?

In the long run, however, and more productively, Congress might more strongly emphasize its mandates for significant parent involvement. Support for parents needs strengthening. To date the parent advisory councils (PACs) associated with such programs as Title I have had only limited success. Much more attention needs to be given to training programs and to the development of more effective, less ambiguous roles for PACs. With increased and more enlightened assistance from state education agencies responsible for distributing and monitoring Title I funds, for example, PAC members might be given far greater responsibility for the development and evaluation of Title I programs as a means of increasing their understanding of education and their political power in support of their children.

In addition, Congress, as well as state and local education agencies, should consider other kinds of parent and community councils that are broader in scope. For too long, we have viewed schools almost exclusively as the center of our educational efforts on behalf of the young. Without denying the importance of schools, we must also acknowledge that other important educative settings in our communities may be equally, if not far more, influential educationally for many children—homes, television, libraries, museums, parks, recreation centers, and neighborhoods, among others. We often concern ourselves with the quality of our schools through official organizations, such as boards of education or parent advisory councils, but take less note of the quality of the out-of-school learning opportunities available to children and young people. These out-of-school opportunities have deteriorated badly in many of our communities. Parks are not maintained; libraries and museums have restricted their hours; volunteer social service programs have declined from lack of attention; child-care arrangements are in short supply, and children are left alone more because parents are working and extended family units are less common.

The resources for out-of-school learning are extensive, but to a very large degree they are untapped. To depend exclusively on teachers in schools for intentional learning is to limit our view of education. How many people with outstanding preparation and experience in mathematics, engineering, medical sciences, business, or the technical and nontechnical vocations are available to children outside of school in any systematic manner? How many practicing dancers, actors, painters, sculptors, musicians, writers, artisans, or craftspersons are currently involved with public school children in or out of schools? What kinds of child-care services exist in our communities? Questions of this sort are innumerable. But they are questions that need thoughtful responses. Community education programs should be more broadly conceived to include school-community councils that view education as broader than schooling; that seek to raise public concerns about the erosion of constructive out-of-school learning opportunities; and that engage far more of a particular community's educational, institutional, and human resources to the benefit of children and young people. Congress might want to develop incentives for communities to organize such school-community councils.

The School and the State Education Agency

The further decision making moves away from the parents, principals, and teachers in a particular school, the more remote becomes the potential for any significant and lasting improvement. To act on this knowledge demands, in particular, a different role for state departments of education and, in turn, a different direction for congressional action. For example, much of what Congress has done over the past decade to strengthen state departments of education, in its efforts toward federal decentralization, has in practice promoted greater centralization within the states. In general, state departments of education wield more power now than ever before. They develop regulations, examine students, direct programs, accredit schools, and influence—if not control—much of what passes for curriculum. The challenge for state education departments in the decade ahead is not more centralization but an increased capacity for providing curriculum, evaluation, staff development, and parent-training resources *to* local school units. The goal must be to increase the competence of individuals within local districts and individual schools, not to centralize competence at the state level.

Rather than directing more dollars to the development of evaluation and related curriculum materials at the state level, as is becoming increasingly the case in many states, we need to direct more fiscal resources toward the development of locally relevant evaluation and curriculum materials. Federal efforts to strengthen state departments should take into account these needs and the changes they demand.

Pluralism, Curriculum, and Testing

We need to reestablish support for pluralism—to acknowledge that we have in the United States individuals and communities with a variety of cultural and linguistic backgrounds. This support needs to include continuing attention to bilingual-bicultural education and to a broad conception of curriculum. The need for multicultural curriculum development, for example, is more critical now than ever before. Moreover, curricular offerings that include the arts, literature, languages, and a broad array of sciences and community studies must also be considered essential. At a time when public confidence in schools is low, however, it seems easier to narrow curricular offerings instead, to fall into the simple paradigm of "basic skills" education.

One impetus for the narrowing of curriculum in our schools, beyond the simple appeal of "basic skills," is the outcome model that has come to dominate our evaluation systems. We tend, in other words, to measure that which is believed most measurable. And much of what is most measurable is often least important. The popular construct for measuring—the standardized, norm-referenced test—tends to limit what can be learned about individuals and schools at the same time as it influences the curriculum itself.

For example, while the tests often purport to measure students' ability to read, it is clear to most educators and parents who examine the tests that they cannot represent reading as reading is commonly understood; the tests are, at best, weak indicators of reading ability. The tests foster, for the most part, a belief that reading is a set of discrete skills that can be—even should be—learned in isolation. Instructional programs that are designed to improve scores on such tests abound, principally, and unfortunately, in programs serving Title I children. Their education is often the narrowest of all.

And what is competency in writing? Is it knowing rules of grammar and spelling, or is it the ability to make oneself clear in a written statement? Most existing tests of writing emphasize the mechanics, the cosmetics of writing. As in reading, there are a number of instructional programs designed to improve test scores in the area of writing. Few, however, demand that students engage in much actual writing. To give as much attention to test scores as we do, in other words, may give the impression that the schools are "doing something about achievement," but the situation is otherwise. Scores on tests may go up while educational quality goes down.

Title II of the Elementary and Secondary Education Act, as amended in 1978, now includes "effective expression, both oral and written" as part of its definition of basics for which states may now write comprehensive plans. How "effective expression" is assessed, however, will determine to a large extent how congressional intent is translated into practice.

In this regard, Congress should review existing federal regulations governing evaluation, many of which encourage the indiscriminate use—if not outright misuse—of tests. Title I evaluation protocols, as they are now being prepared, are a case in point. Students, parents, and teachers are not being served well by evaluation systems that give primary weight to "gain scores" on standardized tests. In Title I and all other areas of education, we need assessment procedures that are more sensitive to students' learning across a wide range of curricula and provide the kinds of information that can be used in the development of responsive instructional programs. Alternative or qualitative evaluation and assessment procedures need greater support, which could come through existing agencies such as the National Institute of Education (for purposes of development and dissemination) and through changes in the regulations prepared by the Department of Education, which tend now to discourage alternative assessment activities.

We also need to press for greater understanding of the strengths and weaknesses of various approaches to assessment (including testing), as well as their appropriate and inappropriate uses. In the past few years, many individuals and organizations have begun to advocate "truth-in-testing" legislation in order to make testing more fair and to bring about greater public discussion of and knowledge about tests and testing. While these efforts are related principally to postsecondary testing, their impact is likely to be carried over to testing at the elementary and secondary school levels as well. Congressional support of such efforts would be a step toward needed reform.

Historical Perspective

Public education in the United States has a relatively long history, yet we lack extensive historical accounts of schools and their interaction with the culture at large. People concerned with schools have simply not seen historical perspective as critical to the improvement of schools. But if we had better descriptions of school curricula, organizational patterns, and instructional processes, for example, as well as the political, economic, and social factors that influenced them, we might have a better grasp of what educational reform demands.

Lacking historical perspective, we often enter into what we think are new directions for reform without a sufficient base for examining earlier, but similar, efforts and their contexts. Competency testing is a particularly good case in point. The history of certifying examinations in the United States goes back to at least 1845, and the overall results up to about 1910 were not positive. Much of what we are seeing now in the new wave of competency testing is painfully similar to our experiences in those earlier years.

This observation suggests an area of investigation that should be added to the nation's research agenda. Unfortunately, however, descriptive historical research has not been considered worthy of public support.

Research and Evaluation: Concerns About Methodology

The worldview that has given form to most of our education research and evaluation efforts (and is thereby considered the "dominant" or "scientific" method) is conceptualized in terms of an "input-output" model. In this model, social and historical contexts, aspects of programs, and individual's lives are treated as "variables" or "factors" to be interpreted through a range of statistical manipulations; reliability is stressed rather than validity; and concern about decreasing variability in teacher-child responses, program implementation, and instructional materials assumes paramount importance. The national evaluation of such programs as Follow Through and Head Start should have provided Congress with sufficient evidence to know that this basic model just does not provide the kind of information that is helpful in policy formation or theoretical understandings of schools and schooling. How such a methodology came to dominate educational research and evaluation in the United States is a matter of educational history; that it continues to hold center stage can be explained to some degree by education's unrequited love affair with science and technology, the belief that we need only apply a little more sophistication to the model to produce significant breakthroughs in our understanding of schools and schooling, teaching and learning. But the more sophisticated the model has become, the less instructive it has become.

While I do not deny that many of the research and evaluation activities carried out within this "scientific" tradition are interest-

ing, far too few of them have added significantly to our cumulative
wisdom or given much direction to classroom teachers. The methodology—the philosophic outlook that gives direction to contemporary practice of this "scientific" tradition—limits the kinds of
questions that are open to investigation, especially in settings as
complex as classrooms. This does not mean that the direction has
nothing to offer; only that its potential is enormously limited.

Alternatives to this dominant, quantitative mode of educational
research and evaluation are necessary if the quality of our educational enterprise is to improve. The alternative directions are
rooted in observation, descriptive analysis, and phenomenological
inquiry—processes designed to get close to data in order to establish meaning. This construct typically acknowledges the improba-
bility as well as the undesirability of controlling variables within
social settings. It operates on the assumption that educational growth
and development are manifest in diverse and unique ways as well
as in shared ways; it gives higher priority to validity than to reliability; and it is cautious about component analysis (Patton, 1975).

I do not wish to argue that what I have labeled here as the alternative has not been a part of the repertoire of educational researchers and evaluators over the years. But this direction has been
given a lower and less credible status within the broad research
community and in the directives of the federal government (the
largest contributor to educational research), to the detriment of our
search for new knowledge. Our agenda for research in the 1980s
needs to be more broadly conceived; less devoted to a research direction that has not demonstrated a capacity for coming to terms with
the complexities of the classroom or with the important issues relating to children, young people, and learning.

The Teacher as Researcher

How does one get close to the classroom to learn about the variety of ways that children come to reading, how they respond to or
extend the use of diverse materials, how they use particular language, what processes they go through in problem solving, the degree of continuity that occurs in their patterns of learning, or why
teachers do what they do, when, and how? A productive route for
responding constructively to such questions, one that makes use
principally of the alternative processes highlighted above, is through
and with classroom teachers. This may not be a simple task, given

the history of research in education and the impact of a related technological orientation in curriculum development, but it is clearly possible. We must reestablish in our schools a capacity for ongoing reflection. John Dewey, among others, thought of teaching as a professional knowledge-producing endeavor. We need now to assume a similar view as we approach the 1980s. Dewey's concern was that teachers needed to maintain a reflective capacity in order to grow, to become individuals who were clear about their intentions and capable of making independent judgments about their classrooms. Teachers with such qualities are capable of informing the research community and assuming in the process a collaborative role. They might also engage in independent research.

Encouraging teachers to assume roles as researchers, with or without external assistance, will, without question, produce a deluge of unique descriptions of practice. While some traditional researchers might pale at the prospect, wondering what form generalizations might take, we should, as a matter of public policy, be delighted. The accrual of such accounts would give us some good directions for inquiry, and it would ensure growth in our understanding of classroom practice. Furthermore, the teachers' own capacities for explicating and understanding practice would enlarge, thus increasing the potential for confidence in the schools, a constructive response to the current concern for accountability.

The Teacher as Learner

Teachers are under intense external pressures now, pushed increasingly into the role of technician rather than teacher as historically defined. In the coming decade, we need to give much more attention to the personal and professional growth of teachers. There is little reason for them to become, as so many do, less effective, less interested in children and young people, less enthusiastic as the years pass. Federal and state programs gave considerable support to teachers and their ongoing learning in the 1960s, but that support has not been sustained in the 1970s. What little remains is fragmented and ambiguous in purpose.

One recent initiative that has great potential if given a broader vision than is now provided by the existing Office of Education leadership is the program for teacher centers. The teacher centers could help consolidate many of the scattered training programs that exist in the vocational, special, bilingual, and parent education areas, to the ultimate benefit of children and young people. They could also stimulate school-based staff development programs that draw heavily upon teachers themselves. But if the promise of this innovation is to be realized, funding for teacher centers needs to be expanded in the 1980s.

In addition, programs for teacher preparation are underfunded throughout the United States. Expenditures for teacher education need to be enlarged, not because we need more teachers but because we need teachers who are better prepared. Teacher education programs at the preservice level demand far more intensity than our mass programs have been able to provide. Public Law 94-142, for example, which was long overdue, places new and difficult responsibilities on schools and teachers and demands a more diverse preparation than has been typical at either the preservice or inservice level. And teacher education institutions need to turn increasingly to the task of supporting the development of teachers in their inservice years. Carrying out this responsibility will be especially costly in terms of time and human resources. While much of the responsibility for funding—particularly in the public institutions where most teachers are prepared and supported—rests with the states, added federal encouragement of experimentation and coordination of teacher education within states and regions would be timely in the 1980s.

Technology and Education

Another issue that should be added to the federal education agenda is the relationship between technology and education. Our society's technological advances have considerable potential for constructively influencing young people's learning. The most maligned of the new technologies is television. While many deplore much of what is offered on television (and correctly, I believe), there is too little praise for the excellent programming that does exist.

The educational potential of television is large and still untapped. In the 1980s, we should commit more energy and imagination to the task of making television more productive for young people and their families. "Sesame Street," for example, is *not* the most promising direction, not because it is lively and creates difficulty for teachers who, as the popular literature suggests, "are expected to *perform* like the characters on the program," but because it presents an inadequate model of education—segmented, unrelated, and ahistorical. The show has entertainment value, but we ought not suggest that its educational value, in terms of school learning, is particularly noteworthy. Changes in the Public Broadcasting Corporation, scheduled for the 1980s, may provide some fresh opportunities. Beyond broadcast activity, however, the in-school use of television as a learning tool is virtually untapped.

The continued development of VCR and video-disc systems, which are likely to be widely available in the 1980s, opens up fresh potential for bringing a wide range of educational programs into schools and the home via the television monitor. Cooperation between the developers of such systems and school personnel would be useful, but we have little history of such cooperation. This may be a useful goal for the decade ahead. In addition, home-computer technology has advanced to a fairly high state in recent years and may in the next decade alter many of the ways children and young people learn. Such technological developments should be encouraged.

I have discussed a number of issues that I believe Congress should take into account as it considers educational policy for the 1980s. More issues such as special education and the needs of the handicapped, vocational education, better use of school facilities and the upgrading of school facilities, especially in our urban areas, and theoretical issues relating to learning could obviously have been mentioned. Education—both in and out of school—must be given a high priority; it must be freed of the polarization (and oversimplification) that has dominated educational policy making during much of the 1970s. We need to learn to respect children and young people again. We need to intensify our resources on behalf of their development and support their parents, who wish for them the very best that our nation can provide. If Congress—and the educational community at large—does not respond positively and constructively to these issues, public education in this country will almost certainly remain mired in public discontent and disenchantment. No society can afford to let that happen to one of its most crucial institutions.

Bibliography

Action goals for the seventies: An agenda for Illinois education. (1972). Springfield, IL: Office of the Superintendent of Public Instruction.

Addams, J. (1902). *Democracy and social ethics*. New York: Macmillan.

Addams, J. (1910). *Twenty years at Hull House*. New York: Macmillan.

Aiken, W. (1942). *The story of the eight year study*. New York: McGraw-Hill.

Alcott, A. B. (1830). *Observations on the principles and methods of infant instruction*. Boston: Carter & Itendee.

Alcott, A. B. (1938). *The journals of Bronson Alcott* (O. Shepard, Ed.). Boston: Little, Brown.

Alcott, A. B. (1960). *Essays on education, 1830–1862*. Gainesville, FL: Scholar's Facsimiles and Reprints.

Apelman, M. (1978, Autumn). Postscript to *Critical barriers*. *Outlook*, No. 29, pp. 27–35.

Apelman, M., Hawkins, D., & Morrison, P. (1985). *Critical barriers phenomena in elementary science*. Grand Forks: North Dakota Study Group on Evaluation.

Armstrong, M. (1980). *Closely observed children*. London: Writers and Readers, in association with Chameleon Press.

Bailey, L. H. (1911). *The country life movement in the United States*. New York: World Book Co.

Barriers to excellence: Our children at risk. (1985). Boston: National Coalition of Advocates for Students.

Barth, R. (1972). *Open education in an American school*. New York: Schocken.

Baudouin, C. (1923). *Tolstoi, the teacher*. New York: Dutton & Co.

Bell, G. (1979). *A survey of placement policies for ninth grade mathematics* (Research Services #61). East Lansing: Michigan State University, Institute for Research on Teaching.

Bellow, S. (1977, Summer). The Nobel lecture. *American Scholar*, pp. 316–325.

Benathy, B. (1968). *Instructional systems*. Palo Alto, CA: Fearon.

Bennett, W. (1984). *To reclaim a legacy: A report on the humanities in higher education*. Washington, DC: The National Endowment for the Humanities.

Bereiter, C. (1972). Schools without education. *Harvard Educational Review*, 42 (3), 390–413.

Beringause, A. (1955). *Brooks Adams: A biography*. New York: Knopf.

Berlak, A., & Berlak, H. (1981). *Dilemmas of schooling*. London: Methuen.

Berlak, A., Berlak, H., Bagenstos, T., & Mikel, E. (1975). Teaching and learning in the English primary classrooms. *School Review, 83* (2), 215–243.

Bestor, A. E. (1953). *Educational wastelands.* Urbana: University of Illinois Press.

Biennial report of the state superintendent of public instruction, 1904–1906. (1910). Bismarck, ND: Department of Public Instruction.

Blackie, J. (1971). *Inside the primary school.* New York: Schocken.

Block, J. (Ed.). (1972). *Mastery learning: Theory and practice.* New York: Holt, Rinehart & Winston.

Bloom, B. (1976). *Human characteristics and school learning.* New York: McGraw-Hill.

Blow, S. (1894). *Symbolic education: A commentary on Froebel's mother play.* (International Education Series, Vol. 26). New York: Appleton.

Blow, S. (1908). *Education in the kindergarten* (International Education Series, Vol. 58). New York: Appleton.

Bobbit, J. F. (1918). *The curriculum.* Boston: Houghton-Mifflin.

Bobbit, J. F. (1924). *How to make a curriculum.* Boston: Houghton-Mifflin.

Bode, B. (1937). *Democracy as a way of life.* New York: Macmillan.

Bode, B. (1938). *Progressive education at a crossroads.* New York: Newson.

Borrowman, M. (1965). *Teacher education in America: A documentary history.* New York: Teachers College Press.

Boyd, W. (1963). *The educational theory of Jean Jacques Rousseau.* New York: Russell & Russell.

Boyer, E. (1983). *High school: A report on secondary education in America.* New York: Harper & Row.

Brookover, W. (1979). *School social systems and student achievement: Schools can make a difference.* New York: Praeger.

Brown, M., & Precious, N. (1968). *The integrated day in the primary school.* London: Ward Lock Educational Press.

Bruner, J. (1966a). *The progress of education.* Cambridge, MA: Harvard University Press.

Bruner, J. (1966b). *Toward a theory of instruction.* Cambridge, MA: Harvard University Press.

Bruner, J. (1971, November). *The process of education reconsidered.* Address given at the 16th annual Association for Supervision and Curriculum Development conference, St. Louis, MO.

Bryan, M., & Mills, R. (1976). *Testing . . . grouping: The new segregation in Southern schools?* Atlanta: Southern Regional Council.

Bussis, A., & Chittenden, E. (1970). *Analysis of an approach to open education.* Princeton, NJ: Educational Testing Service.

Bussis, A., Chittenden, E., & Amarel, M. (1976). *Beyond surface curriculum.* Boulder, CO: Westview Press.

Caffee-Glen, B. (1981). *What works? An examination of effective schools for poor and black children.* Cambridge, MA: Center for Law and Education.

Calkins, L. (1983). *Lessons from a child: On the teaching and learning of writing.* Portsmouth, NH: Heinemann Educational Books.

Callahan, R. (1962). *Education and the cult of efficiency*. Chicago: University of Chicago Press.

Carini, P. (1971). *Recordkeeping*. North Bennington, VT: The Prospect Center.

Carini, P. (1972). *Documentation: An alternative approach to program accountability*. North Bennington, VT: The Prospect Center.

Carini, P. (1975). *Observation and description: An alternative method for the investigation of human phenomena*. Grand Forks: North Dakota Study Group on Evaluation.

Carini, P. (1979). *The art of seeing and the visibility of the person*. Grand Forks: North Dakota Study Group on Evaluation.

Carini, P. (1984). *The lives of seven children*. Grand Forks: North Dakota Study Group on Evaluation.

Carmichael, L. (1981). *McDonogh 15: Becoming a school*. New York: Avon.

Castaneda, A. (1972). Persisting ideological issues of assimilation in America: Implications for assessment practices in psychology and education. In P. Olson et al. (Eds.), *Education for 1984 and after* (pp. 106–120). Lincoln: University of Nebraska Curriculum Development Center.

Cazden, C. (1983, May 13). *Charlotte Winsor as social studies teacher*. Presentation given at Bank Street College, New York.

Children and their primary schools: A report of the Central Advisory Council for Education. (1967). London: Her Majesty's Stationery Office.

Chittenden, E. (1986). *The New York City Science Test*. Princeton, NJ: Educational Testing Service.

Clegg, A. (1972). *The excitement of writing*. New York: Schocken.

Cohen, D., & Stein, V. (1972). *Observing and recording the behavior of young children*. New York: Teachers College Press.

Coleman, J., Cambell, E., Hobson, C., McPortland, J., Mood, A., Weinfeld, F., & York, R. (1966). *Equality of educational opportunity*. Washington, DC: U.S. Office of Education.

Coles, R. (1969). Those places they call schools. *Harvard Educational Review, 39*, 46–57.

Combs, A. (1972). *Educational accountability: Beyond behavioral objectives*. Washington, DC: Association for Supervision and Curriculum Development.

Comer, J. (1980). *School power*. New York: The Free Press.

Cook, A., & Mack, H. (1971). *The teacher's role in the informal school*. New York: Citation.

Cook, A., & Mack, H. (1972). *The pupil's day in the informal school*. New York: Citation.

Cremin, L. (1961). *The transformation of the school*. New York: Knopf.

Cremin, L. (1978). *Public education*. New York: Basic Books.

Cureton, G. (1978). Using a black learning style. *Reading Teacher, 31* (7), 751–756.

Curti, M. (1964). *The growth of American thought*. New York: Harper & Row.

Davies, I. K. (1971). *The management of learning*. New York: McGraw-Hill.

Davis, A. (1967). *Spearheads for reform: The social settlements and the progressive movement, 1890–1914.* New York: Oxford University Press.

DeLima, A. (1941). *Democracy's high school.* New York: McGraw-Hill.

Devaney, K. (1974). *Developing open education in America.* Washington, DC: National Association for the Education of Young Children.

Dewey, J. (1956). *The child and the curriculum.* Chicago: University of Chicago Press. (Original work published 1902)

Dewey, J. (1956). *School and society.* Chicago: University of Chicago Press. (Original work published 1899)

Dewey, J. (1961). *Democracy and education.* New York: Macmillan. (Original work published 1916)

Dewey, J. (1963). *Experience and education.* New York: Macmillan. (Original work published 1938)

Dewey, J. (1976). The relation of theory and practice. In J. Boydston (Ed.), *The middle works of John Dewey* (vol. 3, pp. 249–272). (Original work published 1904)

Dewey, J., & Dewey, E. (1962). *Schools of tomorrow.* New York: Dutton. (Original work published 1915)

Dropkin, R., & Tobier, A. (Eds.). (1976). *Roots of open education in America.* New York: Workshop Center on Open Education, City College of New York.

Duckworth, E. (1978). *Evaluation of the African primary science program.* Grand Forks: North Dakota Study Group on Evaluation.

Duckworth, E. (1986). *Inventing density.* Grand Forks: North Dakota Study Group on Evaluation.

Duckworth, E. (1987). *"The having of wonderful ideas" and other essays.* New York: Teachers College Press.

Dunbar, W. F. (1965). *Michigan: A history of the Wolverine State.* Grand Rapids, MI: William Eerdmans.

Dyer, H. (1971, April 14). Problems with tests. *The United Teacher,* pp. 15–16.

Edman, I. (1955). *John Dewey.* New York: Bobbs-Merrill.

Edmonds, R. (1979). Effective schools for the urban poor. *Education Leadership, 37* (1), 15–23.

Elliot, J. (1978). *Developing hypotheses about classrooms from teachers' practical constructs.* Grand Forks: North Dakota Study Group on Evaluation.

Elliott, J., & Adelman, C. (1975). Teacher accounts and the control of classroom research. *London Education Review, 4* (43).

Engel, B. (1975). *Handbook on documentation.* Grand Forks: North Dakota Study Group on Evaluation.

Engel, B. (1977). *Informal evaluation.* Grand Forks: North Dakota Study Group on Evaluation.

Featherstone, J. (1971). *Schools where children learn.* New York: Liveright.

Frein, G. (1971). Curriculum: A plea for play. *Record* (College of Education, University of North Dakota), *56,* 105–109.

Freire, P. (1971). *Pedagogy of the oppressed.* New York: Herder & Herder.

Froebel, F. (1912). *Education of man.* New York: Appleton & Co.

Gagne, R. (Ed.). (1966). *Psychological principles in system development.* New York: Holt, Rinehart & Winston.

Gardner, D. (1966). *Experiment and tradition in primary schools.* London: Methuen.

Gardner, J. (1964). *Self-renewal: The individual and the innovative society.* New York: Harper & Row.

Glazer, N., & Moynihan, D. P. (1963). *Beyond the melting pot: The Negroes, Puerto Ricans, Jews, Italians, and Irish of New York City.* Cambridge, MA: MIT Press.

Goodlad, J. (1968). *The future of teaching and learning.* Washington, DC: National Education Association.

Goodlad, J. (1969). Studying and effecting change. *IDEA Reporter,* pp. 1–4.

Goodlad, J., & Klein, M. F. (1970). *Behind the classroom door.* Worthington, OH: Jones.

Goodman, Y., & Burke, C. (1972). *Reading Miscue Inventory: Procedures for diagnosis and evaluation.* New York: Macmillan.

Gordon, I. J. (1972). *Children's views of themselves.* Washington, DC: Association for Childhood Education International.

Gordon, J. W. (1970). *Diary of a country school teacher.* New York: Dell. (Original work published 1946)

Grant, G. (1981). The character of education and the educating of character. *Daedalus, 110* (3), 135–149.

Graves, D. (1983). *Writing: Teachers and children at work.* Exeter, NH: Heinemann.

Greene, M. (1978). *Landscapes of learning.* New York: Teachers College Press.

Greer, C. (1972). *The great school legend.* New York: Viking.

Griffith, W. (1971, May 30). A daring educational experiment: The one room schoolhouse. *New York Times Magazine,* pp. 14–20.

Ground Zero. (1982). *Nuclear war: What's in it for you?* New York: Simon & Schuster.

Guide to the elementary science study. (1967). Newton, MA: Elementary Science Study of the Educational Development Center.

Gutek, G. (1968). *Pestalozzi and education.* New York: Random House.

Hall, H. (1971). *Unfinished business.* New York: Macmillan.

Hampshire, S. (1960). *Thought and action.* New York: Viking.

Handlin, O. (1959a). *Immigration as a factor in American history.* Englewood Cliffs, NJ: Prentice-Hall.

Handlin, O. (1959b). *John Dewey's challenge to education.* Westport, CT: Greenwood.

Haney, W., & Kinyanjui, K. (1979). Competency testing and equal education. *IRCD Bulletin, 14*(2), 2–13.

Hawes, G. (1974, June). Testing, evaluation, and accountability. *Nations Schools,* pp. 33–47.

Hawkins, D. (1965a). The informed vision: An essay on science education. *Daedalus, 94* (3), 538–552.

Hawkins, D. (1965b). Messing about in science. *Science and Children, 2,* 5–9.

Hawkins, D. (1978, Autumn). Critical barriers to science learning. *Outlook,* No. 29, pp. 3–25.

Hawkins, F. (1975). *The logic of action: From a teacher's notebook*. New York: Pantheon.

Hector, H. (1971). *Teacher depreciation*. Unpublished doctoral dissertation, Teachers College, Columbia University, New York.

Hein, G. (1970). Children's science is another culture. In *The ESS reader* (pp. 87–98). Newton, MA: Elementary Science Study of the Educational Development Center. (Original work published 1968)

Hein, G. (1975). *An open education perspective on evaluation*. Grand Forks, ND: North Dakota Study Group on Evaluation.

Herndon, J. (1972). *How to survive in your native land*. New York: Simon & Schuster.

Hersch, R. (1981). *Effective schools*. Paper presented at the Western Regional Teachers Center meeting, San Francisco.

Hersey, J. (1975). *Hiroshima*. Toronto: Bantam Books. (Original work published 1946)

Hertzberg, A., & Stone, E. (1971). *An American approach to the open classroom*. New York: Schocken.

Hofstadter, R. (1964). *The progressive movement, 1900–1915*. Englewood Cliffs, NJ: Prentice-Hall.

Holt, J. (1964). *How children fail*. New York: Pitman.

Horne, H. H. (1917). *The teacher as artist*. Boston: Houghton-Mifflin.

Horton, M., & Adams, F. (1975). *Unearthing seeds of fire: The idea of Highlander*. Salem, NC: John Blau.

Hostrop, R. (Ed.). (1973). *Accountability for educational results*. Hamden, CT: Linett.

Howes, V. (1974). *Informal education in the open classroom*. New York: Macmillan.

Hull, W. (1970a). Learning strategy and the skills of thought. In *The ESS reader* (pp. 141–145). Newton, MA: Elementary Science Study of the Educational Development Center. (Original work published 1967)

Hull, W. (1970b). Attribute games and thinking skills. In *The ESS reader* (pp. 146–152). Newton, MA: Elementary Science Study of the Educational Development Center. (Original work published 1967)

Hull, W. (1971). The case for the experimental school. *Insights, 4* (1), 2–11.

Hull, W. (1978). *Children's thinking seminars*. Grand Forks: North Dakota Study Group on Evaluation.

Hymes, J. L., Jr. (1972, December). Overcoming blocks to change: A source of spirit and spunk. *Childhood Education*, pp. 114–117.

Isaacs, S. (1971). *The children we teach*. New York: Schocken.

Jackson, P. W. (1968). *Life in classrooms*. New York: Holt, Rinehart & Winston.

James, C. (1974). *Beyond customs: An educator's journey*. New York: Agathon.

Jencks, C., Smith, M., Acland, H., Bane, M. J., Cohen, D., Gintis, H., Heyns, B., & Michelson, S. (1972). *Inequality: A reassessment of the effects of family and schooling in America*. New York: Basic Books.

Jersild, A. (1952). *In search of self.* New York: Teachers College Press.

Jervis, K. (Ed.). (1983). *Reunion and affirmation.* Cambridge, MA: Windflower Press.

Johnson, H. (1916). *The nursery school.* New York: Bureau of Experiments.

Johnson, M. (1937). Training teachers for the new education. *Progressive Education, 14* (3), 216–221.

Johnson, M. (1974). *Thirty years with an idea.* Tuscaloosa: University of Alabama Press.

Kagan, J. (1972). *Cross-cultural perspectives on early learning.* Paper presented at the annual meeting of the American Association for the Advancement of Science.

Katz, M. (1968). *The irony of early school reform: Educational innovation in mid-nineteenth century Massachusetts.* Cambridge, MA: Harvard University Press.

Katz, M. (1971). *Class, bureaucracy, and schools.* New York: Praeger.

Kerensky, V., & Melby, E. (1971). *Education II: The social imperative.* Midland, MI: Pendall Publishing.

King, R. (1971, October). *Creative heresies in education.* Address given at Southern Oregon College Festival of Ideas, Ashland, OR.

Kohl, H. (1970). *The open classroom.* New York: Vintage.

Krug, E. (1964). *The shaping of the American high school.* Madison: University of Wisconsin Press.

Landrum, R. (1971). *A day dream I had last night.* New York: Teachers and Writers Collaborative.

Lessinger, L. (1970). *Every kid a winner.* New York: Simon & Schuster.

Lilley, I. (1967). *Friedrich Froebel: A selection from his writings.* London: Cambridge University Press.

Living and learning: Report of the Provincial Committee on Aims and Objectives of Education in the Schools of Ontario. (1968). Toronto: Department of Education.

Lott, W. (1977, Spring). Competency testing. *Genesee Valley Personnel and Guidance Association Newsletter.*

McCracken, R. (1973). *The Standard Reading Inventory.* Dubuque, IA: W. C. Brown.

McCracken, R., & McCracken, M. (1972). *Reading is only the tiger's tail.* Seattle: Leswing Press.

Macdonald, J. (1974, Spring). Evaluation in education. *The Urban Review,* pp. 3–14.

Madaus, G., & Airasian, P. (1977). Issues in evaluating student outcomes on competency based graduation requirements. *Journal of Research and Development in Education, 10* (3), 79–91.

Madaus, G., & Airasian, P. (1978, November). *Measurement issues and consequences associated with minimal competency testing.* Paper presented at the National Consortium on Testing meeting, Washington, DC.

Magers, R. (1962). *Preparing objectives for instruction.* Palo Alto, CA: Fearon.

Mann, H. (1891). *The life and works of Horace Mann.* Boston: Lee & Shepard.

Marshall, S. (1963). *An experiment in education.* Cambridge, England: Cambridge University Press.

Martin, B. (1967). *The human connection: Language and literature.* Washington, DC: National Education Association.

Martin, J. H., & Harrison, C. (1972). *Free to learn: Unlocking and ungrading American education.* Englewood Cliffs, NJ: Prentice-Hall.

Mayhew, K., & Edwards, A. C. (1966). *The Dewey school: The laboratory school at the University of Chicago.* New York: Atherton. (Original work published 1936)

Medley, D. (1979). The effectiveness of teachers. In P. Peterson & H. Walberg (Eds.), *Research on teaching* (pp. 11–27). Berkeley, CA: McCutchan.

Meier, D. (1973). *Reading failure and the tests.* New York: Workshop Center on Open Education, City College of New York.

Meier, D. (1981, Fall). Why reading tests don't test reading. *Dissent,* pp. 457–465.

Messarli, J. (1971). *Horace Mann.* New York: Knopf.

Metz, M. (1982). *Magnet schools in their organizational and political context.* NIE Report. (ERIC Document Reproduction Service No. ED 210 400)

Mitchell, L. S. (1928). Making young geographers instead of teaching geography. *Progressive Education, 3,* 217–233.

Mitchell, L. S. (1931). Cooperative schools for student teachers. *Progressive Education, 8,* 251–255.

Mitchell, L. S. (1950). *Our children and our schools.* New York: Simon & Schuster.

Montessori, M. (1967). *The discovery of the child.* Notre Dame, IN: Fides Publishers.

Morrison, Philip, & Morrison, Phyllis. (1970). Experimentation in the schoolroom. In *The ESS reader* (pp. 113–121). Newton, MA: Elementary Science Study of the Educational Development Center. (Original work published 1964)

Morrison, Philip, & Morrison, Phyllis. (1982). *Powers of ten.* San Francisco: W. H. Freeman.

Murphy, R. (Ed.). (1974). *Imaginary worlds: Notes for a new curriculum.* New York: Teachers and Writers Collaborative.

Murrow, L., & Murrow, C. (1971). *Children come first.* New York: American Heritage Press.

Nash, P. (1966). *Authority and freedom in education.* New York: Wiley.

National Assessment of Educational Progress. (1981). *Three national assessments of reading: Changes in performance, 1970–1980.* Denver: Author.

National Commission on Excellence in Education. (1983). *A nation at risk.* Washington, DC: U.S. Government Printing Office.

Naumberg, M. (1928). *The child and the world: Dialogues in modern education.* New York: Harcourt, Brace.

Norris, M., & Hazelwood, A. (1971). *The Open Corridors program.* New York: Workshop Center on Open Education, City College of New York.

Nyquist, E., & Hawes, G. (1972). *Open education: A sourcebook*. New York: Bantam.

Olson, P. (Ed.). (1968). *A pride of lions*. Lincoln, NE: Tri-University Project in Education.

Olson, R. E. (1974). *Marcy open schools: 1973–74 goals evaluation*. Minneapolis: Minnesota Public Schools.

Olson, R. E. (1980). *Evaluation as interaction in support of change*. Grand Forks: North Dakota Study Group on Evaluation.

Page, D. (1964). *Mathematics for elementary teachers*. New York: Macmillan.

Papert, S. (1980). *Mindstorms*. New York: Basic Books.

Parker, F. (1894). *Talks on pedagogics*. New York: Kellogg.

Parlett, M., & Hamilton, D. (1972). *Evaluation as illumination: A new approach for the study of innovatory programs*. Center for Research in the Educational Sciences, University of Edinburgh.

Partridge, L. (1883). *Notes of talks by Francis Parker*. New York: E. L. Kellogg.

Patton, M. (1973a). *Structural dimensions of open education and parental reactions to open classrooms in North Dakota: A sociological view of the diffusion of open education as an innovation in organization of structure and process*. Unpublished doctoral dissertation, University of Wisconsin—Madison.

Patton, M. (1973b). *Parent responses to New School classrooms*. Grand Forks, ND: Center for Teaching and Learning, University of North Dakota.

Patton, M. (1975). *Alternative evaluation paradigm*. Grand Forks: North Dakota Study Group on Evaluation.

Patton, M. (1978). *Qualitative evaluation methods*. Beverly Hills, CA: Sage.

Patton, M., French, B., & Perrone, V. (1976). *Does accountability count without teacher support?* Minneapolis: Minnesota Center for Social Research.

Paull, D., & Paull, J. (1972). *Yesterday I found . . .* Mountain View Center: University of Colorado.

Pederson, C. (Ed.). (1977). *Informal evaluation and record-keeping* (Informal Education Series). Grand Forks: University of North Dakota.

Perrone, V. (1972). *Open education: Promise and problems*. Bloomington, IN: Phi Delta Kappa Foundation.

Perrone, V. (Coord.). (1975). *Teaching and evaluation: New views*. Washington, DC: Association for Childhood Education International.

Perrone, V. (1976). *On standardized testing and evaluation* (ACEI/NAESP Position Paper). Washington, DC: Association for Childhood Education International.

Perrone, V. (1977). *The abuses of standardized tests*. Bloomington, IN: Phi Delta Kappa Foundation.

Perrone, V. (1986). *Johanna Knudsen Miller: Pioneer teacher*. Bismarck, ND: North Dakota Historical Society.

Perrone, V., & Strandberg, W. (1972). A perspective on accountability. *Teachers College Record, 73* (3), 347–355.

Pestalozzi, J. H. (1827). *Letters on early education*. London: Sherwood, Gilbert, & Piper.

Pestalozzi, J. H. (1885). *Leonard and Gertrude* (E. Channing, Trans.). Boston: Allyn & Bacon.

Pestalozzi, J. H. (1915). *How Gertrude teaches her children* (E. Cook, Trans.). Boston: Allyn & Unwin.

Pestalozzi, J. H. (1951). *The education of man* (R. & H. Norden, Trans.). New York: The Philosophical Library.

Petkau, B. (1982). *A prairie puzzle.* Altona, Manitoba: Elim Bible Institute.

Piaget, J. (1929). *The child's conception of the world.* London: Kegan-Paul.

Popham, J., & Baker, E. L. (1970). *Establishing objectives for instruction.* Englewood Cliffs, NJ: Prentice-Hall.

Pratt, C. (1924). *Experimental practice in the city and country school.* New York: Dutton.

Pratt, C. (1926). *Before books.* New York: Adelphi.

Pratt, C. (1927). *Adventuring with twelve year olds.* New York: Greenburg.

Pratt, C. (1948). *I learn from children.* New York: Simon & Schuster.

Pratt, R. (1973). *The public school movement.* New York: McKay.

Rathbone, C. (Ed.). (1971). *Open education: The informal classroom.* New York: Citation Press.

Ratner, J. (1939). *Intelligence in the modern world: John Dewey's philosophy.* New York: Random House.

Read, H. (1960). *The third realm of education.* Cambridge, MA: Harvard University Press.

Read, H. (1970). *Education through art.* London: Faber & Faber. (Original work published 1943)

Rice, J. (1892–1893). Our public school system [series of articles]. *Forum, 14*: Baltimore, pp. 145–158; Buffalo and Cincinnati, pp. 293–309; St. Louis and Indianapolis, pp. 429–444; New York City, pp. 616–630; Boston, pp. 753–767; *Forum, 15*: Philadelphia, pp. 31–42; Chicago and St. Paul, pp. 200–215; Minneapolis and others, pp. 362–376.

Richardson, E. (1964). *In the early world.* New York: Pantheon.

Ridgway, L., & Lawton, I. (1965). *Family grouping in the primary school.* New York: Agathon.

Rogers, V. (1970). *Teaching in the British primary school.* New York: Macmillan.

Rolfsrud, E. (1963). *The story of North Dakota.* Alexandria, MN: Lantern Books.

Rosenshine, B. (1979). Content, time, and direct instruction. In P. Peterson & H. Walberg (Eds.), *Research on teaching* (pp. 28–56). Berkeley, CA: McCutchan.

Rotzel, G. (1971). *The school in Rose Valley.* Baltimore: Johns Hopkins University Press.

Rousseau, J. J. (1962). *Emile* (W. Boyd, Trans.). New York: Bureau of Publications, Teachers College, Columbia University.

Rowland, S. (1984). *The enquiring classroom.* London: Falmer.

Rugg, H. (1947). *Foundations for American education.* New York: World Book Co.

Rugg, H., & Shumaker, A. (1928). *The child-centered school: An appraisal of the new education.* New York: World Book Co.

Rutter, M. (1979). *Fifteen thousand hours.* Cambridge, MA: Harvard University Press.

Sargeant, B. (1970). *The integrated day in an American school.* Boston: National Association of Independent Schools.

Sarton, M. (1959). *I knew a phoenix.* New York: Norton.

Schaffarzick, J., & Walker, D. (1974). Comparing curricula. *Review of Educational Research, 44* (1), 83–111.

Schragg, P. (1970, March 21). Growing up on Mechanic Street. *Saturday Review,* pp. 59–61, 78–79.

Schwab, J. (1963). *Biological science teachers handbook.* New York: Wiley.

Sealey, L. (1966). Looking back on Leicestershire. *ESI Quarterly,* 37–42.

Sealey, L. (1977). *Open education: A study of selected American elementary schools.* New York: Hazen Foundation.

Shalock, H. D. (1976). *Alternative models of competency based education.* Salem, OR: Northwest Educational Laboratory.

Shapiro, E. (1973). Educational evaluation: Rethinking the criteria of competence. *School Review, 81* (4), 523–548.

Silber, K. (1973). *Pestalozzi: The man and his work.* London: Routledge and Kegan Paul.

Silberman, C. (1970). *Crisis in the classroom.* New York: Random House.

Silvaroli, N. (1973). *Classroom reading inventory.* Dubuque, IA: W. C. Brown.

Smith, F. (1971). *Understanding reading.* New York: Holt, Rinehart & Winston.

Spady, W., & Mitchell, D. (1977). Competency based education: Organizational issues and implications. *Education Researcher, 6* (2), 9–15.

Spaulding, F. (1958). *High school and life: The Regents inquiry into the character and costs of public education in the state of New York.* New York: McGraw Hill.

Spring, J. (1972). *Education and the rise of the industrial state.* Boston: Beacon.

Stake, R. (1973). *To evaluate an arts program.* Center for Instructional Research and Curriculum Evaluation, University of Illinois, Urbana.

Stake, R., & Easley, J. (1978). *Case studies in science education.* Urbana: Center for Instructional Research and Curriculum Evaluation, University of Illinois.

Stephens, L. (1974). *The teacher's guide to open education.* New York: Holt, Rinehart & Winston.

Stodolsky, S. (1985). Telling math: Origins of math anxiety. *Educational Psychologist, 20* (3), 125–133.

Strieb, L. (1984). *A teacher's journal.* Grand Forks: North Dakota Study Group on Evaluation.

Taylor, J. (1972). *Organizing the open classroom: A teacher's guide to the integrated day.* New York: Schocken.

Taylor, K. (1928). *The Shady Hill play book.* New York: Macmillan.

Thoreau. H. D. (1953). *Walden.* New American Library.

Tobier, A. (Ed.). (1973). *Evaluation reconsidered.* New York: Workshop Center on Open Education, City College of New York.

Tobier, A., & Dropkin, R. (Eds.). (1976). *The roots of open education.* New York: Workshop Center on Open Education, City College of New York.

Tolstoy, L. (1967). *Tolstoy on education.* (L. Weiner, Trans.). Chicago: University of Chicago Press.

Tolstoy, L. (1982). *Tolstoy on Education: Tolstoy as educator, 1861–62.* (A. Pinch, Ed. & Trans.). Rutherford, NJ: Fairleigh Dickinson University Press.

Traugh, C., Seletsky, A., Kanevsky, R., Martin, A., Woolf, K., & Strieb, L. (Eds.). (1986). *Speaking out: Teachers and teaching.* Grand Forks: North Dakota Study Group on Evaluation.

Tyack, D. (Ed.). (1967). *Turning points in American educational history.* Waltham, MA: Blaisdell.

Tyler, R. (1979, January). The minimal competency movement: Origin, implications, potential and dangers. *National Elementary Principal,* pp. 29–33.

Vonnegut, K. (1971). *Slaughterhouse five.* New York: Dell.

Weber, G. (1974). *Uses and abuses of standardized testing in the schools.* Washington, DC: Council for Basic Education.

Weber, L. (1971). *The English infant school and informal education.* Englewood Cliffs, NJ: Prentice-Hall.

Weber, L. (1973). *The advisory to open education.* New York: Workshop Center on Open Education, City College of New York.

Welter, R. (1962). *Popular education and democratic thought in America.* New York: Columbia University Press.

Whitehead, A. N. (1959). *Aims of education.* New York: Macmillan. (Original work published 1929)

Why do some urban schools succeed? The PDK study of exceptional urban elementary schools. Bloomington, IN: Phi Delta Kappa Foundation.

Winsor, C. (1973). *Experimental schools revisited.* New York: Agathon.

Wolcott, C. (1970). Elementary school biology. In *The ESS reader* (pp. 126–129). Newton, MA: Elementary Science Study of the Educational Development Center. (Original work published 1967).

Yardley, A. (1973). *Young children thinking.* New York: Citation.

Yeomans, E. (1979). *The Shady Hill School: The first fifty years.* Cambridge, MA: Windflower Press.

Young, E. F. (1901a). *Isolation in school.* Chicago: University of Chicago Press.

Young, E. F. (1901b). *Some types of modern educational theory.* Chicago: University of Chicago Press.

Young, E. F. (1903). *Scientific methods in education.* Chicago: University of Chicago Press.

Zacharias, J. (1975). The trouble with tests. *National Elementary Principal, 54* (4), 23–30.

Zimiles, H. (1973). *A radical and regressive solution to the problem of evaluation.* New York: Bank Street College.

Index

About the Author

VITO PERRONE is Senior Lecturer and Director of Teacher Education at the Harvard Graduate School of Education. He is also a Senior Fellow with the Carnegie Foundation for the Advancement of Teaching. He has written extensively about such issues as educational equity, curriculum, progressivism in education, and testing and evaluation. He has been a teacher in the public schools, a university professor of history, education, and peace studies (University of North Dakota), and Dean of the New School and Center for Teaching and Learning (University of North Dakota). Dr. Perrone serves as coordinator of the North Dakota Study Group on Evaluation and is actively engaged in the life of elementary and secondary schools.

damage noted 11/21/07 ✓
RR

DATE DUE

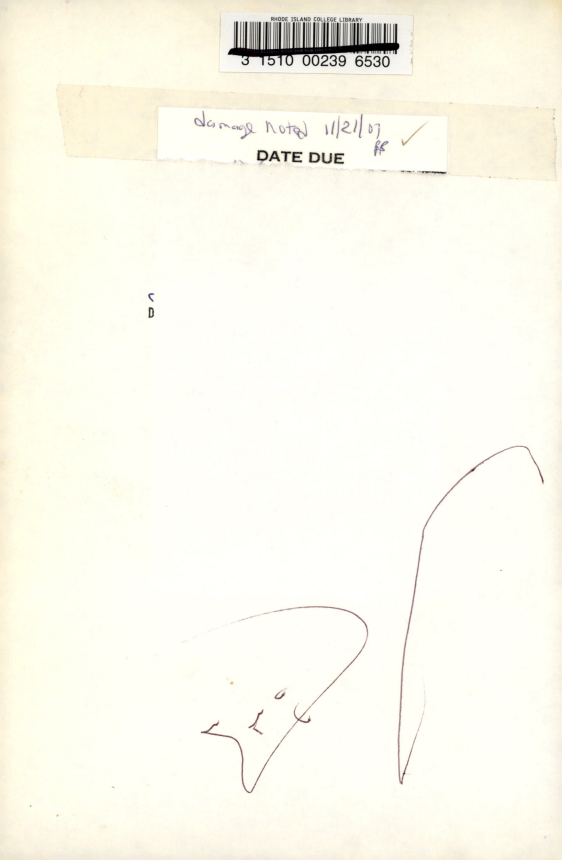